ELLA ELGAR BIRD DUMONT

An Autobiography of a West Texas Pioneer

Ella Bird, ca. 1886. Saunders Brothers Photographers, Quanah, Texas.

An Autobiography of a West Texas Pioneer

ELLA ELGAR BIRD DUMONT

EDITED BY TOMMY J BOLEY

FOREWORD BY EMILY CUTRER

University of Texas Press, Austin

BARKER TEXAS HISTORY CENTER SERIES, NO. 6

First Edition, 1988

LIBRARY OF CONGRESS CATALOGING-IN-PUBLICATION DATA

Dumont, Ella Elgar Bird, 1861–1943.
  Ella Elgar Bird Dumont : an autobiography of a West Texas pioneer
  edited by Tommy J Boley; foreword by Emily Cutrer.—1st ed.
    p.   cm.—(Barker Texas History Center series; no. 6)
  Revision of the editor's thesis (M.A.—University of Texas at
Austin, 1963).
  Bibliography: p.
  Includes index.
  ISBN 0-292-78089-3
  1. Dumont, Ella Elgar Bird, 1861–1943.   2. Pioneers—Texas—
Biography.   3. Women pioneers—Texas—Biography.   4. Frontier and
pioneer life—Texas.   5. Texas—Biography.   6. Texas—Social life
and customs.   I. Boley, Tommy J, 1935–   .   II. Title.
III. Series.
F391.4.D86A3   1988
976.4'06'0924—dc19
[B]   87-33095
                                                              CIP

FOR THE PEOPLE OF
COTTLE, KING, MOTLEY, AND DICKENS COUNTIES
AND FOR ELLA BIRD DUMONT

CONTENTS

James Thomas Bird (left) *and John J. Haynes of Blanco County, photographed by William J. Oliphant in Austin, Texas (Travis County), ca. 1868. Bird was approximately twenty years of age. (Photo courtesy Lawrence T. Jones, Austin, Texas)*

J. T. (Tom) Bird's Winchester '73 awarded to him for tracking down a band of Indians in Blanco County, Texas. The silver shield reads: "Awarded to J. T. Bird by the XIII Legislature, 1873." To the right of the shield appear the silver inlaid J and T, followed by a silver bird, his usual signature. (Photo courtesy Richard Rattenbury, Panhandle/Plains Historical Museum, Canyon, Texas)

FOREWORD

IN 1872, *Scribner's Monthly* dispatched two young men, Edward King and J. Wells Champney, to the southern United States with the assignment to prepare a series of articles accounting for the effects of Reconstruction on that region. When they reached the western end of the old Confederacy, they witnessed what they believed "one of the saddest sights" of their expedition—"the daily arrival of hundreds of refugees from the older Southern states, seeking a home on the Texas prairies."[1] As they accurately assessed it, "the flood of emigration" into Texas from the Deep South was indeed "formidable."[2] More than 100,000 people flowed across Texas's eastern border in the decade following the Civil War seeking new homes to replace those that lay in ruins. In comparison with Georgia, Mississippi and Alabama, Texas at least seemed prosperous. The first settlers to reach the state often sent back glowing reports of what they had found. Thus, it was hardly surprising that, as King and Champney recorded, "old men and little children, youths and maidens, clad in homespun," crowded, not only the railway cars in which the journalists rode, but also the wagon trails, "looking forward eagerly to the land of promise."[3]

The political and economic effects of this migration are well known. Historians have documented the extension of the frontier west of the 98th meridian with its attendant destruction of the Comanche empire, the rise of the cattle kingdom, and the development of a new agricultural region beyond the boundary of the old cotton kingdom. They have traced the biographies of individuals who held political office, owned the biggest farms and ranches, and began the first corporations. Until recently, however, scholars have paid scant attention to the everyday lives of those families who swelled Texas's population in the late nineteenth century.

Historians of Texas are hardly alone in that regard, however. Only during the past decade have American historians spent much time reconstructing the lives of ordinary people. In doing so, they have often found women's first-person, nonfiction accounts among the most useful sources for filling in our view of everyday life in this country. Such archival material has been particularly important in the history of the American West. Women's letters, diaries, journals, and reminiscences have informed much of the recent scholarship on the West and helped to provide a more complete picture of the frontier experience. John Mack Faragher's *Women and Men on the Overland Trail* (1979), Julie Roy Jeffrey's *Frontier Women: The Trans-Mississippi West, 1840–1880* (1979), Sandra Myres's *Westering Women and the Frontier Experience, 1880–1915* (1982), and Glenda Riley's *Women and Indians on the Frontier, 1825–1915* (1984) are only a few of the publications that have utilized these sources.[4] Where more traditional histories of the West have dealt with the activities of the fur trader, miner, cattleman, farmer, and soldier, occupations generally deemed masculine, the newer scholarship, as Faragher notes, acknowledges "with the Chinese, that women hold up half the sky."[5] Thus it has attempted both to restore real women rather than stereotypes to the historical narrative of the West and to give a fuller, more complex view of the American experience.

Similarly, Ella Elgar Bird Dumont's memoir is a major contribution to the literature of the Texas frontier experience. Born in Mississippi in 1861, Dumont was on the leading edge of the great migration that King and Champney wrote about for *Scribner's* when she settled with her family in Johnson County, Texas, south of the nascent cattle town of Fort Worth, in 1867. Her reminiscences not only depict the childish fun she and her siblings enjoyed along the wagon trail, but they also document the hardships and heartaches her family endured as they moved from place to place in search of better economic opportunity during their first years in Texas. As long as she remained with her mother and grandmother, Dumont enjoyed at least some of the advantages of a community—friends, schools, and church. Her marriage in 1877 at the age of sixteen, however, catapulted her onto a frontier that was more wild and unsettled than any she had previously experienced. With her first husband, Tom Bird, she hunted buffalo, lived in a teepee, and endured for "months and months" without seeing "the face of even one woman." When the buffalo gave out, she remained on the plains and watched the cattle industry take over. After the death of Bird and her eventual remarriage, Dumont moved during the 1890s to Paducah, one of the many communities then springing up in the Texas Panhandle, with her new husband Auguste Dumont.

As she wrote her memoirs during the 1920s, Dumont was aware of the panorama of history she had witnessed: "At times I seemed to stand and gaze on the progress of the country almost in wonderment," she described herself as thinking in the 1890s, "Only a little while ago it seemed there were nothing but buffalo. . . . Next the cattle were being moved in, then the ranches, then a long space of time ere the farming and building of towns and schools began, and then the present." Indeed as a woman who in effect grew up with the Texas plains, Dumont saw a virtual telescoping of the American frontier experience. The young woman who skinned a buffalo in the nineteenth century rode as an old woman in a car in the twentieth. Thus, her "true life story," as she called it, provides a lens through which to view the process by which wilderness turns to border-land and eventually becomes "civilized."

Like all lenses, however, Dumont's story has unavoidable distortions. She wrote about her experiences thirty to sixty years after they actually took place. Thus both the passage of time and the very different culture of the 1920s undoubtedly colored her memories of the nineteenth century. These filters are perhaps least important when Dumont is dealing with the externals of her experience. Her descriptions of the methods her husband used to hunt buffalo, her recipe for dressing hides, and her accounting of the different Panhandle ranches and their brands, for example, are straight-forward and remarkably accurate. They are not, however, the memoir's most engaging or unique passages. The information they impart is gener-ally available elsewhere, though perhaps not in such concise or entertain-ing form. The major significance of Dumont's "true life story" lies, instead, outside the realm of purely objective experience. Its value resides in its de-piction of the encounter among the cultural expectations, the stark physi-cal environment, and the individual personality of its author.

Significantly, Ella Elgar Bird Dumont was the product of nineteenth-century American culture and its carefully prescribed ideas about the role and nature of women. As a number of historians have shown, those ideas underwent a significant metamorphosis at the beginning of the 1800s. During the colonial era, when the home was the major center of economic production, women, for better or worse, worked alongside their husbands and children to satisfy the family's needs. The advent of a market economy and then industrialization during the eighteenth century, however, tended to separate home and work and thus to divide men, who went off to facto-ries, shops, and offices to make the family's living, from the women who remained to mind the home and children. Economic change tended also to undermine the values upon which the American nation rested. If many of the country's early leaders espoused an ideology of republican virtue, one which dictated the values of hard work, simplicity, and, most important, sacrifice of self-interest for the good of the community, the emerging economic system fostered an alternative set of characteristics—individualism, competition, and the pursuit of wealth. One way in which the culture reconciled this conflict between theory and practice was through the development of clearly defined gender roles.[6]

While society encouraged men to follow their acquisitive tendencies in the marketplace, it simultaneously decreed that women should guard the national virtues within the home. By the 1830s and 1840s countless books, magazines, and novels were prescribing a moral function for women within the domestic sphere. By advocating that they adhere to a set of precepts that the historian Barbara Welter has associated with "the cult of true womanhood"—virtues such as purity, piety, self-sacrifice, and domesticity—journals like *Godey's Lady's Book* both rationalized women's subordinate status and staked a claim for their moral superiority. The proper subordination and self-sacrifice of a wife and mother could remind her husband and children of values easily overlooked in the competitive public world, they argued, and her role within the family would thus have important social ramifications. As Welter aptly puts it, a nineteenth-century woman was expected to "uphold the pillars of the temple with her frail white hand."[7]

These prescriptions, however, outlined an ideal often bearing little resemblance to the lives of many real women outside the upper classes or the more settled communities of the East Coast. The frontier, in particular, presented a challenge to the ideas of domesticity. The needs of a family far from the marketplace dictated a return to a more self-sufficient life-style and thus at least the temporary collapse of rigidly defined male and female spheres. On the frontier, men and women would often work side by side to feed, clothe, and shelter their families, or when their husbands were off scouting for land or food, women would necessarily assume roles the culture had assigned men.[8]

Yet if the cult of domesticity failed to describe the conditions of pioneer life, it nevertheless presented guidelines against which many women measured themselves. As Julie Roy Jeffrey has demonstrated in *Frontier Women,* nineteenth-century ideas about women's nature and roles continued to influence the way women defined themselves in the West. On the negative side, these notions could cause women to fear or lament the loss of qualities associated with femininity. Frail, white hands often turned strong and brown with hard, outside work. "I am a very old woman," Jeffrey quotes one twenty-nine-year-old woman as bemoaning, "My face is thin, sunken and wrinkled, my hands bony, whithered and hard."[9] At the same time, domesticity could have more positive effects. While women's economic function often reverted to its pre–industrial revolution status on the frontier, their moral role grew in significance. Whereas women had preserved cultural values in the East, they frequently created them in the West. The stereotypical view of the frontier woman as civilizer derives from actual situations. Western women did not merely long for the churches, schools, libraries, and other institutions that fostered the nation's cultural ideals; in countless frontier communities, they organized and staffed them.[10]

Ella Elgar Bird Dumont's "true life story" corroborates many of the standard generalizations about nineteenth-century culture by chronicling how she, as a young wife and mother, fashioned a life for herself in an environment seemingly hostile to everything women of her generation had been taught to hold dear. In one example, Dumont indicates her awareness of ideas about women's domestic responsibilities. When she describes the teepee in which she and Tom Bird first lived, Dumont justifies her crude shelter by noting that a "more clean and comfortable home you could not find in any of the eastern cities." Thus she carefully disarms any criticism that in leaving civilization behind, she had also abandoned its values. She also frequently demonstrates concern that her children not do without those things they might have enjoyed in more settled communities. When she still lived in a dugout, for example, her handiwork bought a lace dress for her daughter, and she moved on at least one occasion so that her children, whom she had been teaching at home, could attend school.

These instances, however, illustrate how Dumont consciously measured herself against her culture's ideas about women's roles. Other passages reveal more subtle ways in which gender shaped the author's experience. By segregating men's work from women's, nineteenth-century prescriptions about male and female spheres also tended to separate men from women emotionally. As a result, one of the most important aspects of women's lives in the nineteenth century was the bonding that occurred between them. Networks composed of family and friends were often a woman's major source of physical and emotional support. Women looked to other women for help with children and domestic chores, and they sought one another in times of joy, sickness, and sorrow. Thus one of the most wrenching aspects of the whole westering experience for women was their separation from mothers, sisters, and female friends and the frequent lack of substitutes in their new homes.[11]

In her memoir, Dumont movingly documents her relationship to what Carroll Smith-Rosenberg has called "the female world of love and ritual." With what may at first seem conventional sentiment, she retells her distress at leaving her mother's home upon her marriage and later she recalls her grief at learning of her sister's death. The language Dumont uses, particularly in the latter case, suggests the psychological importance of these events, however. News of her sister's death, she recalls, "was a blow that I was least prepared for and to which I could hardly reconcile myself. I had always hoped we would be together again and enjoy each other as we had in years gone by." When added to her frequent lament about being lonely in her early years on the plains and to her acknowledgment of a later reliance upon neighbor women to care for her children, these words underscore Dumont's emotional desire for and frequent dependence upon a female network. They also indicate her kinship with women who underwent similar experiences on the frontier.

Dumont's depictions of the landscape in which she found herself follow a pattern as well. In her recent study, *The Land before Her: Fantasy and Experience of the American Frontiers, 1630–1860,* Annette Kolodny examines women's fictional and actual accounts of their lives on the nation's western borders and concludes that women had a very different vision of their physical environment than that of their male contemporaries. Rather than as an Edenic wilderness offering escape or as the raw material of commercial exploitation, women writers, she contends, fantasized about the frontier as a midpoint between the two.[12] The West they envisioned was quite similar to that which Ella Dumont preferred. While Dumont recorded her dislike of the rough landscape near the Palo Duro Canyon and her discomfort in the Wichita breaks, she wrote almost passionately of an environment that synthesized nature and civilization. As for many other women writers, her flower gardens signified her ideal landscape.

In an especially touching passage, Dumont describes a period in her life sometime around the turn of the century that in retrospect seemed idyllic. She had left the prairies and moved into Paducah with her second husband Auguste Dumont. There the couple had overcome tragedy and had begun to live a full and prosperous life with their family of three children. With literary flair, Dumont sums up her happiness by describing the profusion of flowers in her garden one spring, and significantly, despite the passage of time, she recounts what she had raised in great detail. "Trumpet Creepers climbed up over the gable of the house . . . [and] the Moon Vines, Wisteria, and Clematis were twined around every corner," she recalled. These and the many other blooms she named were beautiful, however, for more than the color that they added to the drab Panhandle town; they functioned as metaphors for what was perhaps the high point of her life.

After describing her garden in great detail, Dumont explains what it signified. "This was real home for me," she wrote, "more than I had known in a long time," and she lovingly recalled her young son who was "ever tod-dling at my heels" and her teenage daughter who was budding just like the flowers that she gathered into "many beautiful bouquets." As she wrote, however, Dumont knew her daughter's tragic death and then her hus-band's would soon follow the scene she described. Like her blossoms, her happiness was short-lived. Thus her vision of flowers, home, and children has a special poignance, and it is easy to understand why, like many other women writers, she exercised such care in depicting her garden landscape.

Ella Dumont was not just a "type," however, or a case study whose memoir now fits the generalizations made by historians seeking to find some pattern in human experience. She was, as the passage about her gar-den also demonstrates, an individual with very real hopes, emotions, and conflicts. Indeed one of the most compelling aspects of Dumont's autobi-ography is its depiction of the constant struggle between her inner long-ings and the opportunities her environment offered, a struggle that neither her age nor her writing seem to resolve.

At one point in her reminiscence, Dumont claims that she had "always tried to make the best of life's possibilities," and her narrative is full of ex-amples to support that assertion. She obviously enjoys recounting how she could trap birds, build furniture, or change a wagon wheel as well as any man. Her descriptions of her skill in marksmanship are evidence of self-pride, as her seemingly endless account of suitors undoubtedly is as well. With such anecdotal material Dumont is, consciously or not, persuading the reader (and probably herself) to see her as the stereotypical pioneer woman, the hardy and cheerful soul who successfully coped with the fron-tier by exhibiting strength, initiative, and courage. She is the "Madonna of the Prairies" and Annie Oakley rolled into one.[13]

Yet as Dumont is obviously also aware, the stereotypes from which she drew self-definition were one-sided. Trying to make the best of things, her memoir frequently reveals, was often not enough. Throughout her story, Dumont's words frequently disclose a real anguish at missed opportunities and thwarted desires. From childhood, she displayed what she perceived as a talent for sculpture. Modelling clay and carving gyprock not only filled her many lonely hours as a young wife, but they also satisfied a passion for creativity and form so strong that, when stymied, it found alternate out-lets. When she reached the conclusion that something as unprofitable as sculpture was a waste of time on the frontier, Dumont utilized her artistic talent by beading gloves, vests, and pants that her cowboy friends eagerly purchased. Later she indulged her appreciation of form by collecting ex-otic cacti. Neither, however, was an adequate substitute for what she wrote "my life career should have been." Even in old age, Dumont grieved as she did over her children for the many pieces of sculpture that she had either lost or never completed, and the most eloquent passages of her autobiography are those in which she laments the talent that she had "buried . . . on those broad, barren prairies."

By acknowledging her despair, however, Dumont also affirmed herself as an individual. Throughout her memoir, one is always aware that there was an Ella Elgar Bird Dumont. Alternately funny and tragic, her autobiography does more than confirm our notions of what life was like for women on the Texas plains. By transcending the conventions and stereotypes, it reveals, as only a first-person account can, how personal, complex, and open-ended the frontier experience actually was.

Emily Fourmy Cutrer

Notes

1. Edward King, *The Great South,* ed. W. Magruder Drake and Robert R. Jones (Baton Rouge: Louisiana State University Press, 1972), p. 99.

2. Ibid.

3. Ibid.

4. Julie Roy Jeffrey, *Frontier Women: The Trans-Mississippi West, 1840–1880,* American Century Series (New York: Hill and Wang, 1979), pp. xii–xiii; John Mack Faragher, *Women and Men on the Overland Trail* (New Haven and London: Yale University Press, 1979), p. xi. See also Sandra L. Myres, *Westering Women and the Frontier Experience, 1800–1915* (Albuquerque: University of New Mexico Press, 1982); Glenda Riley, *Frontierswomen: The Iowa Experience* (Ames: Iowa State University Press, 1981) and *Women and Indians on the Frontier, 1825–1915* (Albuquerque: University of New Mexico Press, 1984); and Joanna L. Stratton, *Pioneer Women: Voices from the Kansas Frontier* (New York: Simon and Schuster, 1981). For a sample of primary writings, consult Lillian Schlissel, ed., *Women's Diaries of the Westward Journey* (New York: Schocken Books, 1982) and Jo Ella Powell Exley, ed., *Texas Tears and Texas Sunshine: Voices of Frontier Women* (College Station: Texas A&M University Press, 1985).

5. Faragher, *Women and Men on the Overland Trail,* p. xi.

6. A good summary of the issues involved in the transformation in women's lives during the eighteenth and nineteenth centuries appears in a book by Carol Ruth Berkin and Mary Beth Norton, *Women of America: A History* (Boston: Houghton Mifflin, 1979). See especially Norton and Berkin's introduction (pp. 3–15), Norton's "The Myth of the Golden Age" (pp. 37–47), and Berkin's "The Paradox of 'Women's Sphere'" (pp. 139–149). On republican ideology, see John F. Kasson, *Civilizing the Machine: Technology and Republican Values in America, 1776–1900,* pp. 1–51, and on gender roles and republican ideology, see Kathryn Kish Sklar, *Catharine Beecher: A Study in American Domesticity* (New York: W. W. Norton, 1976).

7. Barbara Welter, "The Cult of True Womanhood," *American Quarterly* 18 (Summer 1966): 152. This essay is the classic statement on nineteenth-century domesticity. See also Norton, "The Paradox of 'Women's Sphere,'" and Sklar, *Catharine Beecher.*

8. A number of books and articles have appeared to point out the limitations of "The Cult of True Womanhood Idea." An early important example is Gerda Lerner, "The Lady and the Mill Girl," *American Studies* 10 (Spring 1969): 5–15. For information on the frontier's challenge to domesticity, see Myres, *Westering Women* and Jeffrey, *Frontier Women,* both of which contain numerous references in notes and bibliography to further primary and secondary sources.

9. Jeffrey, *Frontier Women,* p. 72.

10. Ibid. For more on women's roles as civilizers on the frontier, see Jeffrey, *Frontier Women,* pp. 79–106, and Myres, *Westering Women,* pp. 167–212.

11. Carroll Smith-Rosenberg, "The Female World of Love and Ritual," in his *Disorderly Conduct: Visions of Gender in Victorian America* (New York: Oxford University Press), pp. 53–76.

12. Annette Kolodny, *The Land before Her: Fantasy and Experience of the American Frontiers, 1630–1860* (Chapel Hill: University of North Carolina Press, 1984), pp. 3–13.

13. For a discussion of the standard stereotypes of Western women, see Beverly J. Stoeltje, "'A Helpmate for Man Indeed,' The Image of the Frontier Woman," *Journal of American Folklore* 88 (January 1975): 25–41, and Myres, *Westering Women,* pp. 1–11.

Auguste Dumont in a photograph made by Saunders Brothers in Quanah, Texas. No suggestion of date is provided, but Mr. Dumont appears to be approximately forty years of age, ca. 1896.

Ella Bird Dumont at the approximate age of thirty-five, ca. 1896. Handwriting on the back of the photograph states that her hair was brown, her eyes were grayish blue, and her dress was black. The author had become the wife of Auguste Dumont in 1895.

PREFACE

PUBLICATION OF Ella Elgar Bird Dumont's story heralds a victory. After completion of the manuscript in 1928, Dumont—along with family members and friends—repeatedly tried to get the work published. Numerous potential publishers and editors surfaced, but publication was never realized.

Several forces worked against fulfillment. First, the author and her son Elgar Dumont wanted a contract on their own terms, not those suggested by the majority of publishers and editors. Second, the economic, social, and political disturbances of the nation hindered progress. Third, not enough time had passed since the end of the historical period the manuscript covered to make it valuable as a historical record. Finally, some prospective individuals and companies simply lost interest in the project before they ever went beyond the initial reading of the manuscript. Fourteen years after completion of the work, only the abundant correspondence and a slightly revised edition existed as evidence of attempts at publication. Not until 1985—over forty years later—did the manuscript come to the attention of another publisher, though the work had been researched and had undergone considerable editing for a master of arts thesis in the interim.

In contrast to the unsuccessful publication endeavor, few tasks begun by the talented and resourceful Ella Bird Dumont ever lacked completion. Strong and determined, she endured the harsh blows of frontier life while protecting her family and providing for them. When danger came, she faced it firmly with her reliable Winchester. When need appeared, she met it, killing and skinning an antelope to feed her children or fashioning a pair of stirrups from the poles of a chinaberry tree for her husband. And when she had time to be creative, she designed a mattress from the heavy mops of wool her husband took from the front of buffalo heads, she dressed the ranch cowboys in beaded gloves and vests, and she carved figures from the local gyprock with natural and untrained talent.

With this same zeal Dumont attempted to publish her story of "a time ever to be remembered." From 1928 to 1942 she and her son Elgar corresponded with publishers, editors, journalists, friends, relatives, and anyone else who might aid them. Several contacts seemed promising, but the Dumonts' terms were excessive. First, they believed that they alone should receive royalties on every copy sold; they preferred to pay an editor a flat fee, not part of the royalties. Second, they wanted to see the entire manuscript in print, not a condensed version. In all but one encounter, they held out for these terms, even though most publishers and editors insisted upon splitting royalties and cutting portions of the text and even though the country was experiencing an economic depression, which was followed by World War II. As a result, the story comes to publication forty-five years after the author's death and sixty years after completion of the original manuscript.

The author composed these memoirs in 1927 and 1928. According to Oma Dumont, Elgar's wife, a woman (unnamed) came to Paducah (the author's home), from either Vernon or Wichita Falls to type the handwritten manuscript. This handwritten copy no longer exists, though the Ella Bird Dumont collection at the Panhandle-Plains Historical Museum in Canyon contains the author's introductory handwritten passages on note paper. (It also holds all existent correspondence from 1928 to 1942 concerning publication.) The original typed manuscript, poorly done by contemporary standards, is dated February 1, 1927, on the first page. That the author continued to write in 1928 seems evident late in the book by her counting backward from 1928 to pinpoint an earlier incident.

In the first letter concerning publication, dated February 7, 1928, the author addresses the U.S. Copyright Office, Washington, D.C. She asks whether she should have her work copyrighted first or printed first by a publisher, and she inquires about whether the work needs a title before copyrighting. No reply exists to this letter.

In the first letter from a publisher, dated July 25, 1928, J. W. Pinson, vice-president of Pioneer Publishing Company of Fort Worth, acknowledges a July 23 letter from the author and requests the manuscript. Dumont responds on October 11, saying that she will send the work and that she will appreciate a proposition from the company. No further correspondence from Pinson or from Pioneer exists.

During the same period, Elgar Dumont is advised by Dr. E. E. Violette, a "well-known traveler and writer," in Dumont's words, to send the manuscript to the Stratford Company, a publisher in Boston. Violette had recently been a visitor to Paducah. Elgar sends the work and requests "a proposition" from the company. He also makes three suggestions for a title: "Fifty Years in Texas," "A Half Century in the Panhandle," and "The Autobiography of a Panhandle."

Shortly after Elgar mails the manuscript, Violette writes him on August 15, suggesting that, "in event of an unfavorable reply from The Stratford Press, I believe my own company—Better Books Company . . . Kansas City, Mo. would like to make a bid on your Mother's book. We have heretofore handled only religious and travel books; but I believe we would be willing to go outside of our field on this particular book. In this event, I myself would edit the book, copyright it in your name, and in event of my returning here next year we could sell an entire edition in one meeting."

Elgar's reply on August 28 expresses his enthusiasm for Violette's proposition, stating that it "sounds more plausible than any other we have received." Eight days later, on September 5, Elgar writes to Violette announcing that the Stratford Company has asked the Dumonts "to pay for books published in advance." Dumont holds out to have the manuscript published on a full royalty basis. He believes that one thousand copies will sell in his area, and he invites Violette's bid. In spite of this optimistic correspondence, something went wrong because no further correspondence with Violette exists.

The actual Stratford Company offer, dated August 31, 1928, requests that $2,000 be advanced to the company as follows: $700 when the Dumonts receive galleys, $700 when completed page proofs arrive, and $600 when the completed books are ready. One thousand copies will be sent for sale at $3 each. After the first thousand copies are sold, the author will receive a royalty of twenty-five percent on all subsequent sales. On october 15, Elgar rejects the proposal, asking either for an offer on a "strictly royalty basis" or for the manuscript to be returned. No further correspondence with Stratford exists.

The following year, 1929, reveals two efforts to find help. A letter of March 2 from Elgar to Double Day Doran Company of Garden City, New Jersey, announces that he is sending the manuscript and that he wants the company to make an offer. No evidence of a reply exists today. The second effort that year appears in an undated note to Elgar's mother from Hilton R. Greer of the *Dallas Journal*. Greer will edit the work for $50, providing the author agrees to have Greer's corrected copy retyped should many corrections be necessary. On August 31 Greer writes that he is an editor only, not a typist. His work will be to mark misspellings, errors in diction, and suggestions for rearrangement, and he will also suggest how the author can rewrite sections and lengthen or cut certain parts. Greer's reply sounds as if Dumont had communicated that she expected Greer to put the manuscript into final typewritten form.

Two years and eight months after Hilton Greer's offer, C. C. ("Connie") Renfro, a Dallas attorney (as well as a Paducah native), writes to Dumont on April 28, 1932, announcing the return of letters from Greer. Evidently the author had mailed this correspondence (now missing) to Renfro. Introducing Professor Henry Smith, Renfro states: "I think well of Mr. Smith of the Southwest Press and I would recommend him for the reason that he would be inclined to publish the work if he had edited it." Renfro expresses hope that he can persuade J. Frank Dobie, the famous Texas author, "to take the major portion of your work and handle it like he did Mr. Young' in *The Vaquero of the Brush Country*." Enclosed is a copy of Renfro's April 28 letter to Dobie, which indicates that Dobie has the Dumont manuscript. Renfro notifies Dobie that Hilton Greer and Henry Smith have agreed to edit the work, and Renfro suggests that Dobie look at the material after it is edited with consideration of entering an agreement, providing it will be published by Southwest Press. No further correspondence involving Dobie, Greer, or Smith exists.

On August 9 of that same year, Thelma Smith Yarrow writes to Dumont, asking if the author still needs someone to work on the manuscript. Yarrow informs Dumont that she had read chapters of the work sometime past and that she wants to do "revision and excision" in "the most careful way." Although Yarrow writes from Vernon, where she is visiting (approximately seventy miles east of Paducah), she explains that her home is now Los Angeles, where she has had editing experience with a publisher. This letter is the only existing correspondence from Yarrow.

Later in 1932, on November 15, Renfro writes that a Dallas newspaperman named Gerald Forbes has agreed to rewrite the manuscript up through the part dealing with the author's second marriage and "make it into a straight biography to be signed by you and him jointly." (Evidently connections with Greer, Smith, and Dobie had been severed.) Renfro informs Dumont that he has told Forbes that she "might prefer to divide the royalty on the book rather than be out a lot of expense with times and conditions like they are." Forbes offers to rewrite the manuscript for $25, plus one-half the royalties. Renfro lists additional material that Forbes will want included and adds that Forbes does counsel that "this is not a good time to try to market a book."

Along with this letter is a handwritten pencil copy of an undated note from Dumont in which she agrees to Forbes's proposition. The author suggests that Forbes come to see her to "get a better view and understanding of the manuscript." Dumont asks if she would be expected "to bear his expenses" to Paducah.

On July 7, 1933, Forbes writes from International Correspondence Schools in Dallas: "I am enclosing a start on our book and would like to know what you think of it." Eight and one-half months pass between this letter and Forbes's next existing letter, dated March 22, 1934. During this time a major change has evolved: "It is with a great deal of regret that I send this letter, but after several months of effort I find that it will be impossible for me to continue with our arrangement regarding your biography." Forbes cites an increase in his workload and insufficient leisure as reasons for his withdrawal.

What irony that Dumont finally relaxed her terms for publication, allowing someone to rewrite the manuscript, agreeing to joint authorship, and consenting to division of the royalties, only to have the coauthor default on the project. Is Forbes telling the truth in his excuses for withdrawing? What has transpired since Forbes mailed the early work on the book the past July? The third paragraph of Forbes's final letter suggests a reason when he refers to a letter from Dumont of March 19 in which she asked Forbes to return her manuscript at once. He writes (with spelling, punctuation, and grammar evidently unchecked): "I am pleased to have you say that you will not feel badly toward me for this proceedure, and I trust that you will find a much better person to handle this work quickly, so that you may have the pleasure of seeing the story of your life in print. In closing I want to say that your book is one of the most interesting in material and handling, that I have ever seen and I regret my own limitations which prevent me from carrying out our plans." Evidently Dumont grew tired of waiting for Forbes to produce the revision and elected to move on to someone else.

Next to become involved with publication of the Dumont work was Lewis E. Fite of San Antonio, youngest son of the author's only sister, Lucy Elgar Fite. As early as August 1932, Fite showed interest in helping his Aunt Ella. Five letters written in 1934 reveal his continued interest, and one of these letters acknowledges his receipt of a copy of the manuscript. Not until 1936, however, does Fite report any progress. He writes on May 21 that several publishers have recently reviewed the work, "one of whom seems more interested, and, perhaps, more dependable than the others." Fite adds that a Mr. Lloyd checked the manuscript and showed enthusiasm, but Fite refused to become involved because Lloyd had "one outstanding and condemning evil: namely, he simply would not stay sober long enough to do any work."

Of major interest to Fite is Robert Bellinger of Bellinger Brothers Publishers, who referred the manuscript to John M. Taylor, an editor and author in San Antonio. Fite offers to meet with Taylor and make direct arrangements. Because Taylor suggested that a short book of 20,000 words be made from the manuscript, Bellinger's estimates were based on that length: for 64 pages with cardboard cover, 250 copies will cost $165.00; 500 copies will cost $185.00. If the entire manuscript is published, says Fite, it will make a book of about 164 pages with 70,000 words. Cloth binding will be necessary, and 500 copies will cost $610. Economically, Fite advises, it will be safer to attempt the shorter edition. Taylor offered to edit the work for $50, making the cost of 500 cardboard copies $235, plus the cost of a cover plate, a photograph of the author, and one or two other pictures. To get the project under way, Fite pledges $50, which he states he is privileged to donate.

Enclosed with Fite's letter is a copy of Taylor's letter to Bellinger, dated April 15, 1936. Taylor writes from Southern Literary Institute, Publishers, in San Antonio: "[The manuscript] has real and definite value—but value limited to the historian, the library and perhaps the university. That is, it is not a manuscript that can be made into a book that would interest the general public and, consequently, could not hope for a sale large enough to make anybody a real profit." Taylor emphasizes, though, that the work is "a remarkable family record which should be preserved." For publication, Taylor believes that cutting is a must. "Fortunately," he says "[the author] has written her manuscript in a sort of diary handling, which makes it possible to cut passages, and even long sections, without doing harm." Taylor feels strongly about publication, in spite of his reservations about financial success: "It really would be deplorable for the manuscript to be discarded and not published, for material of this kind—the virtual diaries of eyewitnesses and the first-hand experience of pioneers—should be preserved, as there will be little opportunity to obtain anything of the kind in another few years. In fact, it is the actual duty of a family which possesses such a manuscript to find some means of publishing it, either through subscription from its own members or through advance payment for copies in a number sufficient to defray the cost of publication."

Shortly after Fite sends his lengthy letter introducing Bellinger and

Taylor to the author, Fite writes again on June 1, 1936, referring to a letter he received from Elgar with two letters enclosed. Fite is returning the letters, and he encourages his Aunt Ella to answer the correspondence, which had come from Herbert Gambrell, director of the Historical Exhibits of the Texas Centennial Central Exposition in Dallas. In one letter of December 12, 1935, Gambrell had suggested to the author that she negotiate with a publisher before having the manuscript edited. A publisher, he had advised, could find someone to do the editing without the author being responsible for this work. Gambrell had suggested two possibilities: Turner and Company or Tardy Publishing Company, both of Dallas.

On August 19 of the same year, Fite writes that Naylor Publishing Company in San Antonio will read the manuscript. Although Naylor's prices will be higher than Bellinger Brothers, Fite advises, the Naylors are "very high class people and . . . entirely dependable."

Fite's last letter concerning his Aunt Ella's work, written November 1, 1937, announces that he is returning the manuscript: "I am very sorry that we were unable to interest a local publisher, but they are all very conservative and will not publish this type of work on a royalty basis." For one and one-half years Fite had worked actively to help his aunt publish her memoirs. He had interested two publishing companies, Bellinger Brothers and Naylor, which were high-quality operations in his opinion; and he had obtained the scholarly and practical advice of Taylor, an experienced author and editor. Evidently, Dumont remained firm in her original position: she would settle for no less than publication of her complete manuscript, and she alone would receive royalties. Fite must have felt mixed emotions concerning his aunt's refusal to accept any of the propositions he had been able to arrange: she was stubborn, but he must have appreciated her pride in her work and her determination to see the project carried out as she felt it should be done.

Three additional letters from 1936 reveal attempts by the author to find help. On February 20, L. F. Sheffy, secretary of the Panhandle-Plains Historical Society in Canyon acknowledges a February 17 letter from Dumont. Sheffy agrees to look at the manuscript and make suggestions, though "it deals with a rather local community and, therefore, it will be rather difficult to get a publisher to take it on a royalty basis."

Another letter that year, written on April 21 by Bradford Knapp, president of Texas Technological College, acknowledges Dumont's letters of April 4 and 18. Knapp suggests that the author contact Frank Holland of *Holland's Magazine* in Dallas, Peter Molyneaux of *Texas Weekly*, Amon

Carter, editor of the *Fort Worth Star-Telegram,* and Dr. W. C. Holden of
Texas Tech, a historian. As for being able to offer any personal help,
Knapp explains: "My time is bought and paid for by the State of Texas,
and I am compelled to be almost a perpetual servant of the public."

The final letter of 1936, dated August 20, comes from Miriam Blairs,
secretary-treasurer of Tardy Publishing Company in Dallas. The Tardy
Company had been recommended to the author by Herbert Gambrell of
the Texas Centennial Central Exposition. Blairs acknowledges Dumont's
letter of August 14 and explains that the company cannot consider publication because of a full publishing program for the coming year. In this letter
the manuscript is referred to as *Sixty Years in the Texas Panhandle,* a title the
author must have suggested.

No evidence exists of correspondence about the manuscript from 1937
through 1939. On May 20, 1940, Winnie Allen, archivist of The University
of Texas Mirabeau B. Lamar Library, acknowledges a personal visit with
the author (location unnamed). Allen expresses a desire to read the work
and offers to get J. Frank Dobie's opinion, as well as others. A second letter
from Allen on June 22 acknowledges receipt of the manuscript. On July 5,
Allen writes that a list of suggestions will be coming, especially for "more
details to add interest." Allen's letter of August 7 asks the author for "full
names of the people you mention." The editor believes that the manuscript
"can be revised and made publishable without great effort." Letters of august 22 and October 8 from Allen acknowledge receipt of additional material and encourage the author to make a trip to Austin. On December 17
Allen writes that the autobiography "as we have revised it" is on its way.

On January 20, 1941, Allen acknowledges return of the revised manuscript that she had sent to Dumont, stating that the author should have
kept the complimentary copy of the new version. Evidently Dumont
looked over Allen's slightly revised manuscript and returned it. This second version, currently on file in the Barker Historical Center at The University of Texas in Austin, follows the original typed draft, with seven
clearly marked insertions of material. In addition, two short narratives entitled "Round-ups" and "In the Early Eighties" appear at the end of the
edition. No doubt this new material resulted from Allen's requests for
more details from the author.

Three months later, on April 23, Allen writes that "the entire manuscript
will have to be done over at least once more." And on June 2, Allen announces that work must be done on "the questions" that will soon be sent
for the author to complete. Finally, on September 17, Allen sends Dumont

a carbon copy of notes that the author had submitted in response to the questions from Allen. This typed carbon exists today alongside the original typed manuscript.

Then comes the crushing blow, the final one for the author. Just as momentum has built up with the connection in Austin, just as the author has submitted additional material that Allen believes will make the story more complete, the United States becomes involved in World War II. Allen writes on January 28, 1942: "My staff has been greatly depleted by the war, and I do not know when we will get things straightened out. I am still interested and anxious to get this work in final form and will let you know if things shape up so that this can be done."

No further correspondence with Allen exists. In fact, the January 28 letter above marks the last known correspondence concerning publication of Dumont's manuscript during her life. Fourteen and one-half months after Allen's final letter, on April 10, 1943, Dumont died. Her story lay on the shelf unpublished.

Sixteen years passed with no attention to the manuscript. In the spring of 1959, while a student at North Texas State College in Denton, I enrolled in a course entitled "Life and Literature of the Southwest." Professor George Hendricks announced on opening day that he wanted his students to search their home areas for original material as the basis for the major project paper in the course. I immediately called Paducah, where I had been born and reared, to inquire about any possible sources. My mother replied, "Well, there is that book that Mrs. Dumont wrote." One telephone call from my mother to Oma Dumont, the author's daughter-in-law, gave me permission to use the original manuscript, and three months later I submitted my composition—a thirty-four–page summary of the work. By this time I knew that I must do more with the original. This taste of working with the manuscript was only enough to whet my appetite.

Three and one-half years later, in the fall of 1962, the Department of English at The University of Texas gave me permission to edit and research Dumont's manuscript as fulfillment of the thesis requirement for a master of arts degree. A portion of my preface to the thesis reads as follows:

The editing of Mrs. Dumont's autobiography has been done in an attempt to provide clarity in reading, while maintaining the idiosyncrasies indigenous to the author's style. Some changes have been made in spelling, punctuation, and sentence structure, while many obvious errors have been retained in order to permit the color of the time and the area to pervade the narrative, as well as to give a more correct representation of the author's educational background.

For the first time, the original typed manuscript, the Barker Historical Center addenda to the original, and the author's responses to questions from Winnie Allen were fused. These responses fill seventeen typed pages in their original format. I completed the M.A. thesis in August 1963 under the supervision of Professors J. C. Watson and D. M. McKeithan.

Following the completion of the thesis, I began inquiring among my teaching colleagues about publication possibilities. Reactions echoed those heard by Dumont: the manuscript needed a great deal of cutting; much of the narrative would be of interest only to people in a small area. In 1967, I received one encouraging suggestion from a colleague in the English Department at The University of Texas at El Paso. Two or three interesting articles, he said, could evolve from particular areas of the manuscript, articles that periodicals dealing with western U.S. history would likely publish. Like the author, though, I felt that the full story—or most of it—should be told in one volume, and I discarded the idea of extracting articles from the work. And so the thesis version of the Dumont manuscript rested on the bookshelf along with the two previous ones.

One other typed copy of the original manuscript exists. It appeared in December 1968 as a project of Lyda Kelley's Typing II class in Paducah High School. The finished copy was dittoed in purple ink. Evidently, the Dumont family gave permission for the work to be retyped. Today a copy of the dittoed version is on file at the Cottle County Library in Paducah. Reports of other copies of this version lead me to believe that several copies exist among both current and former citizens of Paducah. Because this version is merely a retyping of the original typed manuscript, I consider it only another draft of the original.

In addition to the three versions and the retyped draft of the manuscript, two articles have appeared in periodicals. First, in 1964, Paducah native Ernest Lee published "A Woman on the Buffalo Range: The Journal of Ella Dumont" in the *West Texas Historical Association Year Book*. More recently, in 1986, Richard Rattenbury of the Panhandle-Plains Historical Museum in Canyon presented "A Winchester for All Seasons" in *Man at Arms*. Also, citations of passages from the original typed manuscript appear in Carmen Taylor Bennett's *Our Roots Grow Deep: A History of Cottle County* published in 1970. Bennett quotes selected passages in her opening chapters on early history in the area.

For the next fifteen years, from 1970 to 1985, the Ella Bird Dumont story lay neglected until Jo Ella Exley published *Texas Tears and Texas Sunshine*. In this series of biographical sketches of pioneer women in Texas, Exley quotes selected passages from Dumont's story of frontier life and the coming of civilization in the latter part of the nineteenth century.

In December 1985, I received a call from the University of Texas Press, inviting me to revise my thesis for publication. I immediately accepted the offer—finally here was the opportunity to present Dumont's story as she (and as I) had wanted it done. At last the book would be accessible to universities, libraries, historians, fans of Texana, young adults, and women interested in reading of the adventures and accomplishments of a courageous pioneer woman.

Actual work on the revision of what would become this edition began in July 1986. At first I had no concept of just how much would have to be done, but one week of work told me that the thorough research it demanded would require much time and dedication. Byron Price, then director of Panhandle-Plains Historical Museum in Canyon, commented in a review of the thesis that although it "provided generally competent notes to accompany the narrative, both the annotation and bibliography should be updated to reflect current scholarship in such fields as women's history, buffalo hunting, ranching, etc." Price listed some twenty or twenty-five additional sources that he felt I should consult. All of these now appear in the bibliography. In the original bibliography in 1963 I cited 43 sources; in this edition I cite 137. My goal has been to add every piece of relevant information that I could find on the people, places, events, expressions, and specialized descriptions presented by the author. In addition, I have attempted to enhance the author's narrative with informative endnotes that cover the era thoroughly.

During my study the most exciting experiences occurred in mid-March 1986 as I performed the major portion of my field research. At the library of the Panhandle-Plains Historical Museum in Canyon, I found the correspondence dealing with the attempts at publication, the pencil-written beginnings of the manuscript, patents and deeds to land acquired by Auguste Dumont in Cottle County, and many other items. And downstairs in the rare rifle collection lay Tom Bird's Winchester '73, the rifle awarded him by the Thirteenth Legislature of the state of Texas. Beautifully displayed, the firearm occupies a prominent place in the museum.

In the same week I met with friends in Paducah who were helping in the research. After a productive morning on March 20, Tom Long, a senior resident of Cottle and King Counties, led me to the original 1877 campsite of Tom and Ella Bird on Bird's Creek in northeastern King County. With the assistance of Ralph Mote, foreman of the Masterson Ranch, we found the campsite around 4:30 in the afternoon. There before us were strewn the rocks of Alec Jones' house, with a part of one wall still standing, and ten yards away lay the remains of what had been the chimney of Tom and Ella Bird's buffalo tepee. Bird Creek, just in front, is now dammed to form a watering tank for cattle. As a person who had frequently relived Dumont's story for twenty-eight years, I was thrilled to see where her life began on the North Central Plains 109 years before.

Most of the work on this published edition, however, was performed indoors—in libraries and in my home office. In editing the original manuscript at the computer, I made three major changes. Since the original format provided no breaks from beginning to end, I divided the narrative into twenty-four chapters to assist the reader in recognizing and separating major events. Chapter division also simplified the numbering of endnotes, preventing a consecutive growth of endnote numbers into the hundreds. Similarly, for reasons of clarity, I added paragraphing where I believed it was needed to provide unity of thought and to prevent confusion for the reader.

Second, I made small changes to prevent unnecessary errors and to remove distracting inconsistencies in style, grammar, and usage, including spelling, punctuation, capitalization, subject-verb agreement, pronoun-antecedent agreement, and fused sentences. Never, however, have I removed or changed any word, phrase, or expression of a dialectal nature. Always I have striven to retain the distinctive tone of the author's voice.

Finally, however, in an effort to keep her voice strong as well as distinctive, I omitted passages from the original in four chapters. In chapter 15, I omitted botanical names of varieties of cactus because attempts to verify without question the types grown by the author failed, leaving little to interest the reader, whether the curiosity be general or technical in nature. In chapter 21, I shortened passages expressing the grief of the author over the death of her daughter, Bessie Bird, believing what is included communicates, if anything can, the depth of that grief. Finally, in chapters 23 and 24, I omitted narrative accounts of the author's day-by-day experiences on trips to New Mexico and California because the material merely was a travelogue, undistinguished by the author's typical style and memorable observations. Otherwise, the author's text remains intact, bringing it into sharp contrast with the condensed version that might have appeared had the work been published during the author's lifetime.

Time, therefore, has done this work several favors. Because Dumont refused to allow severe cutting of her manuscript, readers will now experience the full story. In addition, the one hundred plus years between readers of the story and its beginnings enhance the story's value, a value not recognized in the late 1920s and 1930s. The events, the descriptions, and the expressions were not far enough removed in time to give the story the same fascination that it now holds for readers. A third favor brought by the passage of time appears in the new but firmly established audiences for this work today, such as people interested in women in literature and women in history, as well as young adult readers. Though failing to find the kind of publisher that she wanted brought great disappointment to Dumont during her lifetime, this publication of her memoirs in 1988 will ensure for the author's story the circulation and endurance it deserves.

Plaster models created by Ella Bird Dumont in a Christmas department store display, ca. 1924.

Ella Bird Dumont and Elgar ("Frenchie") Dumont in front of her home, ca. 1938. Mrs. Dumont would have been seventy-seven years of age and Elgar would have been thirty-eight.

A gyprock vase fashioned by Ella Bird Dumont.

ACKNOWLEDGMENTS

EDITING AND RESEARCHING an autobiographical manuscript almost sixty years old, one written largely about the nineteenth century, has required much collaboration. Ella Bird Dumont's narrative, interesting and unusual as it is, involves another story, which had to be added. The author created the background, the foundation for this new material; many people around the country have assisted me in creating the remainder of the story. The result presents a finished picture of "a time ever to be remembered," as the author emphasizes in Chapter 20.

In El Paso, Donna Gene Reardon worked in libraries and in my home office as a research assistant and typist over a period of twelve months. Much of what appears in the endnotes is a result of her meticulous research. In addition, Jon Davis produced the attractive map for the book, while he also initiated Donna Reardon and me into the world of the computer. Betty Davis provided helpful advice and support for her husband, Jon, for Donna Reardon, and for me in editing the manuscript, conducting the research, and producing the map. Roberta Walker edited and critiqued the preface, giving valuable suggestions about style.

In Paducah, Oma Dumont, now deceased, originally assisted and encouraged me in my Master's Thesis edition of the autobiography. During the revision and extension of that work, Oma Dumont's son, J. Verne Dumont, provided the original typed manuscript, pictures, letters, and family statistics. Extensive correspondence and telephone calls to and from Tom Long and Alma Gibson Long provided a wealth of historical data not available elsewhere. Furthermore, a trip to the original campsite of Tom and Ella Bird in King County was possible because of Tom Long's enthusiasm for the project. Grace Jones Piper, director of the Cottle County Library, conducted research for me and furnished special library sources. Mozelle and Clifford Killingsworth also supplied historical information and pictures, as well as transportation to the Bird campsite. Lottie Gibson told me stories about the author in the 1930s and 1940s. Jim Bob, Jo Ann, and Cody Bigham filled in gaps of information, and Ola May Crump provided resources on people of the area. Wayde Smith clarified ranch boundaries. Patsy and Walter Liedtke referred me to a source on knives. Finally, Patty Adams, editor of the *Paducah Post,* published announcements about the progress of the project.

Just south of Paducah in King County, Ralph, Sadie, and Stacy Mote conducted Tom Long, Clifford Killingsworth, and me to the exact location of the Bird campsite on the Masterson Ranch, while offering information about the area in recent years. In Guthrie, Jane Huey supplied additional historical and geographical data.

In Motley County, Harold H. Campbell provided information about the ranch brands and dates of operation of the Campbell Ranch southwest of Matador.

In Lubbock, Wilma Bigham and her son Bill Bigham supplied bits of information about the author as they had known her in Paducah, as well as stories about the era of the narrative.

In Canyon, at the Panhandle-Plains Historical Museum, Byron Price, director, encouraged me to edit the manuscript for publication. As an outside reader of the Master's Thesis edition, Price provided suggestions for specific sources to consult for scholarly information—a valuable assistance in updating my research. Richard Rattenbury, also of the museum, sent excellent photographs of Tom Bird's rifle in the museum, along with an article about the rifle. Claire Kuehn, librarian, cooperated in locating the Ella Bird Dumont collection of material, while Poppy and W. K. Hulsey of Tulia assisted me in my library research.

In Young County, Carol Thornton of Olney helped me to locate Barbara Ledbetter of Graham, who offered original, unpublished material concerning Fort Belknap.

In Central Texas, Ruth Stephens and Mary Pittard Thiele of San Antonio contacted relatives of the author and relatives of their own for historical material. June Bigham of Austin did special research for the project in the Texas State Archives. Gerald Baum of the Texas Water Development Board in Austin provided maps of King County that located Bird Creek, site of the original Bird settlement. Lawrence T. Jones, also of Austin, sent copies of a picture of Tom Bird as a young man in Blanco County; this is the only known photograph of the Texas Ranger and buffalo hunter.

Outside Texas, Glynese and Joe Floyd of Hobbs, New Mexico, assisted me in identifying various flora spoken of in the narrative.

Across the country, J. Bruce Voiles of Chattanooga, Tennessee, produced an article on I. Wilson knives, a subject difficult to research.

Finally, Emily Cutrer of Austin must be especially recognized for composing her elegant tribute to the author and to pioneer women. This foreword sets a tone of dignity for the author's story that follows.

Capp Bird, approximately twenty-two years of age, ca. 1903.

Bessie Adell Bird, known as "Baby" to her family, at approximately eighteen, ca. 1903.

Paducah's first string band (left to right): *Roddie Neff, Oran Kelley, J. M. ("Bud") Barron, Capp Bird, Eastman Campbell, and Charlie Crump (ca. 1905). Behind the musicians stands the gingerbread-trim house on 12th Street built by Sheriff Joe Gober in 1896 and bought by Bud Barron around 1900. Today the house is a Texas Historical Landmark at 1314 Easley in Paducah.*

Ella Bird Dumont and her son Elgar ("Frenchie"), at the approximate age of three, ca. 1903. The white baby dress is now a part of the Dumont collection of the Panhandle/Plains Historical Museum in Canyon, Texas. Mrs. Dumont was approximately forty-two years of age.

Ella and Auguste Dumont's first home in Paducah. In 1898, the family moved from the bottom floor of the Paducah jail into this house, built by Fred M. Campbell, county clerk. On this spot eighteen years later (1916), Mrs. Dumont built her two-story Victorian home. Today the modern home of J. Verne Dumont occupies the spot. Left to right: *Ella Dumont, Pearl Fessenden (Swint), Oma White (Woodley), Capp Bird, Elgar Dumont, and Auguste Dumont (ca. 1910).*

Ella Bird Dumont in front of her second home in Paducah, ca. 1930. Her manuscript was written in this house in 1927–1928.

Elgar ("Frenchie") Dumont, approximately age twenty, in the parlor of the Dumont home, ca. 1920. In the upper center stands a plaster statue of a woman, made by Mrs. Dumont. Flower arrangement on the right displays another of her avocations.

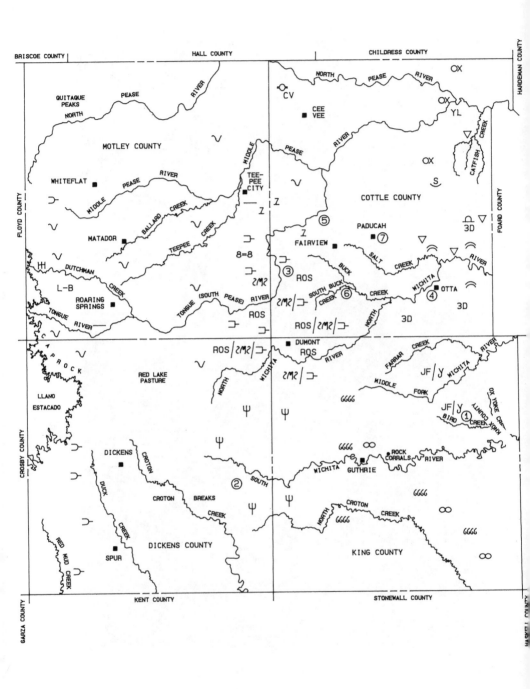

Homesites of Ella Elgar Bird Dumont, 1877–1943.

HOMESITES OF

ELLA ELGAR BIRD DUMONT

1877 – 1943

① BIRD CREEK CAMP 1877 – 1881
② PITCHFORK RANCH 1881 – 1882
③ ROSS RANCH 1882 – 1885
④ OTTA 1885 – 1886
⑤ TONGUE RIVER 1886 – 1889
⑥ SOUTH BUCK CREEK 1889 – 1895
⑦ PADUCAH 1895 – 1943

RANCHES

Z   BIRD RANCH 1956 –
L–B CAMPBELL RANCH 1891 – 1946
ⱈ   CAMPBELL RANCH 1901 –
CV CEE VEE RANCH ? – 1881
∞ EIGHT RANCH 1882 – 1900
ɢɢɢɢ FOUR SIX RANCH 1900 –
JF JF RANCH 1878 (?) – 1898
— JINGLE – BOB RANCH 1879 – 1881
⏝ McADAMS HAT RANCH 1898 – 1921
Ɣ   MASTERSON RANCH 1898 –
∿ MATADOR RANCH 1879 – 1951
-O- MILL IRON RANCH 1881 – 1916 (?)
⌒ MOON RANCH 1879 – 1925
OX OX RANCH 1882 – 1905
Ψ   PITCHFORK RANCH 1879 (?) –
S   PORTWOOD RANCH 1952 –
ROS ROSS RANCH 1879 –1885
8=8 SCAB EIGHT RANCH ? – 1898
Ɔ– SPUR RANCH 1878 –1907
ƧⱮƧ SWENSON RANCH 1907 – 1981
3D THREE D RANCH 1880 (?) – 1916
Ɔ⊣ TONGUE RIVER RANCH 1981 –
▽ TRIANGLE RANCH 1923 –
YL YL RANCH 1905 (?) – 1929

ELLA ELGAR BIRD DUMONT
An Autobiography of a West Texas Pioneer

ELLA ELGAR BIRD DUMONT
An Autobiography of a West Texas Pioneer

One

I WAS BORN in Lee County, Mississippi, near Guntown in 1861.[1] My father's name was Lewis Steptoe Elgar. He died during the Civil War when I was but a little babe eleven months old. He took sick at Corinth, Mississippi,[2] where the soldiers were stationed. Some battles were being fought at that place about 1861. They could hear the cannons roaring from where we were at Guntown. My father's illness was camp fever,[3] I believe. They sent him home, and he died soon after. My mother told me of his death in after years. When his brother sat by his bedside in his last hours, my father requested him to sing "The Dying Californian" of which he did. I don't know if the song is in print now, but it goes something like this:

> Lie up nearer, brother, nearer,
> For my limbs are growing cold,
> And thy presence seemeth nearer,
> When thine arms around me fold.

> I am dying, brother, dying,
> Soon you'll miss me in your berth,
> And my form will soon be lying
> 'Neath the ocean's briny surf.[4]

I think my father must have been a good man, as my mother said she felt at that time she would rather have seen all her children lying corpses before her than he. My father was not an officer in the army. He was a member of the Missionary Baptist Church[5] and was clerk of the church at the time of his death. He was a blond man. He was a farmer and a mechanic, and he also played the violin beautifully, so they told me. He left a large chest of tools and his violin, of which Mother kept up to my early remembrance, as well as a photo. I still have his hammer. It is priceless, of course, and it has some history to it, too. It was given him by his father who made it in his blacksmith shop when his father was a young man.[6]

My mother[7] was a woman weighing about one hundred and thirty-five pounds, slightly heavy, not quite as tall as her mother. She had brown wavy hair and very expressive brown eyes. She was the kindest and most sympathetic of women.

I had one sister five years older than I.[8] We were the only children. My mother, who was yet only about twenty-six or twenty-seven years old, re-married to Thomas Buckle White from New York. I think I was about three years old then. We sold our home and everything and moved to Memphis, Tennessee, where my stepfather's business was mostly jewelry repairing. He also was a mechanic. I do not remember how he looked, only that he had dark hair and eyes. He died of congestive chill.[9] He passed away with the third chill. He only lived two years after his and Mother's marriage. She did not know anything of his relatives as he never kept in touch with them, his mother having died while he was yet at home, and he had a stepmother. He is buried at Memphis, Tennessee. Two children had been born to my mother and Thomas White, two boys, the youngest born two months after his father's death.

We were broken up financially, as many people were, when the war closed. We were left all alone in the city where cholera and yellow fever were raging at their highest at that time, where death and desolation went hand in hand. Hundreds of people or bodies were being buried every day in vats of pure lime in an effort to stamp out the disease. Some boats came in, or rather drifted in, with only dead people on them.

My poor mother wept most all the time. What should we do? She was unable physically to care for her little children. There was to be another baby soon. But it seems there is always a way out somewhere, and with us assistance was nearer at hand than we knew of. My grandmother[10] was a noble whole-souled, generous, good-hearted woman, God bless her. As soon as she heard of our plight, she hastened at once to send my Uncle Charles[11] after us to come back to her in Mississippi. She was also a widow with several children, grandfather having died three years before the war. But she was a shrewd, businesslike woman, industrious, and of great ability in transaction of business. She was a woman of medium size, slightly tall but well proportioned. She weighed about one hundred and thirty pounds, was rather fair complected, and had light hair and gray eyes. She kept up in style when she was younger, wearing the styles of that day and time so my mother told me, but from my first remembrance of her she never seemed to care much for style, after so much responsibility rested on her I suppose. She wanted only plain good substantial clothes. I always thought she looked good and so businesslike in those, too. Truly she was strictly businesslike, yet she was sympathetic and loved her children. She was noted for her fair and square dealing.

I was then five years old. We lived there near her for three years.[12] The little babe came and grew off nicely. Sister Lucy and I named him Lewis for our father. The other little brother was named for his father, Thomas. We were living there very quietly and contented when several of the neighbors began to talk of moving to faraway Texas. One after another would decide to go, and finally all our folks took the Texas fever too. So the move was soon settled on, and everybody was getting busy selling out and preparing for the long journey. On the first of September, all was in readiness, and we hit the road for Texas.

A train of eight wagons all with ox teams, except for a Mr. and Mrs. Walker's buggy with a horse team, was two months on the road, eight hundred miles. A few cattle were driven behind wagons. We had a dim road most of the way. Sometimes it would fade out and would be hard to follow. We followed the old McKinsey Trail a good part of the way.[13] The men and boys kept us in wild meats most all the time. But, oh, the trip was worthwhile. I think everyone enjoyed it, so many young people in the crowd too. They could meet at any of the camps and have real little entertainments every night or two if they chose. There was also a preacher in the bunch named Herrin. He was a good man and had been our neighbor in Mississippi. He was a missionary Baptist. Sometimes we would have church at night in some pretty grove of trees with logs to sit on for benches mostly, as the older ones would corner the chairs.

And the younger bunch of children, to which I belonged, I think we had the best time of any. The wagons moved so slowly along with ox teams, we had all the time to walk and play on the way. So many kinds of wild fruits and nuts, and so many strange things to see. I think we simply combed the country on either side of the wagons all the way from Mississippi to Texas. We had to cross the rivers on the big steamboats and ferryboats which was wonderful to me. There was much wild game on the way. The boys would often go hunting at night bringing in wild turkeys, opossums, and other wild game.

But amid all the pleasures, something serious and sad must happen. Our cousin, Clark Price, got shot. A large flock of geese were flying overhead. He made a rush for his shotgun and was pulling it out back of the wagon, muzzle foremost, when it was discharged, striking him in the breast and ranging back under the shoulder. It was a very serious wound. He had to be left behind which brought sadness to us all. We had just crossed Red River at Helena, Arkansas.[14] That is where we left him with a doctor. As it happened, his sweetheart was in the crowd, and I shall never forget how she cried when we left him. We heard from him several times before we reached our destination. He recovered very rapidly and was soon able to travel, but went south to his other relatives in Burleson County,[15] and we did not see him again for nearly two years afterwards. He and the girl (Suda), who cried so when we left him at Helena, did not marry. They seemed to have forgotten each other to some extent, as it had been so long since they had seen each other.

We were now in the piney woods of Arkansas. As these were the first pine trees we children had ever seen, this is where we got in the biggest scrape yet. We made a rush for the pine rosin. We gathered it by the hands full, rolled it into balls larger than eggs and chewed it. We had it on our clothes and in our hair. Then we carried it into the wagons where we had the bed clothing and everything stuck up with it till our mothers threatened to throw us out, pine rosin and all. We could hardly eat for a week, so much was on our teeth so bad, and it tasted so bitter.

We stopped two or three days in Arkansas and had church in a beautiful pine grove where some of the folks had relatives near. We surely did enjoy this visit in the woods. This is where quite a little romance sprang up between my Aunt Julia and a young man living there, Mr. Sid Smith. They surely did fall for each other in this little time, and it did not end there as most such cases do. It was the beginning of a long correspondence. She wrote a diary of her trip from Mississippi to Texas, and the description of this boy was something sublime and divine.[16] Later on he moved to Texas with his folks. Then the case became more serious. They were together quite a bit, and as the old saying goes, "Intimacy breeds contempt." They soon had a bust-up. She married another man and thus the romance ended. Two other cases developed on the way. One of them married as soon as we arrived, but the other one failed.

We had now gotten over the Texas line and were coming on west of Coffman Town through Grand Prairie.[17] That was the first prairie, the first mule-eared rabbit, and the first norther I had ever seen or felt. From some cause I had gotten behind all the wagons and was gathering sunflower wax I believe, which was also new to me, when all of a sudden the wind rose and began to blow colder and higher every minute. It was a real norther, cold as blizzards, and what do you think? Every one of those old Mississippi steers threw up their heads, sniffed the air, and struck out in a long lope. I could not imagine what in the world was the matter. Those covered wagons were simply flying, and you must know I made tracks in pursuit of them, too. Down the road I went at racehorse gait. All of a sudden I came to a dead halt. What was it? A large mule-eared rabbit ran across the road between me and the wagons. The long-legged animal, with the big long red-looking ears that glistened in the sunshine, almost frightened me to death. Would those crazy old oxen never stop running? I made another break for the wagons, almost outrunning my shadow in overtaking them, and mind you I was never left again.

We finally arrived in Johnson County, Texas, in November, 1867.[18] This was a wild western country where we all disbanded, each family going their way in search of places to settle. I was six years old. I shall never forget my first impression of the soil in Texas. It had been raining and the soil was black and sticky. I was slightly sick when we arrived. The older children were soon out of the wagons examining and experimenting with this black claylike mud, trying to form toys of it and so on. After watching them a few minutes, I began to feel better, so I soon got out of the wagon and joined them in their work. It was the most fascinating of anything I had ever found. Some of the other children said, "Look at Ella, she is beating us all." Another said, "Look what a pretty doll she has made and that pretty horse." Sister Lucy said she wanted that little cat I was making then. This was the beginning of what my life career should have been, clay modeling, first step to sculpturing.

Two

THERE WERE but few settlers in the country at that time. And Indians, oh, horrors! We expected to be massacred at any time.[1] Men wore guns in the fields at all times. They worked ox teams, as the Indians would steal the horses.

We settled there, renting land on the Robinson plantation fifteen miles southeast of Weatherford,[2] and oh, the hard times we had for the next few years with no money in the country. When Grandmother sold out in Mississippi, she had only eight hundred dollars to start with to Texas, and, of course, that would not last long for two families.

When Christmas came on, we children were sad. We knew there would be no good time for us. Now Sister Lucy was always quite clever, so when Christmas Eve came, she sat up until we younger ones were in bed and asleep. Then she got busy making up a good lot of tea cake dough,[3] and of all the fancy things she did cut out and bake of this dough were simply wonderful. There were many fancy flower designs, animals, and dolls with long legs and arms. All the little holey stockings were hanging around the fireplace, of course, so she filled every one of those stockings to their fullest capacity with those cakes. Then she made some marks on the back of the fireplace to show where Santa Claus came down. The next morning just before good daylight, I was the first to wake up. I groped my way through the darkness to make a fire. I could see all those stockings were full. I was so thrilled I could not keep still. There was something sticking out through a hole in one of the stockings, a leg or an arm, I did not know what. I reached over, broke it off, and ate it. My, it was delicious. By this time the other children began to wake up. Then the riot began, everyone grabbing for their stockings. Sister Lucy was surprised and thrilled as much as any of us, of course. Someone said, "Yes, look where Santa Claus came down the chimney." We knew he had been there. Presently someone discovered they had a doll that was minus one leg. They hunted everywhere but failed to find it. I was meek as a mouse, and no one ever knew where it went.

Our wise, good-hearted grandmother kept us ever near her and managed our affairs as she did her own. We were all as one family. I was then seven years old.[4] There were four of us little children then, and our poor mother had to work so hard to support us. My Uncle George Benson, Mother's oldest brother, taught school that year, which gave us some advantage in that line. He left us when the school was over and joined a party driving a herd of horses to Kansas. We never heard of him again from that day till this. We thought he may have been killed by the Indians, but, of course, we will never know.

Sister Lucy was good at many things. She was a natural genius. She was almost a natural nurse, too. She seemed to be able to ease pain when others failed, and she never stopped trying. She and Brother Lewis were the nurses of all the relatives. Brother Lewis, our baby brother, followed nursing from a very small boy, first with the connection and later as a profession. He was not a trained nurse, but he was an experienced one. In later years about all the doctors in Paducah[5] recommended him. They said they would rather have him than any trained nurse.[6]

My mother was an educated woman of much natural refinement, very reserved, and timid. She had never known want or responsibility before, Grandfather having been in the mercantile business all during her raising up. She had never had to work. She was the oldest child and a favorite of her father's. She was petted and made over by him and waited on by the Negro slaves. He never denied her anything. Even up to my first remembrance, she still had bolts of fine ribbons, beautiful cream silk lace bonnets, and some very handsome dresses. To have been reduced to such extreme poverty and want as we were then must have been very trying on a nature so sensitive as hers.

My grandmother's family was mostly girls, there being only one little boy at home, so most of the farm work depended on the girls, except the plowing by hired help. Money was an object extremely hard to get, requiring much labor and energy for a meager amount of pay. Grandmother was thrifty and no doubt did much thinking. Otherwise, we could never have gotten along.

She had a talk with my mother and presented a plan, or proposition, of which my mother hesitated some time before accepting. It was that Mother go out with some of the neighbors who were in need of help, and do work in the home to earn something, be it ever so little, to help tide us over until the crop came in. Now a position of this kind must have been very humiliating to our poor proud mother, but she was willing to do anything that was honorable to save her little children from hunger and want. So the position was arranged by grandmother with a family by the name of Keeze about three-quarters of a mile from us. They were nice people—an old couple, a daughter, a son-in-law, and baby. There was much work to do. Fortunately, Mother's health was always good. Otherwise, she could not have held up as she did. But she was faithful and true, and what would you judge her salary to be? Only $1.00 per week. However, those people became very much attached to our mother and proved some of our best friends in later years. She was as one of the family and not a hireling. They seemed to understand she was not born to a life of this kind. She was always invited same as a guest to everything in the home and often went with them to other places.

But the most pathetic of all were her lonely little children at home. She could only come home on weekends late on Saturday afternoon. We little ones always looked forward to her coming home as that of a ministering angel, or almost as the coming of Christ. When Saturdays came, we could think of nothing but Mother, and could hardly wait for the hour to come when we could run to meet her. A low rail fence crossed the narrow path about halfway to the place where she stayed. The high sage grass covered the entire prairie between this fence and our home with only a narrow path through it. This grass came nearly up to our shoulders, but by close watching we could see our mother when she crossed through the gap in this fence. Then the excitement arose. Today there is a picture stamped on my memory so vividly that it seems only yesterday that this happened. This picture must have been heartrendering to our poor mother. There was a group of four little ragged, tousled-haired children making a wild rush for the little path that led through the high grass, to meet their mother, running, laughing, shouting, crying, "Mother, Mother." On and on we went, Sister Lucy with Baby Lewis bringing up the rear, each one trying to reach her first. And soon the joyful meeting took place, everyone trying to get hold and love her at the same time. On Sunday afternoons when she returned to those people, she usually slipped away from us younger children when she could, knowing how we would cry. Sister Lucy told me in after years that she always went away crying. We lived close to our grandmother, and one of our aunts, Martha,[7] stayed with us at night.

We had been there but a short time when the Indians made a raid[8] and killed two men at Veal's Station,[9] six miles from us. We lived there one year, then moved twenty miles down near Alvarado[10] at Chambers Mill, one mile from town where we children went to school. Our teachers' names were Mr. and Miss Yager. My mother having made some very close friends with the Chambers family, Grandmother ventured to leave us with them and move over to the League.[11] She took up land there six miles east of Alvarado.

This was another place that attracted my attention to modeling in clay. We lived in a woodsy place by a small running stream where we children spent some of our happiest days. We almost lived on this shady creek from morning till night. My oldest brother and I would catch fish in the following way. I would put one of my dresses on him. He and I would seine the fish from the small water holes with our skirts, and of all the fun, we had it. But besides this I had a private industry of my own. There was a spring near the house from which we carried water. The banks of this spring were pure pipe clay in which I worked a great deal. I had my playhouse out in a thick shady place, and I claim it was elaborately furnished, and all with clay toys of every description. Mother would often take her visitors out to see my playhouse.

Alvarado was a wild western town at that time, visited by outlaws and two desperadoes, Bickerstaff and Thompson.[12] They took the town while we were there. They surely did paint it red. They shot up the town, housed all the people, paraded the street, and robbed several of the stores. A murder was also committed soon afterward. Shelf Purdum, a young merchant and only son of his widowed mother, was shot through the head while sleeping in the window. No trace was ever found of the murderer, or any cause for it.[13]

Fort Worth, which was fourteen miles from us, was on a boom at that time. The first railroad was coming there. The Chambers were moving their mill and going to that place. Mrs. Chambers, who had been so good to us, was like a real sister to my mother. She persuaded her to go with them for a short time to help them get straightened up in their new home. So my mother was in Fort Worth when the first train came to that place.[14]

Our Aunt Martha, my youngest aunt, came and stayed with us while she was gone. Grandmother had decided to move again. We only stayed at that place a short while before moving on west to Parker County,[15] where Indians were more plentiful than ever.

Another uncle came to us at this place, my mother's second brother, Uncle Charles Benson[16] from Burleson County. He had come to Texas a few months earlier than we had. He studied law some months at Alvarado. While here, he also taught school of which we had the benefit.

The Indians made many raids and killed lots of people.[17] They killed a preacher and his family in 1868 who were on their way to church four miles from us. A neighbor who attended the funeral gave me a blue silk rosette that the young lady who was killed wore in her hair. I kept it as something very sacred for a long time, but childlike lost it some way.

Sister Lucy married a boy twenty-one years old by the name of Willie Fite. He was a nice, good, moral boy, a member of the church. The wedding took place about two years after we moved to Parker County. His people were neighbors of ours. They were a nice family of people, had only two boys. They lived in a beautiful grove of elm trees near the river. Sister Lucy and Aunt Martha were both young ladies at that time, both nice looking. Sister Lucy was considered the belle of Parker County. Of course, it was thinly settled. She was a perfect blond with large perfect blue eyes and a beautiful complexion. There was not much celebration at their wedding, but it was just a quiet home affair with only relatives and a few special friends. The tables were heavy laden with many good things to eat. Sister's wedding dress was of white swiss, with only a wide blue ribbon for a sash. She wore a beautiful pearl strand of beads. Willie Fite, the boy she married, was nicely groomed. He wore a black broadcloth suit. A very respectable brother-in-law so I thought, and nobody had better say he was not handsome. He is still living today with his youngest son [L. E. Fite] in San Antonio. Willie Fite is eighty-six years old, and is hale and hearty.

I wrote to Willie Fite a short time ago, and just to please him I asked him if his mind ever reverted back to the long ago when we all lived in old Young County. I asked him if he remembered a pecan hunt that he, Sister

Lucy, Aunt Martha, Uncle Truman, and I had taken up on Clear Fork. What a jolly time we had. Got lots of pecans, fished, and hunted.

One night we all had a job each. The dog treed a possum a few steps from the camp. Uncle Truman and I went out and got it. Willie had to clean the big fish, Sister Lucy dressed the big turkey gobbler, and Uncle Truman dressed the possum. Of all the times he had! First he scalded and scraped it, and then he rolled it in the hot ashes. Then he scraped it again until it looked like a little Negro baby. We had the laugh on him. Brother Willie still remembered all of this and enjoyed hearing it over again. I was glad I recalled it to his mind. We got our wagon about two-thirds full of pecans and rolled it home pretty well satisfied.

The country soon began to settle up and the Indians made but few more raids there, though there was one raid in which they stole all the horses in the settlement, killed one of my Uncle Willie Barnett's best horses and left the arrow in him. They killed him because he wore a bell. It made too much noise.

We moved west to Young County [18] in 1873, where my people settled for the last time. They left me in Parker County to go to school. I was then beginning to emerge into the important age of a fourteen-year-old girl.[19] I followed on after the folks when the school was out.

My grandmother's girls had all married off leaving her with her youngest son, Uncle Andy, three years older than I. She was very lonely and insisted that Mother let me live with her. It was agreed on. My mother, after living a widow eight years, had married again to Mr. J. N. Bellamy and was living near. The Tonkaway Indian Reservation was then open for settlers, giving each family one-hundred and sixty acres of land.[20] It was there my people took up their abode, several families of them. The Indians only made a few raids after we moved there. The people were more prepared for them then. They built their stables adjoining the houses with long pickets as high as the house and with padlocks on the doors. They kept the horses in those at night. This was the first place we could feel any peace of mind or safety from Indians since we first arrived in Texas.

Three

THE COUNTRY soon settled up. There were schools and churches and everything like real civilization. Mrs. M. H. Neff taught our first school in a little log cabin up by the hillside. We had hewed logs for seats. Later we were able to build a school and church house of real lumber. A box house loomed up perfectly magnificent as all others were of logs. Mrs. Neff also taught in this house. Mr. Pierce taught our third term here which was the last school I went to.[1]

I was beginning to feel myself some young lady by this time. The ripe age of fifteen was customary for boy company, but my grandmother did not think as I did, so I had to go slow. However, they would bob up on the sly in spite of all, but no serious cases developed. I was yet quite kiddish, of course, and liked my fun, and tomboy ways. I had my quail traps all around the place. I caught quails by the hundred. We ate them until we did not care for them at all and gave many to the neighbors. But my grandmother wanted them caught out of her garden and field, for there were many. So it was only fun and picking for me. My traps were rather a patent of my own. They were something on the turkey pen order without triggers.[2] I would often catch fifteen or twenty at one time. I built up quite a reputation for myself as a bird trapper. You must know I felt quite important, too, when some of the neighbor boys came and asked for my plan of quail trap. With much credit to myself, I proceeded to tell them in a very professional way just how it was done. So we soon thinned out the birds.

My only sister lived just one mile over the prairie hill from us. I visited her quite often. We were real pals and one day she came over and told us a cousin of her husband's had come to visit them. His name was Tom Bird.[3] They had never seen him before. He was from southern Texas, Blanco County.[4] She seemed quite favorably impressed with him. I think she was rather proud of the relationship. In fact, she said he seemed a real splendid young man. He had been three or four days with them. She gave us quite a little sketch of his life, of which her husband had known something before.

He was a fine conversationalist, very jolly, quite witty, and of wonderful personality. He was twenty-nine years old. He was reared on the frontier border of South Texas. He had fought Indians many times before the Texas Ranger Company was organized there.[5] He had with him a fine Winchester rifle of the latest model of that time, which was awarded him by the Thirteenth Legislature in 1873 for an Indian fight. It had a silver shield on it on which his name was engraved with the date of presentation. There were thirty-seven Indians and ten boys. They killed all the Indians but ten which escaped. They did not lose a man, so each of the ten boys received a gun.[6] Later he belonged to the Ranger Company D stationed at Menardville.[7] I believe he also served in another Company B farther up the line until he resigned and came to North Texas, Young County, where we lived at that time.[8]

Sister said her husband had told her about his father, Joseph Bird, who was a captain during the Civil War, who was county judge four years for two or three terms at Johnson City, and who had been a preacher ever since he was a young man. Bird Town in Blanco County took its name for him, where he lived for forty years.[9]

The Birds had moved to Texas sometime before the Civil War. Tom was about twelve years old when they came to Texas.[10] They never lived in Johnson County. They moved from Arkansas to Blanco County, Texas. That was also a wild country at that time, visited by Indians quite often. Mr. Bird later told me of many raids and fights they had with them. One time there were sixteen women forted up in one house. That was during the Civil War. A squad of Indians came along. The women became frightened and broke out to run to another house. The Indians saw there were no men so they simply massacred every one of them but one. They scalped her and left her for dead. Her name was Mrs. Crownover. She got up and crawled and drug herself to another neighbor's. She got well, and Tom said he saw her many times afterward. The Indians also killed a couple of their nearest neighbors, a man and wife by the name of White. They were down on a little creek fishing. They fought the Indians with sticks and chunks till the Indians killed them. They lived with his mother. They had two children. When their mother heard the fight, she took the children, ran out, and hid in the wheat.

There were many raids by the Indians in that country until the boys finally formed a club, laid traps for the Indians, and had runners to spread the news. This country is very rough and mountainous. Only parts of it on the west were passable at that time. The Packsaddle Mountain was one passway by which the Indians could get to that settlement. Those boys laid a trap on this mountain one night for the Indians, stationed themselves in three bunches, one at the entrance, one in the center, and one at the rear. When the Indians reached the center, this bunch was to give the alarm. Then they would all close in on them from both ways. Now there was one little white-headed boy at the entrance who was very nervous and excitable. They knew the Indians were in and would soon reach this mountain, and all was ready for them. So the Indians came in due time and just as they were passing the entrance, this cowardly little fellow rose up and began to yell. So the Indians whirled around and went back by them under whip. Tom said they were all so disgusted that they felt like wringing his neck. They discharged him from their club. At any rate this gave the Indians such a scare, they never bothered but little more in that settlement.

Now if this description of a young man's life should fail to arouse the curiosity of a fifteen-year-old girl, it was not me. Of course, I didn't pretend I was paying much attention to it, but I surely had some curiosity to see this Bird. As it happened in a day or two, Grandmother sent me over to sister's on an errand of some kind, but the Bird had gone to town. It was Christmas time. A light snow was on the ground. I think they had sent him for some Santa Claus.

I was just getting ready to return home when all at once I heard someone call out, "Christmas gift." My brother-in-law, Willie Fite, opened the door, and there I beheld mounted on the most beautiful large black horse I had ever seen, a man, yes, a man in full western costume, that of a Texas Ranger, gallant, and brave in appearance. He alighted and came in. Soon I was introduced to him. He removed his hat and bowed to me most gracefully as if I had been some young queen. I was quite bashful and timid but managed to return the salutation. Of course, I was yet but a kid and felt myself rather insignificant, for he was a real grown-up man and decidedly handsome. He had dark brown eyes that fairly sparkled with wit and humor, and the most beautiful dark brown waving hair that glistened like silk. He was of medium height and well-proportioned. Being related to my folks, he addressed me with all ease and cordiality and seemed a bit interested or inclined to talk to me.

I only tarried a short time after his arrival till I was on my way back home again thinking of some plans I had before I left. First, I was going to try my hand or rather my feet at skating on a little lake nearby the house. Then I had promised my little cousin Dolly that I would make her the cutest kind of a rag doll with real hair and rosy cheeks. Then we were going to make a little house for the old cat and the little kittens, on which my grandmother had already pronounced sentence. They were to be driven out on short order, so, of course, my sympathies were with the cats.

The next three or four days passed over without any special events, but once in awhile my thoughts would revert back to the meeting of Mr. Bird. I wondered secretly if he would ever happen over to our house. No, of course not. How in the globe would he ever frame up any excuse to come over to my grandmother's? Absurd to think of unless a mere accident, so I gave it no more thought.

The next day was Sunday. My Aunt Fannie and little cousins were visiting us for a few days. The snow was yet on the ground and snow birds were plentiful, so I proceeded to look around for a right good plank to make a deadfall, and soon had it in operation.[11] I parked myself just inside the barn door with the deadfall and string outside. I was catching birds by the wholesale, when all at once I happened to look across the prairie on the hill toward my sister's. I saw two men coming walking. I recognized them both at a glance. It was no other than my brother-in-law and the distinguished Mr. Bird. Well, I dropped that string and out the door I went, over deadfall, birds, and all. I hit a beeline for the house, and the whirl of snow that rose up around me as I went was amazing.

The room and everything was in order except myself, for I had not straightened up a bit for Sunday. I made a dash here and there for different things. My aunt said, "Ella, what in the world is the matter with you? You are in such a hurry." I told her I just then thought about it being Sunday. On Sundays we wore pretty much the same as on weekdays with the exception that we always cleaned up for Sunday, though we always kept some nice clothes for special occasion wear, which Mr. Bird later called our "trotting harness." On I went, bathed, combed my hair, powdered my face, dressed, put on my little red sacque,[12] and in less than fifteen minutes, I was sitting back as modest and prim as most any young lady you would meet when the company arrived. I greeted them with a bit of interest, but I was very sedate. Of course, I was tickled to death, but would not have had anyone know it for a million dollars.

It was the middle of the afternoon when they came. They stayed and had supper with us and sat till bedtime. The Mr. Bird was quite talkative, very interesting, and entertaining in a general way. He also talked to me quite a bit. I got pretty well acquainted with him. He was also, I thought, of wonderful personality. He seemed to have a way of leading you into a conversation no matter how bashful or timid you were. I sized him up rather shyly, thinking to myself, "I have caught many birds, but you are about the largest one that has yet crossed my pathway. I might catch you." He seemed to like that part of the country and had decided to remain with his cousin the rest of the winter. Then his plans were to join the Rangers again. The Company A under the supervision and command of Lieutenant Campbell was then stationed near Fort Griffin, forty miles from that place.[13]

The next Sunday my Uncle Andy and I went to church at Goose Neck Bend, as we often did. We rode horseback always, as that was the custom at that day and time. We had to pass near my sister's and usually went by for my brother-in-law. He often went with us, but this time I ordered we should go straight on and let Mr. Willie Fite get to church the best he could. My uncle did not seem to understand what the big idea was, neither did I explain, so he said, "No, we will go by." And by he went. Of course, I had to follow, but very sullenly.

They were both about ready when we arrived. They were soon mounted, and in the twinkling of an eye, the Mr. Bird reined this stunning black horse along by the side of mine and asked the pleasure of my company. Of course, he could not have done otherwise and been very gallant, as seemingly I had gone by especially for him. However, I enjoyed the day very much. He was good company and very interesting, so gentlemanly and respectful. I learned he was a member of the church with all reverence to the Christian faith. He told me his father was a minister of the gospel. I was proud of him as we marched up to the church. My, how grown-up and important I felt.

My brother-in-law and uncle rode on ahead and made fun for us all the way around. My brother-in-law was a perfect mimic. He rode a little mule and of all the antics. There were many cotton-tail rabbits on the way. He would talk about those "cotton-eared" rabbits, as he was too modest and precise to say "cotton-tail" before us, which made it the more ridiculous.

As time went on, it is needless to say, our Mr. Bird made many visits to my grandmother's. He had no trouble to find excuses. A few days later my uncle and I went to a dance at Mr. Bunger's across the river about three miles.[14] When we had an invitation to one of those big ranch dance and suppers, then we donned the swellest rig we had. We had to match up with those Ft. Worth visitors. When we stepped out in our smartest rig, you would hardly have recognized us as from the camps.

Soon after our arrival who should walk in but Mr. Bird. He was always jolly and noted for his ready wit. He was a welcome visitor in any crowd. The dance was well under way but had taken a lull. Just then, so it happened, Mr. Bird picked up the violin and began playing his favorite, he said. This was the first time I had known he was a violinist. I was very much pleased for he made good music, though he did not play for the dancing. He and I were in rather a deep conversation later on, and he asked if I would grant him the privilege of paying his respects to me. I was rather surprised, yet felt complimented, and, of course, answered in the affirmative. He thanked me very nicely. The dance went on. Everybody was jolly and happy. Many times I was invited and joined them in tripping the light fantastic. This was the last dance we attended for some time, as warm weather was coming on and big meetings beginning.[15]

Mr. Bird had begun talking of going to Fort Griffin right soon to join the Rangers. On Saturday we went to South Bend Church, where the big oil field[16] now is and where two of my uncles owned land as homesteads at that time which is now worth millions of dollars. We returned home early that afternoon. Mr. Bird was usually very talkative and interesting with so many brilliant ideas, I thought, but this time from some cause he had become somewhat serious and sentimental, rather bordering on love affairs.

He asked me which I thought was proper, for the girl or the young man to acknowledge their love first. I told him I had never given the matter a thought, but to be sure I thought the man should declare himself first. He disagreed with me and said it was the girl's place. We talked quite a while longer. He said he wanted me to think seriously over this matter till tomorrow as he might ask me a question of this kind. He said he had flirted with many girls, but now to come down to brass tacks and nails, he wanted to settle down, and for me to consider everything, and most especially poverty. Thinks I to myself, "I'm getting into something more serious than the pine rosin in Arkansas. I am no hard-shell, but it seems what is to be is about to happen." However, I soon changed my line of silly thought and began to study most seriously over this matter. I wanted to cry.

That night was a sleepless one for me. Oh, what was I getting into? Did I love him? I did not know. Tears would flow, my pillow was wet, I could not decide. I wanted to go to school some more. I knew I was too young, but I did not think he would wait. He was soon to leave for the Ranger Company. The next day was Sunday and we went to Church at Goose Neck Bend across the river. He did not broach the subject of the evening before until we were nearly home. Then he said in a very simple commonplace way, "Miss Ella, do you love me?"

After some stammering and blushing I managed to say, "I guess I will have to acknowledge the corn."

"That is you do," he said.

"Yes," came very faintly. I thought, "My souls, what is coming next, and how in the world will he say it?"

But it came clear and simple as the above question, "Will you be mine?"

There was no way of shying around this, so I said in the same like manner, "I will."

He removed his hat, thanked me in the most appreciative way, and said I had made him very happy and that he was already a better man. We were nearing home. Then as we alighted at the gate, he was telling me how he had loved me, and henceforth it would be Ella and Tom to look out for and no one else. He said that he would fight for me till he died, dead as a hammer. This latter sentence was one of the strongest phrases of western lovemaking.

I did not see him again until he came to bid me goodbye. He was to leave the next day. We talked for some time. He insisted I should set the date for our marriage, but, oh, this was too much for me. I was so embarrassed I felt an inclination to run but was determined not to show the white feather at the last moment, so we both managed together to set the date as the tenth of October, 1876.[17] He asked if I would write him often. I agreed to do so. He said he had something for me, so he placed on my finger the most beautiful gold band ring with floral decorations and with his initials inside. My, how proud I was of it. He asked me to kiss him good-bye, but I said, "No, never." That was against my religion and my grandmother's teaching. So he had to abide by the consequences, and with only a hearty handshake, he was gone.

I sat for some time in silent meditation thinking, "Oh, what have I done? Am I betrothed? Yes, most assuredly. I have taken refuge under the hallowed wing of the largest bird in Young County."

Four

SOME TEN DAYS or two weeks had elapsed when the long-looked-for letter arrived. I shall never forget. I stole away secretly down on the little branch nearby, and there under the hackberry tree I read my first real love letter. In my estimation it was perfectly sublime and poetical. Possibly I may have read some things between the lines, but it was keen no doubt because I knew it was. He stated he might be able to visit me in two or three weeks, but only [for] a couple of days perhaps as they were soon to go on a scout over in New Mexico.

The days and weeks passed slowly with nothing special to mention, and the appointed time for his visit was near at hand. It was Sunday afternoon. My chum, Ellen Buse, had spent the night with me. She and her beau, Bob Cunningham, and several other young folks were there. We had all made up a trip down to the Graham Boys to get watermelons. The jolly crowd were all just settled in a wagon ready to start when who should ride up but Mr. Bird. He came up smiling, waving us a salute. I thought he was more handsome than ever. With one accord all were welcoming him and giving him an invitation to join the merry crowd. He accepted, of course, on condition that Miss Ella would come and sit on the backseat with him. I hardly could see how it would be done without being teased by this unmerciful, unscrupulous bunch. However, it took only about two minutes till they had me shuffled to the back seat, and all went merrily along. The watermelon trip was a success. All seemed to enjoy it immensely.

A big meeting was going on at Graham,[1] and the next night Mr. Bird and I and Sister Lucy and her husband went, as that was his last day with us. It rained on us coming home. We were all perfectly drenched to the skin, our horses slipping and sliding till we liked to have never gotten home, and of all the "wet rats" when we did get there. I spent the night with Sister, and such a rustling of dry clothes we had. She sent Willie in the other room with his cousin [Tom Bird] to sort out a dry rig for each of them. The lights were poor, and in some way he made a mistake in getting his cousin rigged out properly. One garment did not belong to the male attire at all, but neither of them knew the difference at that time. The next morning Mr. Bird was making a fire outdoors to dry out the wet clothing and was stooping over when Sister came along slightly looking him over. She discovered the mistake and intrusion on her own wardrobe. She rushed back in the house and told us the joke. We were all simply convulsed with laughter and all at the poor innocent cousin's expense. I cautioned them very earnestly. If either of them cheeped it before he left, I would thrash them both. Had they done so, I would simply have died of embarrassment when he came back again.

Laying all modesty aside, I will say that the article of clothing was a plain pair of domestic drawers given my sister by her invalid mother-in-law. She had never worn them. They were made on the airy construction, that is, only a narrow waist band holding the two sections together. We heard him say as he was putting them on, "These must be cut like some of mine." I supposed he meant some of his that were torn from stem to gudgeon.[2] Well, at any rate, the next day while riding along at a pert gait to meet his Ranger boy friends at another station, all at once he felt something give away in the back. It was no other than this narrow waist band that had torn in two, leaving each section to go its own way. Presently he happened to look down and behold something white that was slipping down, so he deliberately dismounted and pulled out each section of this garment over the top of his boots. He then mounted his horse again and went his way rejoicing.

The next time Mr. Bird visited us, Sister was not at home, and the first thing that Willie did was to assail him with the joke. He demanded to know what Mr. Bird had done with the old lady's clothes. The latter denied it at first, but when he found that we all knew it, he rolled over on the bed. Of all the whooping and laughing, they had it.

He made many trips to see me from the Ranger camps. They were not on duty near all the time. Things were becoming more quiet and peaceful on the frontier. During all our courtship, we never had but one little quarrel. It was a very serious one though. I was in the fault and came near losing him, which made me realize for the first time what J. T. Bird meant to me. He was down from the Ranger camp visiting us for a few days. He came in Saturday afternoon, talked to me a short time, and on leaving he said, "Consider your company engaged for tomorrow."

But tomorrow came and with quite a change in the program. My Uncle Nute and Aunt Fannie Smith and some other youngsters came by for me. They were on the way to church at Graham. They were in a large vehicle, something on the order of the old stage. I don't know where he got it, but Uncle Nute was always noted for his freaks and peculiarities. It was quite roomy, convenient, and rather classy I thought. They were hurrying me to get ready, and for my life I could not tell them I had a date. However, I solved the problem. I knew they would stop at Sister's, as they most always did. Then Mr. Bird would either join us, or I would get out and stay there. But my plans failed to carry. Uncle Nute did not even slow up as we passed, and I did not have the nerve to tell him to do so. I knew I was in for it. We remained for the night meeting. Late that afternoon, Sister Lucy, her husband, and Mr. Bird came in. He did not pay any attention to me but passed me by with a very cool "Good evening."

Poor Sister Lucy tried to pave the way for her little idiotic sister as best she could. She told me what all to say to make up with him. A crowd of us took a walk out to the cemetery that evening. They all paired off, and it simmered down till there was no one left but Mr. Bird and I to go together. We walked on quite a distance before either of us spoke. I found that he was very much hurt over the way I had acted. I told him that I was awfully sorry, but I could not think of another thing to say. He spoke as if we had best break up, that I did not care for him as he had thought. I said nothing. We talked but little on the whole trip, but the coldness seemed gradually melting away. I think he considered my age mostly and overlooked it.

My Aunt Julia told me afterward that she felt real sorry for him after I had gone that day. She heard him singing in a low tone, "I'll hang my harp on a willow tree and off to the wars again."[3] He was soon off to the camp again. I did not hear from him for some time. They were detailed on two or three scout expeditions before they returned to camp. It was more than two months before he visited us again.

I had much time to give to home surroundings. My poor little chum, Ellen, was having a world of trouble. Her people wanted her to marry one man, and she wanted another. They did not allow her to meet the boy she loved, Bob Cunningham, but she did meet him many times unbeknowing to them. I shall never forget one eve when she came home with me to spend the night. Grandmother was not at home, but my uncle was there. We were having just a jolly good time. It was rather late, and we were preparing to retire. We had removed our shoes but decided to eat some watermelon first. We found there were none to speak of on hand. There were plenty in the garden about a dozen steps from the house, so we ventured out to get one without our shoes. We had just found a nice one when we heard someone coming down the road in a gallop. Ellen said in a moment, "That is Bob." We made a rush for the house and our shoes. She found hers all right, but one of mine I could not find. Now Ellen was a perfect bundle of mischief and was witty as an Irishman. She ran up in one corner of the room, found a pile of my uncle's little brogan plow shoes, and began sending them at me one by one in a perfect hailstorm manner, saying, "Is that it? Is that it?" We were both laughing till we could hardly speak when her beau came in, but I managed to find my shoe before it was too late.

The summer was waning. September was near at hand, and that eventful date, October tenth, was not far away. I had received a letter calling my attention to the above fact, and that he, Mr. Bird, would be on hand at the appointed time. My Aunt Fannie and Sister came and prepared my wedding trousseau. If it wasn't done right, it was their fault. I had to entertain the children. We romped, made swings in the big live oak tree, played hide and seek in the cane, climbed trees, rode the old gray mare, and had just a plum good time as long as they stayed. I was rather sorry when they left. My grandmother thought I should act more settled and ladylike when I was to be married so soon. I had only one week of grace now. I was looking for my fiancée most any day.

Ellen and I were together a great deal. We had many secrets to confide to each other. She and Bob were to be married in about two months from that time. We talked about our future, where we were going to live, and I told her of our plans. We were to live out near the Rangers' camp for awhile. Lieutenant Campbell lived in a house about a quarter of a mile from the camp. He stayed at home at night but away through the day. His wife was very lonely, and he insisted that Mr. Bird bring me out there for company for his wife. They would be glad to have us with them.

I went home with Ellen, and we came back that evening. We had nearly reached the house when we heard laughing and talking in the front room. We wondered who it could be. On stepping in we saw Sister and her husband, and, behold, the venerable Mr. Bird had arrived.[4] He came forward with his usual jolly laugh, shook hands with us, and looked so pleased and happy I thought. It was as if some truant little angel had dropped down in his pathway, but he was sadly misled of course. We all spent the remainder of the afternoon in talking and telling the news in general. That evening he and I had a long, private, and most businesslike talk. It was only two days till our wedding, and our last talk till then. My good sister and aunties came and arranged everything preparatory for the occasion. My dear good mother was also with us much of the time but was rather sad at heart, for I was her last little girl. I was too young, she thought, to assume the responsibilities I was undertaking. I was only a child of fifteen years old, and I weighed just ninety-nine pounds.[5] I was the last one of the name "Elgar" when I gave it up. There was no one living by that name that I knew of, my father and all of my men relatives of the name having passed away before [or] during the Civil War. I have never known or met anyone of that name since.

The appointed day and hour for our marriage had arrived at six o'clock in the evening. Ellen and Bob were our bridesmaid and best man, Reverend George Black[6] officiating. My wedding trousseau was made of pure white jaconet[7] of the finest grade. The skirt was made with two finely plaited ruffles on the bottom, and it had an overskirt with ruffles on the bottom to match the skirt. This was a pullback, as they were called at that time. It was drawn back perfectly tight over the hips and was pinned. The little cute basque was perfectly plain-fitted very close, with stays in every seam and not a wrinkle in it. It was slightly pointed in the back and front, and it fastened down the back with pretty pearl buttons. On the pullback was a broad blue ribbon sash which was caught up on each side by a ribbon in the back of the skirt. This was tied in a large bow.

After the ceremony was over, congratulations were given, and the old-time big wedding supper was spread with many luscious good things to eat. Everybody seemed happy, enjoying the repast. My husband very naturally was the center of attraction for all jokes, but he stood his ground, for no one was ever known to get ahead of him in a joke. He was the first one to speak very earnestly. "Well," he said, "that was the first time I ever was married." They all laughed. "Honest it was," he added.

The next day we went down to my mother's and stayed with them a few days. Oh, how I hated to part with them. We went back and prepared to take our departure for the Ranger camp near Fort Griffin. How I hated to leave them all. We stopped overnight at Fort Belknap[8] twelve miles from home. We met a scout of Ranger boys there. They gave me many nice presents, including a pair of fine white wool blankets. We journeyed on the next day and arrived at the home of Lieutenant Campbell that afternoon. They welcomed us in and did their part in making us feel at home, but, oh, everything seemed so strange. I was so far away from home. The country seemed wild and unsettled, but I kept a cheerful heart trying to be reconciled to my surroundings. The next day was Sunday. Mr. Bird and I took a long walk that afternoon around to see some of the country. After walking quite a distance, we sat down to rest. I was tired and leaned my head over on his lap, and he began a teasing way saying, "Well, you have left all your people and come away out here with just me and no one else." At this he discovered that I was crying, and you may be sure he changed his tune in a hurry. He began trying to cheer me up, consoling me in every way possible, saying I would soon feel all right and at home. He said that we could be together so much of the time. He kept on and said so many funny things I had to laugh. I finally got straightened up and did not cry anymore for a long time. I could manage very well except when Mr. Bird went on scouts. Then I was awfully lonely.

I took an interest in the Campbell children. There were five in the family, mostly boys. Their names were Tom, Clayton, Willie, George, and the baby, Mattie. We were there only two months when orders came from Major Jones of Waco for Lieutenant Campbell to reduce the company down to twenty-five men.[9] So Lieutenant Campbell called for volunteers if there were any that wished to resign. Mr. Bird volunteered and resigned. He hated to leave the company, but we could have only stayed four months longer, as married men were not allowed in the company. They were allowed to stay six months only after marriage.[10] I felt so sorry for him when he bade all his Ranger mates good-bye. He could never belong to them again. It was sad. I think some tears stole down the faces of several. They seemed to have learned to think a great deal of him. They said he was the life of the camp.

We soon had our things packed, and we took our departure to go back to Young County. We did quite a lot of talking and planning for our future on the way. For a long time Mr. Bird had wanted to go out on the buffalo range. The buffalo excitement was still on. People were making big money killing just for hides. Some of the wealthiest merchants in Fort Griffin made their stakes dealing in buffalo hides, so we decided to go as soon as we could make arrangements to do so.[11]

I could hardly wait to see the folks at home. All were surprised and rejoiced to see us, though they were not expecting us. We visited with them some time, staying till nearly Christmas. They told us about Uncle Jack Benson of Mississippi visiting them while we were gone. He was a second cousin of my mother's and married my father's sister, Aunt Mary. He did not know I was married. He said he was planning to take me back and give me a finished college education. That was an opportunity passed up. It was too late. I suppose they thought they were due Sister and I something. When our grandfather Elgar died, our father took his only two sisters, Aunt Mary and Aunt Martha, in his home, educated them, and made teachers of them. Their children were highly educated. One of them and her husband were teachers and proprietors of a college in Mississippi, the name of which I have forgotten.

Well, such is life! I was too much occupied just then to grieve over any lost opportunities. Bob and Ellen's wedding took place while we were there. We had to serve in return their compliment as bridesmaid and best man. This little visit in civilization, we will call it, was about the last social enjoyment we ever had.

Five

FROM THENCE we began preparing to go out on the buffalo range in the Panhandle of Texas.[1] Our equipment consisted of a general camping outfit, a large buffalo gun, a reloading outfit with plenty of ammunition, several hundred cartridge shells, primers and a keg of powder, fifty pounds of lead, two I. Wilson skinning knives, one Bowie ripping knife, a large steel, and a good pair of rest sticks to hold up the heavy gun while in action. The buffalo gun was a Sharps .45, weighing sixteen pounds. It used a cartridge about five inches long.[2]

We bade farewell to the settlements and bent our course for the wilds of the Texas Panhandle where buffalo, antelope, deer, and many other species of wild animals roamed the prairie and breaks at will. We stopped overnight again at Fort Belknap where Mr. Alec Jones and little family of wife and two children joined us on our trip. We journeyed on a few days when the roads gave out. Then we had to pick our way through the country as best we could. We crossed the Wichita breaks[3] where we came near turning over several times, but we finally made it through. One man had gone that way before and had to take his wagon to pieces three times before getting across. Later as time went on, we made a road through that way that was passable. We traveled on north about four miles and came to a big spring at the head of a creek that led back to Wichita River. There was an abundance of water here and plenty of fish lower down on the stream, so this is where we pitched our buffalo camp on December twenty-eighth 1876.[4] The spot is where Dickens and Cottle counties now join. We filed a claim on this same land later and lived three years on it. This creek takes its name for us. It is on the map as "Bird's Creek."[5]

Mr. Bird and Mr. Jones took a little hunt soon after we arrived and killed some buffalo, but first of all we had to build some winter quarters. Mr. Jones decided to build them a little rock house, as there were plenty of materials at hand already quarried naturally. He soon threw up the walls, chinked with mud and covered with dirt. It was all completed in three or four days' time. Our house was different. It was on the same order that most of the hunters used. They were called tepees, made of buffalo hides.[6] That was before dugout days. They were made as follows: first, we built a frame of small china poles,[7] splitting some for rafters. No nails were used, but rawhide strings instead. We took dried buffalo hides, tied the legs together, and put them around the wall, woolside out. Then another tier of hides was placed over these in the same like manner to break the joints of those underneath. The roof was made on the same like order as the walls, tying down the legs all around the edges. The door was made of a frame of split poles with a buffalo hide stretched over it, legs tied inside. The little rock chimney with fireplace, which was crude, of course, came next. The floor was carpeted with buffalo hides squared-up to fit, woolside up. All was complete, and a more clean and comfortable little home you could not find in any of the eastern cities. The furniture was homemade of the crudest kind. We had no use for anything then but a camping outfit.

In this little home we lived very happily indeed. We cooked on the fireplace and ate our meals in front of the fire, sitting camp-fashion on the floor, which was carpeted with buffalo hides. Our meals consisted mostly of buffalo steak,[8] well-hacked and floured. This steak is far superior to that of domestic cattle, and we never grew tired of it. Mr. Bird would often laugh and tell, when we went back to the settlements, how very heartily we ate. He said that we had a little no. 10 skillet and a no. 12 oven and that we ate each of those full of biscuits and steak at every meal and did not have a bite left. Our other food was plain sugar, coffee, syrup, dried fruit, some canned goods, and flour. We could have wild fruits of different kinds when we wanted them. There was an abundance of wild plums, and they were surely fine. There were also grapes, algerita berries,[9] and mulberries.

Mr. Bird was anxious that I should learn to use a gun. He wanted me always protected when he was away, so he gave me his Winchester rifle that the state had given him. My how I learned to love this gun as time went on. I still have it. No money could buy it.

Mr. Bird and Mr. Jones began hunting regular now. They most always took their wagons to bring the hides and such choice meats as were needed for our supply. They soon built a stack of buffalo hides which had to be freighted to Fort Worth for market. There were a good many hunters in the country, but they were far apart. Some had left, as buffalo were not so plentiful as they had been.

Most every afternoon when they came in off their hunt, Mr. Bird would give me training with my rifle. I would shoot at targets. He said I was an apt scholar, for which I felt flattered. Mrs. Jones and I also practiced together, as she was learning to use a gun too. Sometimes we would go down on the creek and shoot turkeys.

There was one thing I was attracted by when we first arrived at this place. That was the gyp rock.[10] This rock is just the same as marble with the exception that it is not quite so hard. This was about the first industry that took hold of me when we got settled, whittling and shaping things out of this rock.

I would often go out with Mr. Bird in the wagon on his hunts. It was wonderful to me to see them kill the buffalo. The method the men used in shooting the animals was queer. The country was not altogether level prairie, and the hunters could usually slip up within three or four hundred yards of them. When all was ready, the men would shoot the one that seemed to be the leader. The hunter never shot the buffalo behind the shoulder in the heart, or the animal would pitch, buck around and break the stand.[11] It was best to always shoot far back in the body behind the ribs. This made the beast sick. He would hump up, walk around, and lie down to wait a moment until another of the pack led out. The hunter would shoot another leader, and so on until he had shot several. Then the buffalo would begin milling around and around. The hunter had a stand on them, and he could kill all he wanted.

There were many antelope and deer in the country. Herds of them would often play along ahead of the wagons. We never shot at them for fear of disturbing a bunch of buffalo that might be close around.

I still worked at my gyp rock at all odd times and through the day when my husband was away. About the first thing when he came in at night, he wanted to know what I had made that day. I most always had something I had finished. They were mostly toys, but he seemed to admire them. I still practiced quite often with my rifle. I had gotten to be pretty expert with it.

We had been here now about five or six months,[12] and supplies were running short. We had to make a trip back to the settlements for more. We had not had any letters from home since we left. We made the trip all right. We camped overnight on Seymour Creek where the town of Seymour now is.[13] Mr. Bird killed a large buffalo just about where the square[14] is located there. We never thought then of it ever being a town. We stopped at Round Timbers[15] and saw Bob and Ellen.[16] We stayed overnight at Fort Belknap.

Belknap in 1877[17] was a very dilapidated-looking place with all those large brick buildings almost in perfect ruin. Some parts of nearly all of them had fallen down. Others were not so bad. They were built with many

round holes in the wall about one foot in size, used for shooting at Indians, I suppose. We spent the night at a hotel in one of those brick buildings, run down as they were. All those that could be fixed to live in were
mostly occupied. There were only a few others that were unoccupied.
There was but one store, a hotel and post office, and a saloon.[18] Mrs. Tackitt,
whose husband was later sheriff at Seymour,[19] had lived at Fort Belknap in
earlier days. She told me of some of her experiences there. She said at one
time they were surrounded by three hundred Indians in one of those large
brick buildings. They had been there a number of days and [the residents']
rations were growing short, when all at once there rode up a big company
of soldiers. They drove the Indians off. She said she never heard such
shouting from people and that she slapped her hands together until they
were almost blistered.

There had just been a killing when we arrived at the old fort. Mr. Martin,[20] their only merchant, had been murdered. A bunch of drunken out-
lawed men of the country stood him on a box and shot it out from under
him. Then they took him out that night and murdered him without any
cause that anyone knew of.

We made our way to Young County[21] the next day, and found all well
and glad to see us. Of course, we had wonderful things to tell them about
the West, though everything seemed so changed except the home folks.
Several of the younger bunch had married and moved away. We only
stayed three or four days, and then we loaded up our wagon and started
for the wilds again.

We made the trip in due time, and we found the little Jones family anx-
iously waiting to hear from the settlement. We were glad to get home
again. This was our first and only little home, and we had learned to love
it. It is truly said, "Be it ever so humble, there is no place like home." We
were happy. It was a real little love nest. He was ever kind and good to me,
and as the months and years went by, child-wife that I was, it was here I
grew and matured into womanhood and learned to love and even to wor-
ship the only man I had ever loved in life, as I had no father or older
brothers.

I was contented, I enjoyed my carving in the gyp rock, and I never neglected practicing with my rifle. I had begun to have confidence in my
marksmanship. I hardly ever missed a shot. I was about ready to banter my
husband for a shooting match, but I think he was prouder than I.

They were very busy hunting every day, and they most always brought
in hides. I so often thought what a great waste and shame that all this fine
most splendid meat should be allowed to lie and decay on the prairie when

it would have been worth millions of dollars to the people in the East.[22] I believe, though, that they claimed the Indians would never have been civilized had the buffalo remained here where [the Indians] could be independent for a living.[23]

The hides had accumulated now till they must be freighted to market, so Mr. Bird and Mr. McSwain, a neighbor hunter, decided to make a trip to Fort Worth with hides.[24] There was another family with us now. Mr. Jones' cousin, Bence Jones, came up for a short time. It was cold weather when Mr. Bird and Mr. McSwain loaded up their wagons with the buffalo hides. It is wonderful how many hides they could pack on one wagon without danger of toppling over. They were off early the next morning for their long journey. Mr. Bird hated to leave me alone, but I assured him I was not the least bit afraid with my old reliable Winchester always at hand and our camps only a few steps apart.

There were three camps now. I never got lonely. I busied myself mostly with my carving in the rock. I enjoyed it so much. Little Porter Jones and I would take strolls down on the creek and pick up choice pieces of rock that worked beautifully. There were so many different colors and shades.

Mr. Bird and Mr. McSwain had been gone now about three weeks. It was about time they should be coming in. Our supplies were running low. The two Jones men were out hunting most of the time. One day they came in with some news. They had heard there were Comanche Indians in the country. They had been at some of the camps, but they were not hostile. There were about forty of them that had slipped out from the post and come down here hunting buffalo. The buffalo, having been molested and so hard-pressed by the hunters in Kansas and Indian Territory, had migrated down into this part of the country.[25] The buffalo were also being killed out fast here.

The Jones men took a little hunt of two or three days up into Cottle County, which was about fifteen or twenty miles away.[26] We were a little uneasy about those Indians, so Mr. Alec Jones insisted we three women stay together mostly through the day in [the Joneses'] little rock house while the men were gone. I was the only one that had a gun.

On the third day after they had left, we were looking for them in most any hour. We were feeling pretty safe now. We were talking and laughing, when all of a sudden the dogs set up the awfulest raving and barking. We stepped out in the yard to see what was the matter, and, oh, horrors! What do you think met our gaze? Those Indians were coming. They were within fifty yards of the house. We stepped back into the house. I hid my gun for fear they might take it, and so I could get it if needed. Mrs. Jones said she would stand in the door and maybe they would not come in. They dashed up and were dismounted in a moment, almost. The chief led the way to the door. Mrs. Jones did not move. He pushed her aside and six others followed him. Now imagine our plight. This house was about twelve feet square, and it had two beds, five children, three women, and seven Indians in it. We did not have standing room, nor could we understand a word they said.

The old chief was very friendly and tried to talk to us. He was dressed in citizen's clothing. The others wore buckskin and were wrapped in blankets. They were very tall, large, ugly, grim-looking fellows. Some were painted. There was one white man in the bunch. They used him for an interpreter, but it seemed he could not remember enough English to make himself understood very much. I think he must have been captured when a little boy and raised up by the Indians. He looked to be about twenty-five years old. He had dark-brown eyes, rather long curly brown hair, and fair skin. He was dressed in their garb, wrapped in a blanket. Had he been otherwise dressed, he would have been a nice intelligent-looking young man. What a shame his life was sacrificed to those wild creatures.

The object of their visit seemed mainly to trade clothing for groceries. This clothing was given them by the government of which they used but little, preferring to wear buckskin instead. Our grocery stock was short, and we could not accommodate them much. They began prowling through the house as soon as they came. We did not know what they wanted till they found some groceries. They began showing us some clothes, holding up different garments, then pointing to the groceries. We understood but shook our heads. Nothing doing.

They kept on prowling, and behold, they found my gun. They set up the awfulest palavering and talking. Everyone had to look at it. The chief took quite a fancy to it. He had a right new Colt .45 pistol.[27] He offered it to me for my gun. I shook my head. He then began showing me the clothes he had on, first touching his coat, vest, shirt, and so on. I did not understand him and did not make any reply, so he began laying off his clothes one by one. He was taking off his shirt when Mrs. Jones and I looked at each other in helpless dismay. It was useless for us to offer any protest as to our right, for the poor fellow was dead to anything in the line of etiquette or, in other words, what seemed to be about to take place. Our language was dead to him. Finally the truth dawned on Mrs. Jones just before it was everlastingly too late, and she said, "He thinks you have traded your gun for his clothes."

I began shaking my head, saying, "No, no!" He laughed and proceeded to put on his clothes again. She tried to explain to him why I would not part with my gun, that it was a present to my husband by the state. I wanted to add that it was given for killing Indians, but thought it might be good policy to leave off that part of it. However, they did not understand anything she said. She also told them the menfolks would be in that evening. She showed them their clothes to make them understand.

They finally all moved outdoors and sat down with some others beside the house and began talking in low and serious tones, we thought. Mrs. Jones became very frightened and said she believed they were planning to kill us, but sure enough, the Jones men came in that evening before they left. They had struck the Indian trail where they came into the road about one half mile from camp. Mr. Alec Jones said those women would be scared to death. He jumped out of the wagon and made for camp. He came in a dead run. He could talk Indian pretty well himself, having lived near the Cherokees. He met them very friendly with a "How, How."

The Indians seemed rather pleased that the men had come in, I thought. They wanted to trade with them. Bence Jones bought a good suit of clothes for about fifty cents' worth of sorghum molasses. Alec Jones bought a nice dressed buffalo robe for about a dollar's worth of sorghum. He also got a fine green United States Indian blanket for the same above price in sorghum. They did not know what their goods were worth.

They were soon ready to go and started to their horses. One old savage-looking Indian came in, picked up my gun, and offered me an old worn-out vest he had on for it. I shook my head. He started off with it. I followed on after him shaking my head. He finally came back with an ugly grin on his face and handed it to me, and they were gone. I have always believed the chief of this bunch of Indians was no other than Quanah Parker.[28]

Six

IT WAS NOW about five weeks since Mr. Bird and Mr. McSwain had left, and we were uneasy about them. It had been very cold, and we had had a great deal of snow.[1] They were due home in three or four weeks at most. Every evening I would take long strolls over the hills through the scattering brush in the direction they would come, thinking I might meet them, but each time, I would return alone, disappointed, and, oh, so sad and uneasy. It had gone on this way another week or more. I was almost giving up in despair but would go one more time in hope of meeting them. I was about one-half mile from home and looking away across the hills through the algerita bushes about a quarter of a mile away. I saw two wagons coming, jogging along. I knew it was them. Mr. Bird saw me at the same time. He stopped the wagon, got out, and started toward me when he saw me start to run. We missed each other and had to hunt around some time before we met. I was laughing and he was crying. I had never seen him that way before. He was almost crazy from worrying so much. As soon as he could, he told me all the news that had reached Fort Worth while they were there. They had heard that there were nine hundred Indians up on Pease River,[2] not far from where we were, and that they were killing women, children, and all as they came to them, sparing none.

Of course, they started for home at once, but they broke down two or three times and were snowed under at different times till they could not travel for several days. But it was a joyful arrival home to find that we were all safe and well and unharmed.

We certainly enjoyed the new groceries they brought. We had run out of bread about two weeks before they arrived, but where there is a will, there is surely a way. Mr. Jones had a large box coffee mill. He staked it down on the ground so it could not move, and we ground corn on this for bread. Sometimes we ground peas for bread. We had plenty of meat at all times.

The next morning Mr. Bird and I were sitting down on the carpet in front of the fire eating breakfast in camp fashion as we always did. We were enjoying our reunion to the fullest. He was saying, "Ella, if I ever do leave you again, I hope I may be hung higher than Haman." About that time Mrs. Jones stepped up to the door laughing to the top of her voice and in a teasing way. We were plagued, but he had the nerve to say, "I mean it every bit." She and I told him about our turkey hunts down on the creek at night while they were gone. He complimented our bravery and nerve. I also showed him several pieces of carving I had done, which were better than any I had done before. He was proud of this work but like myself did not know the value of it. I only knew that I was the happiest when at work on it. I had many pieces of carving now, and I hoarded them up as if gold, almost.

There was another industry I have not mentioned. I was making a mattress of buffalo mops. Each day when my husband made a killing of buffalo, he would take the skin off the front of the head that contained the long heavy mop of wool. This wool was too heavy and thick to be removed from the skin with shears, so I used a sharp butcher knife instead. It took two or three hundred mops, I think, but I surely had a fine mattress when it was finished. I have this mattress yet, as good as it ever was. I feel sure that it is good for a hundred years. It would take a handsome sum of money to buy it. I don't know of another one in Texas.[3]

The men were hunting steady now. Buffalo were growing more scarce all the time.[4] They were being molested so much it was hard to hold a stand on them. I often went with my husband in the wagon. I felt myself quite a good marksman by this time. I had been practicing quite a lot on prairie dogs. I could shoot the heads off of many without missing a shot. We were out one day and found a small herd of buffalo. We stopped the wagon within about four hundred yards of them, just behind a small bunch of shinnery.[5] I stayed in the wagon. He managed to get to within about two hundred yards of them and held the bunch pretty well till he had killed twenty. Then the stand was broken. They scattered and ran every way. Two of them came by near the wagon, so I just threw my Winchester to my shoulder, and down I brought one of them. Before the other one could get away, I brought it down, likewise.

I think Mr. Bird was more thrilled over my kill than I was. He came up laughing and said, "Now, Old Lady, every hunter must take care of their own kill. I have all I can do, and you must skin your own buffalo."

I said, "But how can I?"

He said he would help me stand them up. This meant to put a chunk under one side to balance them and to stand them on their back with feet straight up. Then they were ready for business. He wanted me to do this just for the name of it, to say I had. Of course, I knew how it was done as I had watched him so often. We both went to work in earnest. We had a good day's work ahead of us. I finished mine in about three hours and helped him some in the way of holding for him. There were some skinners on the range that were so expert they could skin sixty buffalo in one day, but we drove in home that night with twenty-two hides and were very well satisfied.

The art of learning to skin buffalo was very simple. First the hide was cut around all the feet. Next, the hide was ripped from one end of the animal to the other on the under side. Then the hide around the neck was cut, and the legs were ripped down to the body or main line. When this was done, the legs were skinned down to the body, after which the main body was skinned, completing the process.[6]

The staking of hides was done by spreading the hide down on a level, plain place of ground, cutting small holes around the edges of hide, having small pegs ready, then proceeding to stretch the hides tight, driving the pegs through the holes in the hide into the ground.

I will give our formula for dressing hides as follows: first, soak them overnight in cold water, [and] then spread them over a graining horse the following morning. Use the back of a drawer knife to rub all the hair and grain off. It is difficult to get all the grain off, but it must all come off to make a nice hide. When this is done, spread the hide out when thoroughly dry and hard and take about a tablespoon of melted lard and grease the hide all over. Let it stay on overnight. Make an ooze of about one gallon of soft water, one-half bar of laundry soap, a heaping tablespoon of soda, and a tablespoon of lard. Shave up the soap and put all in a kettle and boil till the soap is all melted. Take off and cool to nearly milk warm and put the hide in this to soak overnight. The next morning wring it out as thoroughly as possible, pull it out long, and lay it in the sun to dry, pelt side up. Do not leave it too long. When it begins to dry a little, pull it out all around. It takes two hands to do this. Pull it long again and lay it down as before and let it dry just a little at a time. Then pull thoroughly again, not less than ten minutes at a time. Always pull long before laying it down. Keep on in this way until the hide is nice and soft. In this way you have a good buckskin not eaten up by chemicals that will last twice as long as one that is.

The two Jones families had been thinking for some time of leaving the buffalo range, as buffalo were playing out fast. They were getting very scarce now and taking mostly to the breaks. Only occasionally would we see a bunch on the prairie. The Joneses were preparing to leave, so they took their departure back to Parker County, their old home. It was 1880, I believe.[7] We were left now to hold the fort alone.

Mr. McSwain and Mr. Bird hunted together some. Mr. Bird and I would often take trips of two or three days around in other parts of the country. I would drive the wagon, and he would hunt along through the country nearby. I had learned to drive quite well now. I had been driving some ever since we had been in the country, though I had never tried to harness or unharness the team. We were coming in home late one afternoon and had just gotten into the edge of the breaks four miles from home. We saw a small bunch of buffalo not far away. They were on the travel.

Mr. Bird said, "We will strike camp, and I will follow them. I must hurry, or they will be gone." He asked me if I could unharness the team.

I said, "Sure, I will try." So he was off at once, and I began my task. I thought I would never get the harness clear of the horses. I think I unhooked, unbuckled, and unsnapped everything that was detachable about the harness and did not know where to lay each part when I got through. I proceeded to get the lariats and stake out the horses. I made a fire and prepared our evening meal.

It was getting dark, and my husband had not returned. I seated myself in a chair by the side of the wagon to wait. We had three dogs, hounds they were. They lay down around me. As the black darkness came on, the hoot owls began their nightly serenade. It seemed the breaks were alive with them from the fuss they made. The coyotes were howling on every side. Occasionally a loafer[8] would chime in. We had fresh meat in the wagon. That was the attraction. I was more amused at those hounds, cowardly as they always are, who were so frightened that they did not even cheep. They crowded up so closely around me that I could hardly move. I was not in the least afraid, as my gun was sitting beside me, and I had confidence in myself. I was lonely, however, for I had waited almost two hours.

Soon I heard a gunshot. This was always music to me. I rose up and fired my gun in answer to it. Often Mr. Bird was out at night, and when he was not quite sure of the direction to camp, he would fire off his gun. I would answer him with mine. He followed those buffalo quite a ways and made a pretty good killing, but being afoot [he] took some time to get back to camp.

The next morning when he went to harness the horses, he was astonished at the plight of the harness. He was surprised but more vexed to think I knew so little about harness. Now I knew the names of some parts of them and the wagon, and just for fun, I played more ignorant than I really was. I proceeded in a very innocent way to explain just how I managed them. I had tried to fix them just like he did first. I unhitched the surcingle and hung it on the rocking bolster. I then unloosed the swivel from the clevis pin and laid them over on the hames. I took off the martingales and hung them on the thimble skein. I put the singletree on the hounds and laid the tugs on top of those.[9] By this time he was laughing till he could hardly stand up. He finally got everything arranged, and we were soon off after those buffalo hides that were yet to be skinned. We drove in home that afternoon. We were tired but glad to get home. Mr. Bird staked out the hides, and we were ready for a rest. Everything was so quiet now. No one was nearer us than fifteen or twenty miles. Most of the hunters had left the range.

We had been thinking of another trip to the settlement, perhaps the last one for a long time for it was a tiresome long journey. We wanted to lay in sufficient supplies for a whole twelve months. It had been four or five months since the Joneses had gone, and it had been three months since we had had our mail.[10]

We were now ready to start for Young County. We camped the first night on the far edge of Wichita breaks. It was there I came near being killed by a buffalo. After we had struck camp, it was early, and Mr. Bird went out about a quarter of a mile and killed two buffalo. We ate supper early and started over to skin them. They were just on the other side of a deep, narrow canyon. We had crossed and were just approaching them. We were within about twenty steps of them. Mr. Bird said one of them might not be quite dead. He had no more than said the word till it was on its feet. It bowed itself, gave a snort, and took a beeline for me. I don't know whether I rolled, ran, or flew down that hill, but I was down, the first I knew. Mr. Bird did not move. He was a crack shot. He took in the situation as a life-and-death affair, of course. He threw his .45 to his shoulder, and with dead aim, he brought down the monster before it reached the brink of the hill. We soon collected our rent off of them and drug the hides back to camp. We journeyed on the next day and camped in The Narrows[11] that night. Nothing of special event happened from there on.

We reached Young County on the sixth day, and there was another happy reunion as usual. However, it was the last one for a long time. We visited with them several days. It was summertime, and we ate watermelon and fried chicken, went to church, saw many of the old-timers, and enjoyed civilization to the fullest.

My brother-in-law wanted me to demonstrate some of my "expert shooting," as he called it. So as it happened, the hawks were very bad after the chickens. I turned in on them and killed three and crippled the fourth one, all in one day. We hung them on a live oak tree, and they were not bothered with hawks for some time afterwards.

I always took my collection of carvings when we went back to the settlement to show them off. Many of the acquaintances would come in to see them.

We were now loading up our wagon to return to our little home on the Wichita again. We stopped over one day at Seymour and visited one day with Ellen and Bob, who had moved there. They had two children now. Seymour was just starting up. The people there tried hard to induce us to locate there. They would give us many lots, but we could not be persuaded. We were bound for the far west.

Seven

THE COUNTRY had begun to settle up a few miles west of Seymour by the ranchmen. There was the Millett Ranch, the Oxford, the Bedford, and others.[1]

We were soon clear of any settlements or even roads. There were only a few wagon tracks that were hard to follow. We finally reached the Wichita breaks, crossed the river, and camped. Mr. Bird went back across the river where we saw buffalo tracks. He killed a buffalo cow with a little calf. We went over the next morning for the hide. The little calf was still by its mother. It was pitiful. It was very gentle. When we were through, it followed us back to camp. We took it home and tried to raise it, but having no milk, it only lived a few days.[2]

Mr. McSwain came over. He and Mr. Bird went in partners hunting. They made up a trip out on Double Mountain Fork at Brazos River, Croton,[3] and so forth. The buffalo were now about all gone, so they turned their attention to smaller game such as antelope, deer, wolves, and other small game for the hides. They had gotten quite a collection of hides. They could dress those and get a good price for them.

We camped several days in different parts of the country. The men were out hunting all day leaving me in camp alone. I did much carving in the gyp rock. I was never lonely in the day. If I grew tired of my work, I took my gun with belt of cartridges and roamed the woods around. I was always a lover of nature and had much curiosity. I would walk two or three hours over the hills, up and down canyons, gathering fancy specimens of rock and other curios. Sometimes I would kill a nice fat turkey on my rounds and have it cooked nicely for their supper when they came in.

For the past few days, Mr. Bird was having to ride at great disadvantages. He had broken or worn out both of his stirrups and was having to use rawhide straps for a substitute. One morning as they were starting off he said, "Old Lady, you take the drawer knife and saw and cut down one of those little china trees, split it, and make me a pair of stirrups today." Of course, he was joking, but after they had gone, I wondered if I could. So just for an experiment, I thought I would try. I landed in to it and soon had my material in good shape. I had the old ones for a pattern and also the fittings for the new ones. I finished them up that afternoon, and they were a genuine, substantial pair of stirrups. I was rather surprised at my own success.

That night the men were sitting and talking when I passed along carelessly and dropped the stirrups down between them. They first looked at them in astonishment; then of all the laughing I never heard. They said I didn't do it. I said, "Sure, I did." They surely filled a much-needed place and did good service for several months.

One day the men came in with some serious news. There were Indians in the country up on Yellowhouse Canyon. They had killed some people there.[4] We were camped over in Croton Breaks[5] on a canyon that led back to the river about one mile. At the head of this canyon were large deep holes of fresh water with springs. Just above this where the branch was shallow, we pitched our camp. We hung a wagon sheet above for protection from wind.

We had been here several days. They had good luck hunting. One cloudy day late in the afternoon, it was misty, dark, and dismal. I was busy on a special piece of carving, but it seemed I could hear an occasional twig crack or a slight noise not faraway. I rose up, walked up on the hill a few steps, looked up the branch, and there about one hundred yards away I discovered a large body of something stooping, creeping slowly toward camp. I was not excited just then. I looked carefully to be sure I was not mistaken. My decision was [that] no other than a bunch of those Comanche Indians [were] slipping into camp. I turned and walked down the hill very leisurely, as if I had not seen anything, but when I was securely behind the wagon sheet, there was some fast work going on. I grabbed my gun, filled it with cartridges, filled up my cartridge belt, buckled it around me, took my gun and an extra box of cartridges, made about three bounds, slid down the bank by the big water hole, and took down the creek to the river. I ran with all my might. I felt sure they would follow in pursuit of me. I had gone down the river about one mile where a large deep canyon followed it to the head which formed a large basin about four hundred yards across. I went up on the side of this basin and found a good hiding place. A shallow sink covered over with high grass completely hid me.

Night was coming on. It was between shadows and dark. I could see all around the top of this canyon back toward camp. I was sitting there waiting and listening for any sound. I was, oh, so uneasy, for fear the men would be killed when they came into camp. Pretty soon the form of a man appeared out on the edge of this canyon in the direction of camp. Of course, I knew it was an Indian in reach of me. He was about four hundred yards away. I could see him in the sky light, and he looked large and savage. I thought at first I would kill him, which would have been an easy matter. I drew a fine bead on him once, twice, and the third time came near pulling the trigger. Then I hesitated. If I killed him, it would only give away my hiding place, and perhaps I'd lose my life as the result. Therefore, I changed my mind and kept quiet. He turned and walked away pretty soon.

In about twenty or thirty minutes, I heard three or four gun shots and my husband yelling and shouting to the top of his voice. It was dark now. I sat in frenzied suspense. I felt sure the battle had begun. Pretty soon off in another direction, four or five more shots were heard, and the shouting continued. Then farther away, six or seven more shots in succession, all with the big buffalo gun that sounded like a cannon in those breaks. I supposed the Indians were using bows and arrows, as I could hear only one gun.

Several minutes elapsed when I heard horse's feet coming in my direction. They stopped just on the hill above me, not ten steps away, and of all the yelling he did. It was my husband hunting for me. Then I knew there had been no Indian fight at all. He was only trying to attract me, and when I failed to answer him with my gun, he felt sure I was faraway or that something very serious had happened to me. When he stopped his big fuss, I deliberately walked up the hill and asked what he wanted. His horse scared at me and nearly threw him off. He said, "Ella, what in the world are you doing out here at this time of night, and why did you not answer me?" I asked if he had seen any Indians. He said, "No." But he became very serious and interested. He had never known of me taking a scare before. I related to him what I had seen, and till this day I cannot understand what motive those Indians had in slipping up on our camp, then turning back before they had quite reached it.

The men examined next morning, and the tracks were there where they had retreated and disappeared in the hills. The only conclusion they could come to was that the Indians might have seen them coming into camp and perhaps thought there were more of them. The Indians did not care for a fight, so they turned their course backward.

But there was a very serious incident that occurred in this affair that made me shudder and almost tremble when I thought of it. The Indian or man that appeared at the head of this canyon where I sat and the one whom I came so near shooting was no other than my husband looking for me. Surely kind Providence must have stayed my hand. Otherwise, I would have committed an act that would have caused me a life's remorse.

The next day we loaded up our camping outfit and started for our home on Wichita. We found everything all right and were glad to get home again.

Mr. Bird and Mr. McSwain now entered into a new industry for awhile, that of dressing hides. They dressed many deer and antelope hides, also some wolf and other smaller furs. They worked hard and faithful on those nearly three weeks and certainly had a valuable lot of fine dressed buckskin ready for the market.

We had now stayed at home a little longer than usual at this time of year. Mr. Bird and Mr. McSwain were planning another hunt, a short trip of a couple of weeks out west [to] Red Lake, about twenty-five miles away.[6] I had never seen this place before. It was a shallow sunken basin of about two acres of ground perfectly dry. It never held water. It was filled with many beautiful shade trees. I was delighted with this place. It was a natural and most ideal camping ground. I spent many pleasant hours while here. I busied myself mostly with my preferred occupation, carving in the rock. A good portion of this western country is sandhills covered with shinnery, which are small post oak bushes. At that time this shinnery was heavy laden each year with large acorns, making it a most splendid place for hogs. There were a few hogs being brought into the country now west of us. There were one or two ranches, I think.

We had been at this place about one week. We were sitting around the campfire one evening after supper when two men came in and visited with us. They certainly found a hearty welcome. People were now becoming so scarce here, we were glad to see anything in the shape of a human being. It had been near twelve months since I had seen a woman. One of these men was young, about nineteen or twenty I should guess. He was a blond, a fine-looking boy. He was large, portly, and quite handsome. He was out here only for a short time. His name was Tom Goforth. The other man was more settled, about thirty I think. He was just the reverse to the above one. He was French Canadian, and he was not handsome but [was] rather attractive. He was small in stature though well built, dark complexioned, and had quite intelligent eyes. He gave the appearance of a man steady, staunch, and true, and was well educated. He had traveled extensively. He conversed well and was quite interesting to talk to. Mr. Bird was a great talker himself, so the rest of us did little but listen. Just here I will say little did I think at that time what this man might figure in my life twenty years hence, for his name was no other than A. Dumont.[7] He and another man, Mr. Crego, were the owners of a hog ranch a few miles from this place. They stayed and talked till late. My husband insisted they spend the night with us, but they said they could not so took their departure.

After another week's hunting, we returned back to headquarters. Game was getting more scarce, and Mr. McSwain decided to quit the country and go to Phoenix, Arizona. He took his departure in a day or two, and we never saw or heard from him again.

We were sure left alone now. We spent most of the spring and summer in perfect solitude. My husband was so lonely at times that he would say, "I would be proud to see even one of our old neighbors' dogs come in." We fished, gathered wild fruits, plums, mulberries, algerita berries, and so forth. He would hunt sometimes. We had plenty of nice fresh meat at all times, such as deer, antelope, turkey, and quails. Once in a long time when we meandered around, we would strike a fresh wagon track. We would be so enthused we would follow it two or three miles trying to overtake it and see who it was. One day when we were out, we discovered something very strange. We were about two miles away. We drove till we came to it, and, behold, it was a bunch of real domestic cattle. There were about fifty head. We learned later that they had drifted away from a herd that was being taken up where Duck Creek now is.[8] We had been out here more than three years, and this was the first cattle that had ever been in the country.[9] They looked as strange to us I think as a bunch of buffalo would look to people now. They were mostly yearlings. They were on the travel and had drifted down into the breaks of Wichita. They were scattered and finally all killed and eaten up by the loafer wolves.

One day when everything was quiet and lovely as usual, we were met with a great surprise. Three wagons with families and a good-sized herd of cattle came driving into camp. It is a wonder we did not take fright and run, but we did not. We were real glad to see them. These were the first women I had seen in about twelve months. They were the Dykes, the boys Billie and Dan, Mr. Yarbrough, Mr. Pots and two boys, cousins of the Dykes, and three women and a little girl. It looked to us as if the population of this part of the country was complete. They were hunting a location for their cattle. They wanted to pitch their camp here with us, so all was agreed on. That afternoon three large tents loomed up around us. It seemed almost like living in town. These ladies were all nice jolly good company. Two of them were near my own age. They had been married only a short time. We were soon acquainted and enjoyed each other's company fine. We were together a good portion of the time.

The time had come, however, when we had to make another trip east, for supplies were running low. We had not had any mail in four or five months. So we bade adieu to the folks, for they too were going east for the winter. They left the Curtis boys to take care of the cattle.

We made quite a visit this time with the folks. We stayed nearly three months. Sister had moved up to Round Timbers near Seymour, but she came and was with us a good portion of the time. About the first of September,[10] we prepared to take our leave for the west again. Right here I will divulge a secret. There was to be a baby in the Bird family. We were keeping very quiet about this and did not want my mother to know, as she would be so worried and uneasy when we were gone so far away.

We made our way back to our little home all right, but it seemed deserted again. The folks had all gone east for the fall and winter. However, we were not upset, for we were proof against everything that came up, especially a life of solitude. We just settled down in the same old way and were contented. We had brought with us a fine pair of Chester White pigs[11] and about two dozen chickens. This made things seem more eastern like.

Mr. Bird deer hunted a good deal and killed many deer. He also dressed a number of hides. I did several more pieces of carving in the rock. We often put up a target and trained our guns. I always hit the nearest to the mark. He was given up as the best marksman on the buffalo range, but he said he would hand over the championship to me, as I had beaten him. We also did some trapping of wolves. We dressed the hides and made a fine wolf robe of twenty hides lined with a blanket, which we used for several years afterwards.

Eight

MR. BIRD had planned for some time to take a bear hunt out at the foot of the plains. He had heard that they were plentiful there, so according to his plans the time had arrived when we should go. We soon had everything arranged in camp and struck out for the foot of the plains and Canadian breaks.[1]

There were now a few scattering cow ranches around in the country, but they were far apart. We made our way rather northwestward in an ox wagon. We only saw one person on the whole way, a cowboy. We met out in the mesquite as we were driving along. He belonged to the Shoe Nail Ranch[2] I believe, as well as I remember, but was on the Matador Ranch later, at any rate. We were real glad to meet with him just to have someone to talk to. He was real nice and friendly. He insisted that we camp there for awhile and offered my husband an extra horse to hunt on. He said there was much game there, such as deer, antelope, and so forth. This boy was no other than George Cluts of whom we knew so well in after years and thought a great deal of. Owing to circumstances, we had only a limited time for our trip, so we thanked him very nicely for his kindness and journeyed on.

It was getting well up in the winter now, and cold weather was coming on. In a few days we reached the east edge of the breaks at the foot of the plains. As it happened, we struck one of the line camps on the Goodnight Range, a small dugout[3] with only one man as occupant. This was about ten miles north from the headquarters.[4] I don't think he had seen anyone for two or three weeks. He seemed as glad to see us as if we had been some old acquaintance. He invited us in and made us feel perfectly at home. We were certainly fortunate in finding this place. It was just night and had begun to snow. This dugout was nice and cozy as could be with a fireplace and everything convenient. It was sitting right on the brink of the canyon. About six feet from the door was the edge. It was near one-hundred feet to the bottom. It had banisters around the front of the yard.

The next morning we were simply snowed under and could not leave this place for more than a week. This old boy said he was "plumb glad of it." He said he had been so lonely he could hardly live. His name was Joe Green. He was certainly lovely to us. He turned over everything to me to do just as I pleased. He was out on the line all day. Mr. Bird hunted some. When they came in at night, I always had a nice supper for them. He, Mr. Green, could never stop praising my cooking. He said a man could not cook at all. I made him a nice pair of fur mitts while we were there of which he seemed very proud. He threatened in a mischievous way to push my husband off some of those high bluffs and have him a good-looking woman.

I really enjoyed the stay there. From this view the country was picturesque. All those deep canyons and breaks clad in snow were wonderful and beautiful. It finally thawed up, and the snow melted off so we could travel again. We went on our way. The breaks were about four miles across. Mr. Green told us of a large good dugout near the other side where we wanted to go. There were bear there. We never heard of Mr. Green again.

After much hunting our way through, we found the dugout, and of all the rough country, I had never seen anything like it. Deep canyons and gulches were on every side, one after another. Many of these were a hundred feet deep with only a narrow passway to get out.

Mr. Bird went out the first afternoon about two miles and killed a large bear. He was after night getting in. It seemed almost an age before he came. The loafer wolves were howling, and twice I heard a panther scream. After a while I heard a gunshot, and I knew he was coming. I answered him with mine, and I was not lonely anymore.

He had an awful time getting his bear in the next day. The country was so rough we did not like that place very much, and he did not kill as many bears as he expected. I don't remember the exact number, but it was less than a half dozen, I think. However, he was satisfied, and we were thoroughly ready to get out of those hideous breaks. We finally got back on level ground again and bent our course homeward. In a few days we arrived safely and found everything O.K. We did not have a neighbor now nearer than thirty-five miles of us.

Mr. Bird had killed a number of antelope and some deer, and he had many pairs of nice hams to cure for the winter besides the bear meat. So he was occupied for a while. I did quite a bit of sewing, embroidering, some carving, and so forth. We remained here until about the first of January. Then we decided to go down to Seymour and spend the remainder of the winter. That place had grown to be quite a little town now.[5]

We loaded our wagon with many nice cured hams and other meats sufficient for the winter, and also a lot for the market. We were soon on our way. We stopped the first night at [the house of] Mr. Chess Tackitt, the first sheriff of Seymour. We had no trouble in securing room in a residence with some nice people there by the name of Harding. John Harding was one of the earliest residents there.[6] We enjoyed staying in this home very much. They were young people and had only one baby, which was born soon after we were with them. We were acquainted with a number of people here, as this was on our route back farther east. The neighbors were all nice and friendly as most always is the case in new towns. Everything was pleasant and agreeable, and I rather enjoyed staying here.

We had been at this place some two months, when on the first day of March, 1881, something out of the ordinary happened. A nine-pound boy was born to us. We had wanted this baby very much, and the newly made father, who was quite humorous, was so elated that he became rather poetical with it. On meeting some of his friends uptown the next day, this is the way in which he broke the glad tidings to them:

> Last night as old Saint Peter slept,
> He left the doors of Heaven ajar;
> When through the gates an Angel crept
> And came down with a falling star.
>
> When all was calm and serene,
> I, slumbering peacefully by my bride,
> Awakened from some pleasant dream,
> And found this angel by her side.
>
> God, grant but this, I ask no more,
> That when he leaves this world of pain,
> He'll wing his way to that bright shore,
> And find his way in Heaven again.

Now the naming of this wonderful baby was the greatest problem yet. So, womanlike, I unloaded the whole responsibility on his father. However, I think he rather liked it but did not say so. After studying a while, he said, "His name is Capp Jay."[7] I may not have given him that name, but it had to go. He was named with my permission.

We only sent out one announcement, which was to my mother. She or none of the relatives knew of this expected arrival of the baby except my sister, who got word of it and came up to see me the next day after the baby came. She could hardly forgive us for keeping it from them all, but it was only to save my poor mother of worry.

As soon as I was able, we went down to Sister's at Round Timbers for a few days. Then we all went on to our mother's in Young County and visited them for a week or two. Then we came back to Round Timbers and prepared for our journey home on the Wichita. We were so eager to get home that we hardly slowed up as we passed through Seymour. We stopped one night each at Millett, Oxford, and McCuin's ranches on our way.[8] We arrived home safely, and the baby stood the trip fine.

We were surprised and pleased to find our neighbors had all returned, but the greatest surprise of all was that each of us three younger women returned with babies, and neither suspecting it of the others. Things were more interesting now than ever. We were well entertained and could have a baby show every day if we chose, which we most always did. We all had little truck wagons made for our babies, partly covered with bows and sheets for shade. We were just as proud of those as if they had been fine baby carriages such as we used in later years. It was comical though to see us strike out through the woods berry hunting with our little train of wagons. We spent many happy hours together.

We were all interested in the same way and were perfectly congenial, and thus the summer passed away until August, when quite a change took place. The Dykes, Yarbroughs, and Pots all sold out their cattle to Mabry and Glasgow of the JF Ranch, which was adjoining us.[9] So in a very short time the cattle were all gathered, rebranded, and delivered. All the folks but ourselves took their departure for the east again.

We were left again to hold the fort alone. My husband had been riding around and met some of the ranchmen. They were much in need of a hand and wanted us to move on the ranch in order for Mr. Bird to take a job as line rider.[10] He came home, and we talked it over and decided to go. We had torn down our buffalo tepee house some time previous to this and had moved into the old Jones camp house, which was part rock and part dirt. We stored all our camping outfit, a box of large books which had belonged to my father, and a box with all my priceless carvings, now numbering sixty pieces, in the house. We wired and nailed up the door securely, we thought. We did not expect to be gone more than three months at most.

We started for the Savage Ranch, now the Pitchfork.[11] We arrived that afternoon without any trouble. Our little babe was now six months old and was quite a young cowboy. Everything seemed so strange and different to our past mode of living, though very quiet for a ranch. There were only three men on the ranch, my husband making the fourth. Women were scarce in this country at that time. They were more appreciated, I think, than in later years when there were more. Those men were perfect gentlemen and treated me with the highest respect. They seemed rather pleased at my presence, I thought, and tried to make everything as pleasant for me as possible.

The ranch house consisted of two large dugouts with no furniture whatever, except bedsteads and some benches. It was a camping outfit and nothing more, but this was customary. No one expected anything better. The wealthiest cowmen's families lived in dugouts when they first came here. Mr. Savage, the proprietor of the ranch, was very refined and a gentleman. He was an Irishman and had been in the United States only a short time. His foreman on the ranch, Mr. Mike Sullivan, was also Irish, but he was a native of this country. Mr. Savage was here only for a short time to see after his interests. He had married just before leaving Ireland and was anxious to get back. He meant to keep this a secret for fear of being teased, but his foreman betrayed him to my husband and me. I thought we did not dare give it away.

It was rather lonely for me. The men all left early in the morning, each on his line, and they did not return until late in the afternoon. There were no fences then. Each cattle range was laid off in so many sections, and each man had his own line to ride, keeping the cattle in their own range.

One day after they had all gone I was looking around the place. I noticed some large-sized goods boxes. We had been using two of those large benches for a dining table. I made up my mind I would make a table. There were plenty of tools, a hammer, saws, and so forth. The baby was asleep, so I went to work. I had good luck with it. Everything measured out, and by the middle of the afternoon, I had a first-class table on foot with a large drawer for cold victuals. For knobs on the drawer I sawed a large spool in two and attached [the halves] with two horseshoe nails in each, and I bradded them on the inside of the drawer. All was complete, and I was rather proud of the job if I did do it myself. It was substantial and very good looking. This same table was still in use eight or ten years afterward.

That afternoon when the men came in, Mr. Sullivan was the first. He asked who had been here.

I said, "No one at all."

He asked, "Where did the table come from?"

"I made it," I said.

He laughed rather incredulously, as he thought I was joking. I could hardly convince him that I really did make it. He examined the drawer and everything and said it beat anything he had ever seen made by a woman. He went out and brought in Mr. Savage to look at it. He would hardly believe it either at first. He said there was not a man in the country that could do half as good a job. They gave me such a "blow-up" that I rather got plagued out and almost wished I had not made it.

That evening when the others came in, I had supper on the table with a nice tablecloth on. They shied around as if they didn't know whether to come in or not. Mr. Bird simply put on a show, at which he was an expert. He was such a tease, and he did so many funny, crazy things that it made it more absurd than anything else. Everybody was dying laughing. I was so plagued and embarrassed, I wished I had never heard of a table.

They had a roundup a short time after we were there. The men did most of the cooking. My job, they said, was to take care of the baby and put the finishing touches on the dinner. I suppose they were pleased with the dinner part of it at least. Mr. Savage made me a present of ten dollars the next day for my services. Of course, this included my husband's help also. I liked the ranch life pretty well. It was not hard on me. They were all so nice and good to help around the place. I did not have dinner at all to prepare, but it seemed changes were taking place all the time. We had been on the ranch not more than one month when Mr. Savage sold out to D. B. Gardner of the Pitchfork Ranch today. Everything changed altogether. Some left and others came in.

Mr. Savage was soon off for the old country. Before going he asked a little favor of my husband. He said by chance he had seen in a drawer some beautiful artificial flowers that I had made of silk floss. He wanted a sample of them to take back with him to show what could be done in this western country where they believed everything was wild and uncivilized. We fixed him up a little bouquet in a little tin can for which he thanked us over and over. He said it should occupy a prominent place in the decoration of their new home. So I guess some of my bungling went to old Ireland.

Mr. D. B. Gardner, my husband, and Mr. Jeff Scott were all that were left now with the exception of a Negro man, Cal, the horse [wrangler] and dishwasher. We spent the remainder of the summer here with nothing special to mention. The care of the baby and other work took up about all my time. It had been so long since I had done any carving in the rock that I longed to get back to it again, but I could not as I had no leisure whatever. I did not mention it to anyone as I felt they would think it a silly, foolish occupation.

Mr. Bird was out on the line all day but hunted a good deal on his rounds. He would bring in from one to three deer and antelope hides every few days, and the hams kept us in fresh meat a good portion of the time, as well as saving us from killing beef. Mr. Gardner was planning to move his headquarters down east about ten miles from this place, near the Wichita. They had begun working on the dugouts already. We moved in October and spent the winter there. Another boy was added to our list, John McKeen. This was in the breaks of Croton.

I did one piece of carving that winter. I made a small Bible, a present for Mr. Bird's mother and father. I carved their names in raised German text letters on it.

Another family was added to the ranch that winter, Mr. Dan Morrison. They were on a line camp on Croton. We stayed there till the last of February when Mr. Bird decided we would leave the Pitchforks and go on the Ross Ranch.[12] They wanted a family on a line camp, and that suited us better. However, we liked the Pitchforks all right.

After a drive of about twenty miles, we arrived at the Ross headquarters. They were all strangers to me, but I rather liked the appearance of the folks and all the surroundings. Our camp was to be over on Tongue River, ten miles north of headquarters.[13] They did not have it finished when we arrived. Mr. Bird helped complete it. I liked this camp. It was on and near the bank of the shallow river in a shady grove of cottonwoods. There were many interesting things here. We raised lots of chickens, kept cows, and had all the wild turkey meat we wanted, for the woods were full of young turkeys of all sizes. There were lots of deer and antelope, and much wild fruit, such as plums, grapes, and berries which were extra fine. I did quite a lot of preserving and canning. Mr. Bird dressed a good lot of deer hides. We bought a sewing machine, and I made a good many pairs of gloves for the cowboys. I also made some buckskin pants and vests. I had many more orders than I could fill. My health was not very good at this time.

Mr. Bird had to make a trip to Seymour on business of some kind. He went by our old camp on the Wichita where we had left our things, and what do you think? When he came back, he told me that everything we left there had been taken, the door was torn down, and even the cattle had been going in the house. All my carvings had been stolen, and no trace of them was ever found from that day to this. It almost broke my heart when I found I had lost them. I simply lay awake nights and grieved about them. There was at least two years' solid work on them without any stops. There were sixty pieces in all. It was all my first work and improvements.

How I would have liked to have laid everything aside and worked in this rock and nothing else. I wanted to be a sculptor. It bore on my mind incessantly, though I said nothing about it to anyone, for I felt that we were not able for me to devote my time to something I could not see any profit in. Of course, I was inexperienced and knew nothing of Eastern life, arts, or any advantages in that line, no matter how gifted I may have been. I was barred from any development whatever other than what I could just work out myself. Though I was never any hand to worry, I feel thankful that I have always tried to make the best of life's possibilities. It is usually hard enough, at best.

Nine

IT WAS LATE summer now. We were preparing for a trip down east to my mother's, and right here I have another little secret to divulge. There was to be another baby with us. Mr. Brack Garrison was staying with us at that time, and we were leaving him to take care of things while we were gone. We were soon off to Young County and landed there without any trouble. We found all well. It was such a pleasure and privilege to be with my mother again. It had been some two years since I had seen her. We stopped with my grandmother mostly on this trip. She was always a dear faithful friend to the afflicted. To all the relatives she seemed as a magnet to which they were all drawn in case of distress or affliction of any kind. Sister came down from Round Timbers a few weeks after our arrival and stayed two or three weeks with us. And during her stay on one eventful day there came to us the cutest little blue-eyed, fair-haired, six-pound girl imaginable. Her father said she was a perfect little nymph, a professional beauty. We named her Arra Jimmie. This was a part of both of our names.[1]

We did not make a very long stay this trip, as cold weather was coming on and we wanted to get home.[2] Some of the relatives had been talking of moving to New Mexico, which made me a little uneasy, as they all usually took the moving fever at the same time. That would mean to leave me behind. However, I gave it but little thought. We were soon on our way home rejoicing that all was well with us, and we had one more little sunbeam added to our little family.

We moved camp that winter and built another large roomy dugout farther up on the hillside a few yards from the old one, as the walls of the first
shelter were too sandy and were inclined to cave in. From this new one we
had a better view. It was fine winter quarters, well built, [with a] good
fireplace, [and it was] canvassed and papered all inside with carpet on the
floor. We had nice pictures and other fancy things on the walls. The door
was hinged at the top when raised and fastened to the ceiling overhead.
My husband often explained in a joking way that every night when the
door was dropped down, it trapped four birds, two old ones and two
young ones. This dugout was cut back in the hillside, as most of them
were. This left only a small yard in front about ten feet wide, with a deep
canyon below. A narrow path led out each way. Below and above on the
flats was the only passway we had to the lots. When the cows came home,
they had to pass right through the yard, and some were wild and rather
vicious. Our little boy, Capp, often played out on this path, and we had to
keep watch for the cows.

We had quite a little excitement one evening for a few minutes. Mr.
Bird's brother, Bill, was with us then for a short visit.[3] I was busy working
on gloves. He and I were talking when all at once we heard Capp screaming to the top of his voice. He was about thirty yards down the road.
When I looked out, the old blue cow, the worst one, was just passing the
door. I made a dart, and out I went and took even breaks with her. Of
course, it scared her, and she ran with all her might. I stayed right by her
side, however. It was a close race, but I won it and reached Capp just in
time to save her from running over him. The next day some of the boys
were speaking something about a horse race, when Brother Bill spoke up
and said he would put Ella against any racehorse they might trot out. He
said that I went out at the door like a blue darter and beat that old blue
cow a flat-foot race of thirty yards, fair and square.

Bill was quite jolly, and we enjoyed his visit very much, though he was
preparing to leave us at that time. I made him a nice pair of fur mitts. I also
gave Mr. Bird a surprise birthday dinner, which came in about the right
time as Bill was leaving the next day. In planning the dinner, I could not
find a place to hide the cakes, pastry, and other foods, but finally I did. I
emptied the tray of my large trunk, laid paper in it, and had plenty of room
for everything. No one would suspect what was in it. So when my husband and Bill came in at noon, they were astonished. They wanted to
know where I got all this nice dinner. They surely did praise and enjoy the
dinner. Mr. Bird had not thought of this being his birthday. I poured out a
little glass of wine and set by each of their plates. They did not know I had

this either. They said this just touched off their dinner complete. That was the last time we ever saw Bill, though he lived many years afterward.

The boys often visited us from headquarters, which kept us from being so lonely, but there were few women in the country. I was quite busy most of the time making gloves. We were saving up a little now. We were starting us a little bunch of cattle, and they gave me a yearling for each pair of gloves. Cattle were cheap then. Mr. Bird also bought a bunch from Ed Shafer, or Deer Trail they called him. He also bought a bunch from Mr. John Abbott.[4] This gave us a little start by which I have profited all the way down until the present time. [The cattle] have bought all the land we own today in the country.

Our little babe was so sweet and good that I had much time to work through the summer.[5] I made many fancy fringed and beaded vests of buckskin, for which I received twelve dollars each. The beaded gauntlet gloves were seven dollars each. Often when Mr. Bird went to the round-ups, he would take three or four of my vests, wrap and put them in a flour sack, and tie them on behind his saddle. They always sold readily. He would bring me back about fifty dollars or more.

This summer Colonel Kit Carter, the owner of the ranch, came up and spent a few weeks with his son, Sul Carter,[6] who was foreman of the ranch. He, Mr. Kit Carter, visited with us while there, and he gave me an order for three small books carved out of gyp rock. His daughter, who was in college at Thorp Springs,[7] wanted them as presents for some girlfriends.

This was a change in the program of my late line of work, but when I got them all finished, they looked so beautiful to me I did not want to go back to glove making. I wanted to keep on working in the rock, but I could not, for my work was much needed elsewhere. Thus, by degrees as time went on, this continual longing for sculpture, which I did not understand myself, must gradually burn itself out to some extent. Otherwise, I could never have gone on with success at any other industry. But today I realize fully that I have, though unknowingly at the time, buried a talent on those broad barren prairies of the Texas Panhandle. This was a talent which perhaps might have been worth hundreds of thousands of dollars, as well as a world of pleasure to me. Many people have told me that I was dropped down in the wrong place, but I suppose the good Lord knew what he was doing when he allotted me to a western life. At any rate I feel my life has not been entirely misspent. I hope I have done some good, besides enjoying some pleasures aside from the many sorrows and disappointments that came to me. As time went on, that fall and winter I did a lot more glove and vest making.

We had a very sad thing occur the latter part of that summer. It was the death of Mr. John Coker, one of the boys on the ranch. The Murphy family was on the ranch then,[8] and their little boy, Harve, and Mr. Coker were both very seriously ill at the same time with typhoid fever. We were all gathered there to do what we could, but that was little, as we had no doctor. The poor boy, Mr. Coker, passed away, and the little Murphy boy was laying lifeless. Poor Mrs. Murphy was walking the floor wringing her hands. It seemed there was no hope, but he finally rallied and recovered. There was no lumber of which to make a coffin for Mr. Coker, so they took some plank out of a shed room. From this, Mr. Mathis made a very nice coffin, lined and covered with black cloth. We put Mr. Coker away very respectable, considering everything. We all returned to our camps sad at heart. This was the first death we had had in this country.

Mr. Bill Pressley spent the winter with us, as another man was needed on that part of the range.[9]

I shall never forget a wolf hunt or excitement we had one night. The loafer wolves were so plentiful. They would howl around near the house every night. Mr. Bird was gone on a trip to Seymour. He had two fine young hounds. We had to watch to keep the wolves from catching them away from the house. The names he gave those dogs were Garfield and Guiteau. This was the year Garfield was assassinated.[10] Mr. Pressley and I were sitting up one night. I was finishing a pair of gloves, and it was about ten o'clock. The loafers were howling down on the sandbar of the river about fifty yards away, when all at once we heard the fight begin. Our dogs had ventured too far and the wolves had caught them. Manfully, Mr. Pressley grabbed a gun and ran with all his might to rescue them. He was passing a big hole of water just before he reached the scene of battle, when he met little bobtail, Guiteau, running like a streak of lightning with a bunch of loafers right at his heels. He rose and jumped in the middle of this hole of water, swam out on the other side, and saved himself. But poor Mr. Pressley, where was he? He had been left standing amid this big bunch of loafer wolves. With raised bristles and snarling teeth they were all around him. He fired two shots at them, and the gun had only two loads in it. They scampered off a little at this, and he made for the house. All the time I was loading up another gun. Out I went with a belt of cartridges and gun, headed for the battlefield. I met Mr. Pressley about halfway. I asked him three times what was done, but he only said with shaking voice, while trembling from head to foot, "Give me that gun!" I gave it to him, and we went back down the road. The wolves had gone. We found Garfield on the sandbar. He was nearly dead. He was torn to pieces. We carried him to the house on a piece of canvasing, but he died before morning. Mr. Pressley said those big loafers looked as large to him as yearlings.

Mr. Bird was very much disappointed at losing his fine dog. He said he guessed it was sent on him for naming them as he did, though he did not mean any disrespect to our poor unfortunate President Garfield.

The Matador Ranch had grown to be quite an immense piece of property. It employed one hundred men, using five hundred head of horses.[11] They were putting on a little social affair just then. It was a grand ball, something out of the ordinary in this country. We had an invitation. I took much pains in preparing suitable costumes for myself and the babies for this occasion. There were so few ladies in the country that there were a few who came out from Fort Worth. It was certainly a success. The house was decorated and beautifully furnished. I felt rather timid, as I had not seen so much luxury and splendor since we had been in the country. The table fairly groaned with its burden of luscious good things to eat.

Mr. H. H. Campbell was the foreman and a shareholder in the company. Mrs. Campbell, being a wonderful hostess, made us all feel so very much at ease.[12] I soon forgot my embarrassment. Mr. Bird, of course, was acquainted with most all the boys. I don't think I ever saw a lot of people enjoy anything so much as they did this affair.

We moved camp again in the spring on the east side of the range. We had very good quarters here. We had a large rock house partly sunken in the ground with a dugout for a kitchen. It was very comfortable.

For the past year we had been planning to visit my husband's people in southern Texas, at Round Mountain in Blanco County.[13] We had been married for seven years,[14] and I had never seen any of his folks except his brother.

I did much sewing in the spring preparing for the trip. Our little girl was then two years and ten months old. She was a perfect blond and our boy a brunette, which we thought was just right. Their father was almost vain over them. He was so anxious to have his people see them. I took much pains with our little girl's clothes. One dress especially was a dream. It was of a solid handmade lace, touched up with blue ribbon. I had worked days and days on this dress. Oh, had we seen the dark cloud in the distance that was hovering nearer and nearer over us, our hearts would have sunk and all vain pride left us. But thanks to the merciful God who had so ordained that we do not penetrate the future. Much of it comes all too soon anyway. We were so intent on our visit that we gave but little thought to anything else at that time.

My sister was living at Seymour. They had built a home there. We planned on visiting with them a few days. Then we were to take the stage for Fort Griffin and go on to Albany[15] to take the train for the rest of the trip. We were soon on our way to Seymour and had no trouble in reaching that place in due time. They were expecting us, and we were all rejoiced to be together again. We had not seen each other in nearly three years.

Seymour had built up wonderfully,[16] but we learned that there was much sickness in the town, mostly a slow fever that was very fatal, especially to children. We decided to shorten our visit. We had been there three days when our little girl, Jimmie, took the fever. [Our children] were both the picture of health, but this fever was something distressing. We watched over her with anxious, praying hearts only to see her pining away day by day. Then our boy, Capp, took the fever, and our anxiety was doubled. We called in another doctor for him, the one who had always claimed him and who was with me at his birth. We sat by them day and night, almost in breathless despair. For a time it seemed both of them would be taken, but Doctor Wilson[17] was fine in this fever. He finally brought Capp through till he was out of danger. But our darling little Jimmie seemed slowly but surely slipping away from us.

Oh, what should we do? We pled to God with all our hearts to spare our little one to us, but the Death Angel was already hovering over her. The little pure soul was preparing to take its flight. On the tenth morning from the time she was first taken sick, all was over.

We had never had a death in our family before, and naturally it seemed impossible for me to take it calm and quietly as I should. When the first moan of anguish escaped me, I felt the pressure of arms around me. I knew it was Sister. She was kneeling by me pouring out words of sympathy and consolation as only a true sister to a sister can. I seemed to have swooned and lost consciousness. The next I knew I was lying on the bed. Sister was bending over me bathing my face, still talking and weeping with me. Oh God, why must we suffer these heartbreaks? Why, oh, why must our hearts be rent asunder and laid bare at thy feet when we have lived a Christian life to the best of our knowledge and understanding? Why with all thy power were we not made strong in mind and with all fortitude to bear these things?

I was led into the front room by the side of the little white casket to view her remains for the last time. Dear Sister had dressed her so beautifully. She looked like a little sleeping angel. She wore the same little lace dress that I had spent so much time and happy hours in making, the one I expected to have so much pleasure in seeing her wear. I was truly glad I had made this dress, but, oh, how our fondest hopes of expected happiness and bliss can so soon be changed into the bitterest gall. We thanked God fervently that even one of our little ones was spared to us.

In a few days after we had rested, we continued our visit, though not in the spirit we had expected. The world seemed dark and dreary without our little gem, as we deemed her. She had been a perfect little sunbeam in our home.

We went by way of Austin and stopped over one day there to select a tomb for our baby's grave. There were many beautiful monuments. The man took us into his display room where there were many beautiful statues. This was the first real sculpture work I had ever seen that amounted to anything. I was so enthused over it that I could have stayed there for hours and days. Mr. Bird told the man that I was interested in this line of work. He said he would show me a fine piece. He took us back and opened the door of a fine mahogany case, and there we beheld a lady statue, an angel, in life-size, holding a bunch of grapes. It was so beautiful I almost fell on my knees in front of it. Oh, how I wanted to do this work. My whole soul was in it. This statue cost one thousand dollars and would be twice that now. If I could only have begun then, I felt that I could have done wonders with it. However, this pleasure was not mine. This ambition had to be crushed. Other duties of a household nature were calling me in the opposite direction.

We journeyed on the next day about fifty miles west to Round Mountain, the home of my husband's people. It was a happy meeting with their wandering boy. They had not seen him in seven years. The brothers and sisters came flocking in. There were eleven of them living and one dead. Bill Bird was the oldest, and then the boys Tom, George, Joe, Julius, and Frank followed in succession. The sisters were Mary, Martha, "Dochia," Kate, and Sussie.[18] They had a regular jubilee. The house was a large two-story building All the surroundings and everything seemed so homelike and comfortable, and they were all so nice to me that it was pleasant to be there. They had lived at this place for forty years. My husband's father was conducting a big camp meeting out in the country a few miles away, but they were in that night. We drove out there the next day and all remained there till it was over. Many people were out from Burnet Town.[19] It was a great revival. There were fifty conversions.

Our little boy, Capp, was four years old then. He had never seen a Negro till we were on the train.[20] He asked his father what it was. He told him it was a bear. There was a family of Negroes at this campground. They

were carrying water up on the other side of the camp. Capp was out playing on the grounds when all at once we heard him screaming and running
with all his might saying, "Yonder comes a bear, two big bears and a whole
lot of little bears." He was very much frightened. He said, "And, Mama,
they were carrying buckets with their forefeet." He had seen a real bear
once before. They had quite a laugh over it. His grandmother took great
interest in him and said he was just like his father when he was little.

The meeting was over, and we all went back to the Bird house. We enjoyed a rest and recreation for a while, [and] then we visited quite a lot
among my husband's relatives and friends. Of course, we were yet in
mourning for our little one, but we tried to cheer up and be as pleasant as
we could. It was good to see my husband enjoy his relatives and old
friends. But there was no place I enjoyed more than in the home with his
mother and father. They were wonderful, I thought. His father was interesting, and his mother was so kind and sympathetic with me in my late
trouble. We remained with them about one month.

We decided to return home by private conveyance, so we bought a hack
and team.[21] Everything was soon arranged. On the following morning,
we bade farewell to all the homefolks. This parting was final with their
son and brother. They never saw him again on this earth. Neither have I
ever met with one of them again from that day till this, more than forty
years ago.

We came back by Burnet Town and stopped over two days with my husband's sister, Mrs. Saulter. Her husband was sheriff at that place then. This
was his favorite sister, and I thought when I met her, "No wonder!" She
was just beautiful and so fine looking without ever seeming conscious of it.
Her hair was simply wonderful. It was rather heavy dark brown, wavy, and
reached nearly to her knees. She was splendid company and so jolly.

When we left Burnet, we bent our course for Young County to see my
people before we returned home. We made the trip without any special
events. We found all well and happy but took them by surprise. They were
not looking for us. We only spent a few days with them on this trip. We
were anxious to get back home again, though we enjoyed the little visit
with them.

We stopped at Round Timbers and visited with Sister and family two or
three days. They had sold out in Seymour and had moved back to the
ranch. I always enjoyed the visit with Sister. She and I seemed just two to
ourselves.

We journeyed on to Seymour, but the thoughts of this place only brought
sadness to our hearts, this being where we had laid our little one to rest.

We only stopped a few hours here,[22] [and] journeyed on our way home to the east camp on the Ross Ranch. We found everything all right after a three months' absence.

Ten

MR. BILL PRESSLEY stayed with us again that winter.[1] I made more gloves and some vests. This was a lonely winter for me. Time grew heavy on my hands. My one little boy was a source of comfort and company to me, but the vacant little chair still held its place in our home. The Carters visited us sometimes on Sundays. We sometimes drove down to Otta, a store and post office kept by Mr. John Abbott and family, which was six miles east of us.[2]

We had some news from my relatives in Young County. They were planning for another move. They were going to the Sacramento Mountains of New Mexico around Cloudcroft. Some had already gone. Sister Lucy, my grandmother, and all except my mother's family were going. There were five families in all. I was certainly grieved over this move, most especially Sister and Grandmother. Many of them I have never seen again, and several I will never see again on this earth, as they have passed away to the great beyond.[3]

But changes are taking place continually. The Ross Ranch, or the Carter Cattle Company as it was called, sold out to a northern company. All the cattle were shipped away north. The land was also sold, and the Ross Ranch was no more. For a time our little bunch of cattle and another one or two small ones were the only cattle on this range.

We moved again in the spring down to the post office at Otta. Another family, Mr. Al Crawford, had moved there, which made three families of us. I was not lonely any more. Mrs. Abbott and I were good friends of some years past, and all three were very congenial.

Mr. A. Dumont was one of our nearest neighbors then. He and his partner, Mr. McGaughey, still owned a hog ranch in connection. He was quite often at Otta, and we all became quite good friends.

The spring passed off into summer without any special events to speak of. I was doing much sewing and embroidering. We were preparing for another trip to my mother's in Young County. I have another secret to confide. There was to be another baby. We were soon on our way. We landed in Young County all O.K. My mother had ordered this trip for us and, of course, was expecting us.

Everything seemed changed up. All the relatives were gone except my mother's family. I missed my sister, oh so much. Several of the old friends had moved to California, including one of my girlfriends that I loved very much, Bell Jones. Ellen and Bob had moved to Arkansas several years ago. Such is life, however. Nothing can remain the same. It is continually on the change. I felt very thankful though, for my dear mother was left me. She, of all the relatives, I wanted most.

My stepfather kept the ferry boat on the Brazos River. It was interesting to be near the river and enjoy so much nice fresh fish, which we always had. It was fun to watch the big rises coming down and the large cable boat shooting to and fro carrying people back and forth through the angry rolling waves and drifts that seemed impassable.[4]

The summer was fast waning, when on the twenty-second day of July there came to us another fair-haired, blue-eyed baby girl, weighing six pounds. We were so proud of her. She looked so very much like our little Jimmie. It seemed almost like she had been restored to us. On the way home three weeks later, we discussed the naming of this girl. Her father wanted me to select the name, so my selection was Bessie Adell.[5]

We arrived at home with the brand-new baby and found everything O.K. and all as glad to see us as we were them. That fall and winter Mr. Bird spent in seeing after our cattle, hunting a part of the time, and dressing deer hides. I made more gloves, vests, and pants.

That winter was [when we saw] the last buffalo that was ever seen in this part of the country. It was killed in Mr. George Brandt's pasture, now the 3D's.[6] That has been just forty-two years ago from this date.[7]

After the passing of the buffalo, the stockmen went on out into the vast domain that had been known as the "buffalo range." The Lasaters and Hensleys were among the first to locate ranches there. The Lasaters moved in, in 1877 or 1878. They located on the South Wichita River and built what is now known as "Rock Corrals," two miles east of Guthrie in King County. This was about the same time that the Hensleys located on Duck Creek in Dickens County.[8] From that time on, they came fast. In 1879 C. L. (Kit) Carter located the R O S Ranch on the head of North Wichita,[9] and about this same time, H. H. Campbell moved in the V cattle. He later sold out to a Scottish company, and [the ranch] took the name of the Matador Land and Cattle Company.[10] They bought out several brands that had located in their part of the country, such as NN, T41, O, and other smaller outfits.[11] The Frying Pan or Jingle Bobs,[12] as they were known, [were] trailed there from the noted Chisum Ranch on Pecos River in New Mexico by R. K. Wiley, a noted West Texas cowman. He was ranching on the head of Tongue River a few miles above Roaring Springs[13] in 1877 or 1878. They were the first highbred cattle to come into the country, being mostly all reds or roans. They were thoroughbred Durham Cattle. Jim Hall located his cattle on the headwater of the North Pease River about ten miles south of Quitaque Peaks in 1878, and later sold out to an English company that took the name of Espuela Land and Cattle Company. They made their headquarters on Duck Creek in Dickens County, and they bought out many smaller ranches adjoining them.[14]

The famous old Pitchfork brand was trailed from southern Texas in the early seventies, making many stops before locating in King, Stonewall, and Dickens counties. It was originally owned by a man named Savage. I am unable to say how many times the brand changed hands before it became the property of D. B. Gardner, who bought it in 1881 or 1882, and later formed what was known as the Pitchfork Land and Cattle Company, with headquarters located on the headwaters of the South Wichita River. It was managed by D. B. Gardner as long as he lived.[15]

The Scab Eight brand was owned and trailed to King County by Sam Lazurus, who later sold it to the Louisville Land and Cattle Company, John A. Lee, general manager. Lee headquartered on Newman Creek, and later sold to Burk Burnett who ran the brand into his own 6666 brand.[16]

The JF Brand was owned by [John] Farrar in the northeast part of King County. It was sold to Mabry, Crawford, and Glasgow in the eighties, who later sold the brand to King County Livestock Company.[17]

The Moon Brand was trailed from Shackelford County in 1881. It was owned by Charlie Cannon. He was killed in 1883 in Seymour by Henry Jones. The ranch changed hands many times, and was owned later by W. Q. Richards. This was his headquarter ranch at the time of his death.[18]

The 3D brand was owned by W. Q. Richards. It was trailed to Cottle and Foard counties in 1880. The ranch was located near the east line of Cottle County by George Brandt.[19]

The OX brand was owned by [A. J.] Forsythe. The ranch was located in Cottle, Childress, and Hardeman counties. The headquarters were in Childress County, twelve miles north of the mouth of Catfish Creek and five miles southeast of the town of Childress.[20]

When the lease law was passed by the regular session of the State Legislature in 1883, there was a scramble for lands. Each outfit tried to get hold to keep from being moved out of business. It was a case of the big fish catching the small ones. It put many little cattlemen out of business, and broke lots of the big ones. Up to that time, it was a free-for-all country, and one had as much right as another.[21]

Then fencing began in earnest. Some few had fenced in widely separated parts of the country. Now every ranch began fencing, but none close up to their pastures, as the law required them to pay lease on all lands they enclosed. To beat the law they would make gaps. Others would build drift fences to turn the drifting cattle around or off their ranges. For two years starting with August 1, 1883, there were thousands and thousands of miles of fence built up and down the West Texas border.[22]

The winter of 1884 and 1885 was one of the worst winters this country has ever passed through.[23] Lots of snow and cold weather caused the cowman a great loss from poverty-stricken cattle. Lots of outfits lost two-thirds or three-fourths of their cattle. Ranchmen who were ranching the Yellowhouse and Blanco canyons that ran up into the plains had cattle to get out in the open plains. The blizzards drifted them across the plains to the Pecos River by the thousands. It was reported that an engineer on the Texas and Pacific Railroad said he had to stop his train for two hours to let the cattle pass. He said that there were cattle as far as he could see in every direction.[24]

After the prairies were cut up into pastures, cow work was some easier. Even at that the life of the cowboy[25] was full of hardships and exposure. The cowboys were usually scattered out over different parts of the pasture from fifteen to twenty miles apart. Their jobs were to repair fences, water gaps, pull cattle out of bogs, and keep an eye open for cattle "rustlers" (thieves). The cowboys always lived in dugouts, which were very warm in winter, and strange as it may seem, were cool in summer. Some were fixed up very artistically, the dirt walls being white-washed with gypsum, which was very plentiful. Very few of the cowboys were married, and when a woman was met, there was much bowing, scraping, and rattling of boots and spurs. Reading matter was very scarce, and when received, it was passed from one ranch or cow camp to the other. Two comic novels read by most old-time cowboys were *Sut Lovingood* and *Peck's Bad Boy*,[26] which were considered very classic.

Cow thieves or "rustlers" were very troublesome in those days.[27] One of the most hated human beings on earth was a horse thief. Very often, when captured, he was tied up and hung on the spot and left hanging as a warning to others. I heard two old-time cowboys, Dick McDuff and a man by the name of Thompson, relate their experience with a cow thief. This thief had stolen some of McDuff's and Thompson's best cow horses, and after following him several days, they captured him. They bound his hands and feet, tied one end of a lasso (rope) around his neck, and threw the other end over a limb of a tree. Before drawing him up, they decided [that] on an occasion like this they should do something sanctimonious like singing a religious song or a prayer. Each insisted on the other performing the ceremony. Neither one could think of anything in the way of a prayer. They couldn't think of but two songs, "My Darling Nellie Gray" and "The Old Gray Mare Comes Tearing Out of the Wilderness." At last one of them said, "Oh, Lord, take this bow-legged, white-livered, hoss-thievin' son-of-a———. We ain't got no use fer 'im down here. Amen!"

Eleven

THESE WERE the days back in 1885 up into the 1890's. There were two main events—the spring and fall "roundups." The spring roundups usually took place in the months of April, May, and June. These are the months when most of the calves are born. The fall roundups brand all calves missed in the spring and all calves born during the summer.

The old-time way of handling cattle was quite different from the modern way. There were no pens or chutes to brand in. All this took place out on the bald prairie. It would have taken two regiments of cavalry to force one of those old lanky cows into a pen.

These roundups were carried on very systematically. Before roundup time started, all the cowboys stationed at cow camps over the pasture were notified to meet at the ranch house at a certain date. The adjoining ranchers were also notified so they could each send a man to get what cattle had broken over the partition fence which divided the ranches. The men from adjoining ranches were called "stray" hands. The ranch owner had a special range boss who told the cowboys what to do. Each cowboy had a "mount" which consisted of from eight to ten horses. Four or five of these horses were well trained, and the rest were broncos or "willer trails,"[1] which were used on "drives." After all pots, skillets, tin plates, tin cups, branding irons, bedding, slickers, and "chuck" (food) were loaded into the chuck wagon, the cow outfit was ready to head for the open range.

After moving out from "headquarters" or the ranch house, they would go to some part of the pasture which had been selected in advance to start the roundups. The roundup ground was usually a smooth prairie as free from timber and ditches as possible. The cow outfit would usually strike camp near a creek or water hole in the evening and prepare for the roundup early the next morning.

While the cook or "culinary-buckshot" was preparing supper, the horses were rounded up in a close huddle to be "hobbled" out to graze for the night. This was a very hard job, and some of the cowboys would often lose their religion. To hobble a horse was to tie the front feet together, leaving a space of eighteen or twenty inches between feet, so that the horse was compelled to take very short steps and was unable to stray very far from camp during the night. This was done with a special short length of rope about three feet long. The older horses were not very troublesome to hobble, but there was always a large percentage of young horses that were on their first "cow work." Of course, they didn't know what this was all about and would have to be roped and manhandled severely.

Each man had a night horse which was very gentle. This horse was staked out to ride next morning to round up the horses which had been hobbled out the night before.

After supper the cowboys would gather around the camp fire and proceed to have some cowboy songs, which could be heard almost as far away as some lonesome lobo wolf. Another camp fire pastime was telling tall stories or shaking nickels in a tin cup. Each man would put a coin in the cup, and the man that [guessed] the most heads after shaking got the contents, which would sometimes be as much as a dollar or more depending on the number of men in the game. After the fun was over, each man would proceed to spread out his bed, or hot roll as they were sometimes called, using their trousers, coats, or slickers for a pillow.

Next morning very early when it was light enough to see, they would saddle the horses they had staked and ride out and bring in the horses they had hobbled the night before. After the horses were unhobbled, which was almost as big a job as the hobbling, they selected the horses to ride on the "drive." Now another real job began. That was to saddle and ride those wild horses. It was a free rodeo every morning. A great many of these horses were of Spanish or mustang extraction and were very mean and tough.

When the horses got the "raw edge" off, the men would divide up and go in all directions. This was called the "drive," which extended out several miles from the roundup ground. When the cattle were driven in, a fire was built out some distance from the roundup to heat the branding irons. The expert ropers would now go into the cattle and rope the calves and drag them to the fire where they were "bull-dogged" or thrown on their sides to be marked and branded. To "mark" a calf was to split one ear and cut off the tip of the other for identification. Each cattle owner had his particular mark.

When this roundup was completed, the cow outfit would move to another place, and the same thing was repeated until all calves were branded. Some pastures were so large that they had more than one outfit working at the same time.

Then there came the time when the calves were a year old, called "year-lings." They were collected and driven to the nearest railroad, which was at one time very far away. These "trail herds," as they were called sometimes, consisted of several thousand cattle and were several miles long. This was a long tiresome journey, as the cattle had to be driven in a very slow walk. Water was sometimes far between.

"Cuttin'" and "ropin'" horses were very highly prized. There was quite a rivalry between the owners of good cutting horses. A cutting horse is a very intelligent horse trained to be ridden into a herd to cut out a special cow, and once this horse finds which animal is selected, all worry is over as far as the rider is concerned. The horse will do the rest. About the biggest worry for the rider is staying on the horse, especially if the cow does very much dodging and darting. Cutting horses are very active on their feet and are very hard to ride when in action. A great "show off stunt" is to reach over and pull the bridle off and let the horse take the cow out of the herd without any guidance whatever from the rider.

A great many things had nicknames in cowboy lingo, and one not ac-quainted would not know what it meant. One favorite dish most relished by the cowboys was called "County Attorney" in the presence of ladies and preachers, as the real name like some of the horses' names would not look well in print. Sometimes, however, it was referred to as Son-of-a-Gun. The cowboys would usually cook a big oven full of this dish when they killed a beef on the roundup. It is made as follows. Certain parts of the beef, liver, sweetbread, marrow fat, and so forth are used. The marrow gut, as they called it, is the last intestine that conducts the fat to the body of the animal. Mr. Carr, one of my neighbors and farmers,[2] took dinner one day with the boys at the roundup. When they passed this favorite dish around to him, he said, "No, thank you. So long as there is plenty of meat, I do not care for any of the guts." The boys had a big laugh.[3]

Another bit of cowboy slang was referring to a horse herder as a "horse wrangler." "Broncho busters" were also called "peelers."[4]

Mr. Dumont and Mr. McGaughey spent the winter of 1885–1886 at Otta. Mr. Dumont took care of the post office, and Mr. McGaughey made boots at times when not busy with the stock. That was his profession be-fore coming to this country. Mr. Bird was away from home a great deal, and Mr. Dumont was always so nice and thoughtful of me and the babies. He kept us supplied with plenty of wood at the door and always divided milk with us, as he and the other boys came by from the lot. These little kind favors and acts we never forgot.

We were out of dressed buckskin at that time, and I wanted four dollars to order some trimming for the baby's dresses. How I was to make this money I could not figure out. I walked around the house and spied an old dried-up wildcat hide hanging on the fence. Now Mr. Webb, a boy on the ranch, had ordered a pair of gloves some weeks ago and was waiting for them, so I looked this hide over and decided to dress it. I put it in to soak that night. The next morning I spread it over the graining horse, took the back of the drawer knife as I had seen my husband do, and rubbed all the hair off of it. I put it to soak in the dressing ooze that night and dressed it the next day. It was spotless white and looked like a fine kid skin. I went to work and made a pair of gloves of it with long gauntlets, fringe on the sides and fancy-colored silk stitching over them. A nicer pair of kidlike gloves you would not find anywhere. They were much more tough and durable than kid. Mr. Webb came down to the post office the next day and gave me four dollars for them, so I ordered the trimming for the baby's dress at once.

All would have moved on peacefully and quietly, but it seems there is always something disagreeable that must come to take the joy out of one's life, or the life of a friend. For some time there had been a feud between Mr. Abbott and another man, Bill Trumble, who was a young cowboy. There had been several gunplays and shots fired, but friends had prevented any loss of life. Their gunplays were becoming more serious all the time, and everybody had to look out for number one. When Trumble came to the post office, the row usually began.

One special time there were several freighters there, bone haulers with ox wagons. The bone hauling business was very profitable at this time, although it did not last very long. They were all gathered pretty soon after the passing of the buffalo when the bones had dried and bleached.[5]

There was also an Irishman there who had just come from Missouri. He was prospecting for a homestead. He was a large, portly, good-looking man who was quite talkative, though he did not know anything of the West.

About the first thing we knew, shooting began in the store. Some shots penetrated the wall between the store and the Abbott dwelling, and they shot one of Mr. Abbott's fingers. Bullets were whistling in every direction. We women were all gathered in Mr. Crawford's picket house about twenty steps away. All the freighters began rushing out of the house, hiding behind wagons and everything. We women were crowded in and around the door looking to see what was going on. Trumble was then on his horse out in front of the store waving his gun in the air, daring Mr. Abbott and all his friends to show up. He would fight them all. About this time this Missouri Irishman (Wells was his name) gave a leap out at the door. He was pale and ashen, and he took a beeline for our picket house. He did not even slow up when he reached it. He just made a high dive right through the bunch of us, never stopping until he got to the back of the room behind everything. About this time Mr. Abbott came out at a side door with a Winchester rifle, but two men were holding it and would not let him shoot. Some other men out on the front got around Trumble and persuaded him to leave, as Mr. Abbott was not allowed to fight him. All was calm once more. Mr. Wells came out rather sheepish looking but with a little western experience. He told Mr. Bird later that Trumble was the bravest man he had ever seen in his life, and that if he were in Abbott's place, he would go to him like a man and tell him he was afraid of him and wanted to call it off. This would be using good judgment.

Spring was near at hand now. Mr. Bird had been looking out for a location for us, a permanent home. He decided on a piece of land joining the Matador Ranch, twelve miles away.[6] He built a large dugout with a picket house in front, which he intended to use for a barn and stable in the fall when we built a good house. The picket house was made with long split poles, one end in the ground, the other end nailed to the top frame or wall, covered with either dirt or hand split shingles. So we were settled for a while.

We had been here but a short time when the sad news reached us one day that Trumble had killed Mr. Abbott that morning. He had shot him three times while Mr. Abbott was at the spring getting water. It was about four hundred yards away from the house. Mr. Abbott's little three-year-old boy was left standing by his father, talking about "poor Daddy" when some of them came up.[7] We got ready and hurried down to Otta that afternoon. Poor Mrs. Abbott was almost frantic with grief, as we knew she would be. Two other ladies were there, Mrs. Austin and Mrs. Colthorp who lived a few miles away. We did all we could to console Mrs. Abbott, but of course, there is not much we can do when the grief is at its earliest. She had him buried there near the house where she could tend his grave, which she did for several years afterward.

Trumble received a life sentence to the penitentiary but was released in fifteen years. He died two years later of tuberculosis contracted while in the penitentiary.

Our little bunch of cattle, which numbered one hundred and thirty head then, were still on the Ross range, and remained there for several years afterward. Mr. Bird worked through the range with the other cattlemen.

We had been at this place some two years. Mr. Bird's health had been failing for some time. He had some very serious attacks of cramps, and the doctor said he could never survive another.[8]

He had wanted to move to the mountains of New Mexico, so he decided to go out there and look at the country. The first of October, he started on the long journey in a wagon. I dreaded so much for him to be gone from home so long. It was so lonely for me and the two children. Capp was then only seven and Bessie two years old,[9] but we made it all right. Mr. Bird was gone three months. It seemed ages. He was fully in the notion of moving to New Mexico the next fall.

Mr. Jameson and Mr. Wells were our nearest neighbors. This was the same Wells we met at Otta. Mr. Bird had been at home only about two weeks when he and Mr. Wells took a trip to Quanah[10] for supplies and feed. The weather turned awfully cold, with snowing and sleeting. They were gone several days when Mr. Wells came in, but Mr. Bird was not with him. They started out from Quanah together in the evening, he said, but became separated some way. He drove on ahead and finally camped thinking Mr. Bird would come on, but he did not. The next morning he harnessed up, drove back a few miles, but did not find him so he came on home. He said he thought Mr. Bird must have gone back to Quanah for something, which he spoke of doing after they had started home.

The weather was still bitter cold. We waited three days, then Mr. Jameson and Mr. Slaughter, the latter an old friend of Mr. Bird's, went in search of him. They rode till they came to Groesbeck Creek about twelve miles this side of Quanah.[11] They first came in sight of his wagon where he had camped in the shallow, flat bottom of the creek above the crossing. They did not yet suspect anything serious but rushed on. The first thing they beheld was Mr. Bird lying on the side of a little bank. They thought at first he was asleep; but, oh, horrors, when they reached him, yes, he was asleep—his last sleep—he was dead! He had died all alone with no one to attend him. We believed he had an attack of the cramps.

They searched everything around him. There were thirteen empty cartridge hulls in the spring seat. By these shots it seemed he was trying to attract the attention of Mr. Wells. A few yards back showed where he had turned his wagon around and started back to Quanah. It must have been dark, for he missed the crossing, going above it and getting down in the bed of the creek. The banks were too steep to get out. It showed where he had cut his wagon around different ways trying to get out but failed and had unharnessed his team. He had tied them to a tree on the hill. His bed was made down, but he was not on it. Everything showed he was perfectly rational. It seemed his dog had gotten poison. A bucket of lard was sitting near where he had been doctoring him. The dog was laying a few steps away, dead. The team was almost perished for water and feed. If the dumb brutes could only speak, revelations might be made that we have never guessed. I believe my husband passed away the first night he was left alone, from the cramps.

One of the men hurried on to Quanah to give the alarm. They brought an ambulance out for him and carried him back to Quanah and prepared him for interment as soon as possible. They had no way of communicating with me, and it was so far they could not wait.

The news came around by Matador and on to me by Mr. Fult Hardy. It was a shock that almost drove me insane. It was too bad to be true. It seemed that half of my life had passed out. I could not comprehend it at first. My first thought was, "Oh, what will become of me, with no one but my two little children left me." It seemed the three months that he was away in New Mexico must have been intended to prepare me for this trial and to make me more resigned to my fate, to make me know that I could live alone. It may have helped some, but, oh, I felt so desolate and lonely for a long time. The weary weeks and months that seemed to drag were almost unbearable.

My oldest brother, Willie,[12] who was visiting our mother at that time, came and stayed with me the remainder of the winter, [and] then went on to his home in New Mexico. This was a help to me.

Twelve

THERE WAS one thing I had in mind from the first. That was to make a tomb for my husband's grave. I intended to make it out of gyp rock. I began on this a few weeks after his death. It seemed this work relieved my mind of worry more than anything else. It was steady employment. It was a long tedious job that took more than three months to complete, but my whole soul and interest was in it. This tomb was beautiful, as I had determined it should be. It stood about five feet high. It represented the form of a large church and was cut back in the rock about six inches, leaving a deep heavy frame all around with pillars and steps on each side. There was a large lily carved. It looked as if it was carelessly dropped down on two of the steps. In the back of this deep frame, the inscription was made. It was raised above the surface about one-third of an inch and was carved in large German text letters. Over the top of this front was carved a beautiful heavy wreath of ferns. Across the top of this, a deep slab was laid, and a large vase sat on this with a cloth thrown over one handle and draped down over the slab. This was all in pure white marblelike stone.

It was all completed and was ready to be carried to Quanah to be erected. But oh, how was I to get it there? I did not know. I had only two neighbors who lived one mile and two and one-half miles away, Mr. Jameson and Mr. Bailey. The next was Mr. Wells, four miles away. Mr. Bailey came up one day and told me that Mrs. Bailey would go with me to Quanah.[1] I was certainly relieved and began preparing for the trip at once.

My team was in fine shape, having been used but little in several months. One horse had been rattlesnake bitten near the mouth, but that was about well. Early the next morning, Mrs. Bailey and I loaded up our wagon, packed the monument securely, and started to Quanah, which was about fifty miles away. We had gone but a few miles when we came to a small creek. Our horse that had been rattlesnake bitten balked on the hill. They had always pulled true before. We tried every way, unloaded some of the things, but they would not pull; so we took a stake rope, tied it to the end of the tongue, and put the team up on the hill with the double tree tied to the end of the stake rope. I took the lines, and Mrs. Bailey watched the wagon. I had no more than said the word when they pulled it right up without a bobble. We were all right then.

We drove on, but they tried to balk at every little hill. We crossed South Pease River at the mouth of Catfish.[2] It was about dry, but when we struck the sand bar, we stalled again. We were not heavy loaded, but the old horse would not pull a pound. He just balked. We worked and worried with them more than an hour and finally got across to the other side.

We were going up through the breaks having all sorts of trouble when Mrs. Bailey stopped the team short and said, "We will try another remedy." Mrs. Bailey was a woman of much good sense and sound judgment. She got out, took a small rope, made a halter, removed the bridle from the horse, and put on the halter instead. We then started them off again, and you never saw a horse pull better than this one did. We never had any more trouble with him. Mrs. Bailey said his mouth was tender from the snakebite, and he would not pull against the bit. We drove on and camped that night between the two rivers, North and South Pease. We had three children with us, Mrs. Bailey's baby[3] and my two.

We drove into Quanah the next afternoon and stopped with Mrs. Ashford, a friend of Mrs. Abbott's, whom the latter had recommended to us and whose husband would help us with our work the next morning. She was a very pleasant woman. Mr. Ashford drove out to the cemetery with us and erected the monument to my husband's grave.

This visit to the cemetery was a sad one for me indeed. It was the first time I had seen my husband's grave. It was hard for me to realize that he was lying there and that I should never see his face again on this earth. I called my little girl, Bessie, to my side and told her all about her father. I so much wanted her to remember him, and she did for a long time. As she grew up, however, his memory gradually faded from her mind entirely. Poor Capp was brokenhearted over the loss of his father.

The monument is completely in ruins now, being of gypsum rock which could not stand the weather when exposed to the rain and sun.[4] The rock was partly underground when it was quarried, and I never thought of it ever cracking and falling down. It was a great disappointment to me after so much work and pains.

We drove out in town that afternoon and did some shopping. We loaded our wagon with groceries, taking several hundred pounds of flour and a lot of barbed wire. We drove back and spent the night again with Mrs. Ashford.

We got an early start the next morning and were going to try and make it in home the next day. We had gone about one-half mile and discovered that we had left our wagon sheet. Mrs. Bailey took one of the horses out of the harness and rode him back to get the sheet. We hit the road once more. We crossed Pease River and had to unload the flour. We were making it all right but had a long road through the sand and sagebrush, a different but nearer route than the one we came.

Our team was getting pretty tired. We missed the road and drove a few miles out of our way. It was getting late and one horse was almost given out. We were more than ten miles from home yet. We drove till dark and saw we could not make it, so we camped in a big swag[5] amid the sandhills. We were tired, worn out, and hungry. We had no light, neither did we have any bread. There were only some crumbs of bread and cake. We opened some canned goods and ate the best we could. Hidebugs were plentiful then.[6] It was comical to see us feeling around in the dark for those crumbs, fearing we would get a hidebug instead. We staked out the horses, made down our bed, and had a good night's rest on the sand.

The next morning as we were getting a little breakfast, a bunch of antelope came up in sight on the hill about four hundred yards away. I pulled out my Winchester and slathered[7] into them and killed one, so we had another white elephant on our hands. We carried one of the horses out after it, the one Mr. Bird had always hunted on. He snorted and made a big to do at the first sight of the antelope. Mrs. Bailey said we would never get it on him, but I said he had carried too many of them. He walked right up and stopped by it, and we loaded it on his back. She held it on while I led him back, and we put it on the wagon.[8]

We were soon on the way again. We struck the good road and were traveling at a pretty brisk gait. We were in good spirits now. Mrs. Bailey said, "Well, after all we have not had such a bad time. We have gotten along very well." We were rather congratulating ourselves, and just then we were crossing a little ditch in the road when our wagon wheel ran off. Our axle went flat in the road. We sat a moment in bewilderment. Mrs. Bailey said, "I will swear! We have the hardest luck of any two humans that ever started out." I thought a whole lot worse than that but did not say anything. We had to unload some of the things, get prize poles, and raise up the axle before we could get the wheel on. It took about one hour.

We hit the road once more for the last time and soon drove in home. We stopped at Mrs. Bailey's and had a good breakfast and unloaded her part of the freight. We skinned our antelope and divided the meat. The two little ones and I were soon at our home.

And now the long and lonely hours and weeks began for me again.[9] We lived near the river, Tongue River, where there were many cottonwood trees. The bottom was only slightly timbered with low undergrowth, but it was very wide. It was rather a lonely kind of place. We had moped all day. Late that afternoon when Capp had gone down on a little flat near the house hunting rabbits with his dog, he had treed one in a hole and came after me and the gun to kill it. We failed to get the rabbit, but while there we happened to look across toward the river a few hundred yards away. We saw a man coming toward us with a gun on his shoulder. It was something unusual for someone to be traveling around at that time of day, but through curiosity we waited until he came up. We scanned him over as he approached. He was quite tall, broad shouldered, and held himself very erect. He was dark complexioned and was rather an attractive looking man, but what could be his business?

He came up, removed his hat, bowed very politely, and introduced himself. I will call him F. P. He told me he was traveling with a friend from East Texas. He had been visiting relatives and was returning home to Roswell, New Mexico, but one of their horses had gotten slightly crippled, and they had to lay over a few days. They were camped down the river near Mrs. McDonald's, and she had told him I was taking a paper, *The Nogal Nugget*.[10] This was from near his hometown, and he wondered if I would loan it to him. I said sure I would, so he took my gun on the other shoulder, and we walked back to the house.

I was in deep mourning, and he seemed to understand my situation. He may have learned it from Mrs. McDonald. He talked freely and with all ease in a general line of conversation. His voice was deep but with the kindest of tone. He spoke of the country in a general way. He seemed to wonder why I was living all alone as I was, with so few people in the country. He conversed well and was interesting to talk to. On leaving he said it might be that they would move their camp farther up on the river where they could get better water, as it was very sorry where they were.

The next day they moved up just a few hundred yards from my house. Game was plentiful, and they did much hunting, mostly for turkeys at night. I never met the other man, but Mr. F. P. came out to the house quite often and talked awhile, sometimes bringing turkey meat. He said they were so lonely that they could hardly wait to get started on the road again. I learned that he was a carpenter and a saddler. He was a widower, his wife having died not very long after their marriage. He was reared in southern Texas not far from Mr. Bird's old home, though they were not acquainted. He came out one morning and said they were preparing to leave and that he wanted to give me an order for a pair of gloves. He would wait till he got home to send me his measurements. He bade us adieu in the kindest, sympathetic way in our loneliness, and they were soon on their way rejoicing.

In a few weeks I had a letter from him, though he did not mention the gloves. It was just a friendly letter. He said he had thought of me many times living in the lone little chocy, which was "dugout" in Spanish, I believe.[11] He said that he did not understand how anyone could live in such perfect seclusion and solitude as I, and that he would forget how to talk. He told of their trip home. His letter was interesting but somewhat brief. I did not answer it for nearly a month, but he was very prompt in answering mine.

I had been at home only a short time when I had a bad attack of ulcerated throat. I suffered with it several days and finally had to go to the doctor at Childress[12] for treatment. I left the baby with Mrs. Jameson and took Capp with me. My throat grew worse, and I suffered untold agonies. There was a large rising down inside that almost choked me. I was there at the hotel ten days. They told me that almost every day some of the boys from the neighboring ranches would call and inquire how I was, and that if I needed any money or anything whatever, to let them know. They told them I did not. If there was a married man with them, they would send him in to talk with me and find out how I was. I thanked them kindly and told them how very much I appreciated their interest in me, but I did not need anything at that time. These boys were friends of my late husband, some of whom I did not know, but they knew him and wanted to do something to help me.

My throat continued bad. It got so I could not talk. Poor little Capp would come to me every little while and say, "Mama, do you reckon you will die?" I was rather in doubt myself. My fever was raging at its highest. I did not feel that I could last through the night. My throat was almost closed, and I was gasping for breath. I wanted to wire my mother but could not tell them. All at once it seemed to take a lull and was growing easier. I knew what had happened. My throat had broken. I rose up, and it all passed out. Such relief I never felt before. In one hour's time I felt almost well. I had a good night's rest and was able to sit up the next day.

One of the Ross boys came in to see me. He was one of the home boys and had stayed with us some. When he went to leave, he asked if I needed any money. I told him I did not, but he took out some bills and just left them anyhow. He said I might need them.

Mrs. Griffith, the landlady, wrote the folks that I was ready to come home. I saw Doctor Albert and asked him for his bill.[13] He had been very kind and attentive to me. He said he would not make any charges, but he had heard that I did beautiful carving in gyp rock, and that if I would make him a small piece of some kind in this work, he would prefer it to a doctor bill. I told him I would. Before I left, Mrs. Griffith gave me a talk. She said, "Now whatever you do, don't go back to any hard work. There is a fortune in store for you if you will only take advantage of it." She had heard much of my work in sculpture and told me never to bury such a talent as that. If I could have only taken her advice, but I had no inducement whatever. One of my neighbors came for me in a day or two. I arrived home feeling fine. About the first work I did was to do this piece of carving I had promised Doctor Albert. I decided on a napkin ring. It was made as follows: it lay on a small base two inches by five inches nicely carved. The ring also was carved with a spray of wild roses around it. By the side of it, a small squirrel sat, its back leaning against the ring. Its tail lay on top. The squirrel was holding an acorn in its paws. I sent it by Mrs. Jameson who was going to Childress to visit her sick sister, whom Doctor Albert was tending. She said he was highly pleased with the napkin ring and said he had much rather have it than a doctor bill. He told me later that he had been offered ten dollars for it several times.

It was now getting well into the summer, and I wanted to visit my mother.[14] I had to make a trip to Childress for groceries and dry goods. I made a pretty quick trip of this. I got back and began sewing and preparing for my visit east.

One afternoon I had rather a surprise, a visit by an old man from one of the nearby ranches. He was an old bachelor. He had just fallen heir to about ten thousand dollars, and it seemed to have put him strictly on the carpet for marriage. He talked a short time but soon landed straight to the point and asked me if Tom White gave me the message he sent me. I told him he did not. He said he told him to tell me that he was looking out for a wife and would be down to see me soon. I gave him to understand Mr. White knew better than to bring me a message of that kind, and if that was his motive in this visit, to please drop the subject at once, as I did not want to hear it. But he was not so easily turned off. He kept on and on. I told him he must leave at once, but he would not. I finally told him if he did not leave I would take the gun to him, so he took the hint at last and left. After he had gone, Capp said, "My, Mama, why did you talk to that old man like that?" Capp did not understand his business, so I explained it all to him. After studying a little, he said, "Mama, do you reckon that old fool did want to marry us?"

He came twice more. He was a little goofy, otherwise I would not have borne with him as I did. The last time he came, I stepped out in the yard, gun in hand, and waved him by before he had gotten off his horse. I told him not to stop. This bluff was the last resort; but it had to be done, and it worked very effectively. He turned and rode off at rather a brisk gait and did not come back anymore.

I was quite busy now that I had gotten through with my sewing, but I was having some trouble over another job I had on hand. I had gotten my hack top broken off by a hard wind, so when I was at Childress I laid in a supply of material such as bows, oilcloth, and everything sufficient to make a new top, thinking that any of the neighbors would make it for me. The first one I called on said that he could not make a hack top at all, the next one said that he would not dare undertake it, and the third one said he could not do it himself but could tell me where I could get a man that could. He was in Matador, thirty-five miles away.[15] I made up my mind then and there that I would not go thirty-five miles to get a hack top made. I would make it myself. The next morning I sailed into it. I had the old one for a pattern. I made all the woodwork, curtains, top, and everything complete, ready to attach to the hack. I was a little surprised at my own success, as I had never tried a job like that. I sent Mr. Jameson word to please come down and put my hack top on. He came down and said, "Well, you sure did get it made and a nice job, too. Who made it for you?" I told him I did it myself. He said I didn't do anything of the kind, nor would he believe it for a good while.

I was all ready now for my trip to Young County, and we were soon on the road. I had never made this trip by myself before, nor had I camped out alone. I was not in the least afraid, however, as I always kept my gun near me and felt perfectly safe at all times. We spent some nights with acquaintances on the road but rather preferred camping out mostly.

We reached my mother's home in due time. This was rather a sad meeting, as I had not seen them since Mr. Bird's death. It seemed to bring back my old trouble anew.

This was the time of year when the Old Soldier's Reunion was held in Young County up at the mouth of Clear Fork. Everybody was preparing to go, as this was always a very special occasion. My folks were going, and, of course, I was glad to go with them, as I always met all the old acquaintances and so many people. There were about thirteen thousand people on the ground. They always had such interesting programs too.[16]

On the last day of it, my mother and I were sitting near the grandstand on the end of a bench. On the other end there were several men, speakers and preachers, mostly. One of them, an old man, kept leaning over looking toward us. Mother knew him, but I did not at the time. He was a preacher from Fort Worth. When the program was over, he came around and spoke to us. He seemed to take special interest in me. We had met him several years before, and I was slightly acquainted with him. We gave him no more thought, and we were soon on our way home. But when we arrived, we learned that he was already there with some of the near neighbors awaiting our arrival. He wanted to talk to me. I kept out of his way for about two days. My mother finally told me I might as well talk to him and have it over with. He would not leave without it. So I went into the front room. He came in soon and began his little story of marrying. I felt hurt and insulted. I was still in mourning, and it was so soon after my husband's death. I told him I thought it was people's duty to respect the feelings of others in cases like that. I told him I did not appreciate his mission there, and I asked him to kindly drop the subject at once. He begged my pardon over and over. He said he did not mean to offend me, so he tipped his hat, bade me adieu, and was gone. I spent the remainder of the summer with my mother. I also visited with my Uncle Charles' family in Graham.[17] His second wife and I were good pals, near the same age.

I enjoyed the fruits and melon on the farm, as we had nothing of that kind in the West. I also enjoyed being with my mother more than anyone else.

During my stay we had a sad message from New Mexico. It was a death message, that of my dear grandmother. Besides our own sorrow, it seemed to have brought sadness to the entire settlement where she had lived so long and had nursed so many through sickness and sadness. The church was built on the land she had donated. The first Sunday after the message was received, the church was draped in mourning. The minister, Brother Black, could hardly deliver his sermon. He would nearly break down every time he spoke of her. She had nursed many times in his own home.[18] They all loved her.

The summer was waning, and the time was drawing near when I must return home. Yes, return home all alone with only my two little children for company. The thought of this made me very sad. My poor mother could hardly bear to think of it. She and my stepfather wanted me to remain with them, but I thought it best to stay where my interest lay mostly. So we were soon on our way home.

My father-in-law in Blanco County wrote and asked me to come and make my home with them. I appreciated the offer but could not think of breaking up and leaving my home. There was no other place that would ever seem like home but here. Yes, here among my friends and my late husband's friends, the cowboys. I must say, God bless them, they were true to their comrade. They never forsook his little family. From the very first when I was left alone, they came and bade me look on them as brothers, in order that I should not suffer for anything that they could supply. You must know how I appreciated their friendship. It made me feel strong when otherwise I should have felt so weak to face the world alone. They seemed to feel that we were left in their care, and they surely proved themselves worthy of the charge. They cared for my cattle and interests as their own and would never accept a penny of pay for anything they did. They always kept me supplied with plenty of wood. This was not only for a short time, but faithful, enduring friends they were all during my entire widowhood of nine years. They never grew neglectful of me. Yes, to the cowboys I offer a tribute, and if it should be as high as the sky, it would not be too much for them. I have always held a warm place in my heart for these friends who can never be forgotten.[19]

There were some other friends I must not fail to mention who were lovely to me, Mr. Sul Carter's family most especially. They visited and cheered me in my loneliness. I thought of them as near relatives and enjoyed visiting in their home so much. They were so good and thoughtful of me. So often when I visited them, when I was ready to return home, I would find my buggy loaded up with everything good to eat. Mr. Carter was truly a good man. He passed away some twelve months ago at Corpus Christi. I felt very much grieved to hear of his death.[20]

Thirteen

I WAS NOW settled down at home again, but, oh, I was so lonely. It seemed I could hardly live, at times. Of course, I had my two little children left me, God bless them. I thanked Heaven for that, but they could only exchange childish thoughts for those of a sad and desolate mother.

Mr. Bird and I together had planned that I should make him a book of gyp rock, a small Bible for a birthday present which was the fourteenth day of February. But when I was denied this pleasure, I decided to make the book in remembrance of him. It is a small Bible with his name, age, birth, and all, carved on one side in raised letters. On the other side is carved Holy Bible, and on the corners, In God We Trust, in German text letters. There is much other fancy carving on the book, clasp, and elsewhere. This book is the most tedious and difficult piece of work, and has had more compliments than anything I have ever done. It is an heirloom and will be handed down to my children. I spent much time on this and passed many lonely hours.[1]

Another piece I have, and the last piece of carving in gyp rock I have ever done, is a large vase made many years ago. It is about fourteen inches high. The handles represent large limbs off grape vines, and the whole vase is a mass of carving in high relief of wild roses, berries, and leaves. It has a large carved base. This is another heirloom. I made it sometime after the book.[2]

It had now become necessary that I should do work that would bring in some revenue as a help for our support, as my cattle were not yet quite sufficient. My mind must be employed too. I could not be idle, so I hastened to begin glove and vest making again. I had on hand a good supply of material, sixty nice dressed buckskins. Mr. Bird had killed and dressed these hides all along at odd times before his death. It seems as if he must have had a premonition when he prepared this material that I was to be left alone, making it possible that we should not want for a while at least. It certainly did this. It supplied me for more than two years with material to work with, which made us a very comfortable living until the increase of revenue from my cattle began coming in. Then we were safe and secure for a living. I made many pairs of gloves and some very fancy beaded vests. I always had ready sale for these from the boys on the nearby ranches. I was always busy. I had begun to feel more confidence in myself now, and I was reconciled to living alone.

I could always ride well. I could attend to my own affairs around the place, such as the horses and the milk stock. I made a full beaded buckskin suit for a man on the Matador Ranch, Mr. George Walker. It was certainly an elaborate costume. I received a very nice little sum for this, but such a suit would now bring not less than two hundred dollars. I received an order for a rock book from a young Irishman, Mr. McLauthin, a boot-maker at Matador. He wanted it for his girlfriend up north. The inscription he gave me for this was "Hiawatha, to Minnehaha." They had read this novel together. This book was very pretty and was something similar to the one described elsewhere, but not nearly so elaborate. I sent it to him requesting him to set the price on it according to his idea of its worth. He sent me a check for twenty-five dollars. He was highly pleased with it and said he could not begin to tell me what he thought of its beauty. I also received another order from a Matador boy for a seven-dollar pair of gloves for his girlfriend. He wanted those extra fancy. I trimmed them in gold and silver beads, adding fringed gauntlets. They were some flashy!

The next order that I had was a little different. It was from a boy on the CV Ranch.[3] I was well acquainted with him. He wished to know if I would correspond with a man at Childress, a friend of his. I consented to do so merely for [a] pastime. I had never met him.

I saw Mr. Dumont very often in his travels around in the country. He always stopped to see how I was and to have a talk over old times. He was always at my service. In case I needed anything, I did not hesitate to call on him, as I had known him so long. He still lived at Otta. I always saw him when I visited Mrs. Abbott. He sometimes helped me in a business way on such matters as the drawing up of legal papers, or anything in that line.

We had another close neighbor now, Mr. Austin. He lived on the Pane farm adjoining me. I thought a great deal of Mrs. Austin. She was a good woman and a true friend. There was an Indian trail or passway between her place and Mrs. Jameson's that led from Oklahoma down south. The Indians were friendly then, but really too much so. They would stop at noon out at Mrs. Jameson's well, and some would come to the house and beg for things to eat. They saw one day that Mrs. Jameson was alone. She became frightened at them and came down to my house almost in a run with her baby in her arms. She said she held the fort as long as she could, but she just had to run.

It was now about October.[4] Mr. Carter had sent two of his boys from the ranch over to put up my feed and to haul up plenty of wood for me. They had finished it, and I was now heeled for the winter. I worked at glove making when not busy at other household duties. I often made trips horseback through the mountains to Teepee City store, five miles away, for my mail and other small articles.[5] I left my little ones with Mrs. Jameson.

I received another letter from Mr. F. P. He had bought stock in a copper mine and was getting quite a good profit from it. He was working at the saddler's trade then. This was about the fourth or fifth letter I had from him, but this one was different. It had a little sentimental touch occasionally, but in my reply I did not pretend I understood. However, he was a good correspondent. I enjoyed his letters. They were interesting and educational, as well as [a] pastime and company for me.

I had also received three or four letters from the Childress man, but I had never met him. I did not take much interest in him.

Wintertime was coming on now. It was cold weather. I seldom saw anyone but a passing cowboy now and then who would stop to see if I was in need of anything, talk with us awhile, then go on his way.

My little boy, Capp, was learning to play the violin. His father's violin was left him, of course, and he seemed determined to learn. He made pretty good progress from the first. I also began teaching him some in his books that winter. There were no schools in that part of the country.

I did not like that location much either for a home, for I could not get as much land as I wanted. I had prospected some over on the prairie near the Ross Ranch. I had also figured on the section where Paducah is now built. Mr. and Mrs. Gober were with me.[6] That was some years before there was any thought of such a town as Paducah. Mr. Gober said that I could never get water on this section, as some of the ranchmen had tried. However, I rather preferred the section near the Ross Ranch on Buck Creek.[7] It was a fine piece of land. It was one mile and a half from the Carter home. But owing to circumstances, I could not move before another year.

The winter passed off without any special events, with the exceptional visits with the nearest neighbors when the weather would permit. I did not get my mail regularly, as the weather was cold, and there was not much passing. I had an occasional letter from my two correspondents, besides relatives. I also had a letter from a man in New Mexico asking if I would correspond with him. I had never heard of him before, but suppose he must have gotten my address some way, perhaps from some of my relatives. At any rate, I did not reply to his letter as I cared nothing about it.

It was springtime now, well up into April.[8] We were needing some milk cows, so Mrs. Bailey and I saddled up our horses and took a little round. We brought in some pretty good milk cows, so we were heeled in that line.

I had a business trip to make to Matador. I was going the next day. It was Sunday, and we were about ready when one of the Matador boys from the Pane farm came down and asked to drive the hack for me. I thanked him just as nice as I could but told him the team was perfectly gentle, and I did not mind to drive them at all. I took it solely as a charitable offer, but down in my heart I knew better. He did not take any exception at my refusal. He was a nice good boy. I thought well of him as a friend. I will call him J. B.

The weather was getting nice and warm now. My boy was hard to keep indoors. He wanted to stay out on the river with his dog and hunt all the time, keeping me uneasy. The river was dry, but high sandbanks were dangerous, as they would cave off. This is where he insisted on staying mostly. I had hunted for him almost two hours one day, up and down the river, when at last back in the deep canyon I heard his dog. I rushed on and had to climb up a high bank, but I finally reached the place. The first thing I saw was a huge sand bank just freshly caved off. The dog was caught in behind it and was barking and whining and trying to get out. Capp was nowhere in sight, but his tracks were thick all around. Now any sane person would have known or guessed at a glance that he was nowhere else but under that sand. I rushed in and began rolling back clods with all my might, huge ones that would have been beyond my strength had it been any other time. I was growing weak. I had to raise up to get my breath, when I noticed there had been just a few sprinkles of rain on this bank since it had fallen. This gave me courage. I rose up and began to look around and back toward home. I saw my boy, his head just above the weeds, going in home after me to help him get his dog out. It seemed he had been rescued from the dead. Somehow I was down on my knees thanking the good Lord fervently for sparing my boy to me. But this was only one incident out of many, though they were not quite so bad.

He came in one day and said that there were three wildcats up in a tree, and he wanted me to go and kill them. I thought he must be mistaken but went on with him. Sure enough there were three, an old wildcat and two half-grown ones all up one tree. I shot them all three, and we carried them to the house and skinned them.

He often went bathing in the river, a small hole of water by the bank, but I could not risk him to go alone. I would sit on the bank and read or work at something until he was through. One afternoon I told him to go on, and I would be on in a few minutes. It slipped my memory for nearly thirty minutes, but when I remembered it, I rushed down to the water hole. His clothes were lying there on the bank. His tracks were all around the water, but he was nowhere in sight. Now you must know I was frightened again. I called him at the top of my voice, but no answer. Oh, could it be he was in the bottom of this hole of water. I picked up a large brush and began to drag it through the water. I kept on until I was thoroughly convinced that he was not there. I ran on up the river two or three hundred yards, calling as I went. I finally heard him answer away out in the brush. I pulled through the cockleburs high as my head, until I finally found him sitting up in the top of a small cottonwood tree. He was just as well contented as old Adam ever dared to be. He said, "Oh, Mama, when I was in swimming, I saw some of the most beautiful birds fly over here and light in this tree. I followed them and tried to catch one." He wanted me to stay and help him out of the burs. I told him to get out just like he got in, and I dared him to leave the house again for the next three days. If he did, he would need more clothes on than he had right then.

I was busy now with some more gloves. I had orders from some of the boys. I also made a beautiful fawn skin vest for the foreman on the "8" Ranch, Mr. Jeffers.[9] It had the hair on with the white specks and was nicely fringed. It had fancy buckskin facings on [the] pockets, and the front was trimmed with brown beads and fancy buttons. I had many compliments on this vest. I had just finished this one afternoon when Capp came in and said, "Mama, there is a bunch of turkeys just across the river from here. Come and kill one." I took the rifle and walked out on top of the hill. They were about four hundred yards away going down a little path from me. So I took a long range shot at them and killed three of them at one shot. Capp sailed in after them like a birddog and came lugging them all in after a while. He was about given out, for one of them was a large gobbler.

The next day was Saturday, and I went to Teepee City. I got quite a lot of mail. When I returned, I was opening it up, and one letter most especially attracted my attention. I could not quite locate from where it came, but on opening it, I was somewhat surprised. It was from no other personage than Mr. A. Dumont. He addressed me very timidly and modestly. He said he had intended to talk to me on a subject the last time he was at my home but had no opportunity. He said his object in coming had been to ask me to make him happy by accepting him for better or worse. He said he had always respected and admired me for my bravery and kind disposition and many good qualities, which is usually the theme of everyone's life. And now he had conceived a deep affection for me which would be as enduring as life. He said that he could scarcely hope that his love was returned, at least in the same degree, but by kind attentions and deep devotion, he believed he could gain my respect, as it would be the care of his life to make me happy and contented. But in case I should not accept his proposal, it would not change his feelings toward me. He said he would ever be ready to render me any service I might need, but he hoped almost against hope that I would answer his proposal favorably.

When I had finished this letter, I felt very sadly indeed. Oh, why had this subject arisen between us? He had been my friend, my counselor. I had always thought of him more as a kinsman, an uncle, or someone like that to whom I could carry my trouble and be assured of sympathy and advice. He was my advisor in any business matters. I had never thought of him in any other way. He was the last person I wanted to bring disappointment to, but things had come to a climax. They must be met with honest candor. To answer this letter was a task. I addressed him in the kindest and most sympathetic way. I told him how I had always appreciated his friendship and hoped never to lose it, and that I realized in full the honor he had bestowed upon me. He had paid me the highest compliment any man could ever pay a lady. He had offered himself, his all. But to come straight to the point, I told him in the kindest way that I could not answer favorably. I had never considered a second marriage. I did not want to marry any man, and were he a king my answer to him would be the same. I said that I hoped our friendship might remain as it had been in the past.

Fourteen

SUMMER WAS well on now, and the time for my annual visit to my mother was drawing near.[1] We had begun to arrange things in shape to leave. Our chickens were the greatest problem. The varmints had been bothering them already. I had just gotten up the night before and killed a polecat that was raising a disturbance.

Late that afternoon I was busy in the house. A large flock of geese were flying overhead quite low down. Capp rushed in after me to go and kill one. I stepped out and ran down the path toward the river a short distance in order to get a good shot. Capp and his little sister ran after me. I fired two or three shots but missed every time. We were coming on back to the house rather dejected at my failure, when Capp asked the question, "Mama, if you had killed one of those geese, would they have been good to eat?" I did not answer him. Now little Bess, or "Baby" as I called her, always held herself an authority on any question that might be asked. She would answer it in some way or another, and she had her father's ready wit. Capp asked again, "Mama, if you had killed one of those geese, would they have been good to eat?" She threw back her little proud head of yellow curls and said with all authority, "No." Capp asked meekly, "Why?" She answered, "Just because they've got guts." Capp did not say another word. He was simply crushed.

We had quite an exciting time over a polecat a few nights after this. It had been slipping in under the door several times, and when anything would move, it would run out. We were laying for a chance to kill it, so this time it came up into our bedroom. We had two small dogs. One of them was in this room, and this nervy skunk got by the dog and was climbing up on the foot of the bed. I felt it and gave a slight kick. It went off and ran outdoors. Now there was but one way for it to get out. A path led by the side of the house, or dugout, to the lot about fifty yards away. There was a window just over our head and just even with the top of the ground. I awoke Capp and said to him, "Let's get out at the window right quick and catch this polecat as it comes by."

Out we went in our nightclothes, barefooted. The moon was shining, but not very bright. I picked up a hoe that was lying near, and sure enough, up came the polecat in the path to the lot. I ran with the hoe and overtook it about half way. It stopped and came back toward me. Now, the nature of a polecat is to bluff, run at you a few steps, and then run off. I was never afraid of them and had killed many, but this one was different. It did not stop but kept coming toward me. I kept backing, and on it came. I threw down the hoe, and turned and ran. Each time I looked back it was a little closer and had nearly overtaken me. I was running for dear life when I reached the house. I looked back, and it nearly had hold of my heels. I was laughing all the time, and yet I was scared and surprised at this [bold] skunk. Capp was standing there. I gave a little shout as we passed by. It almost scared him to death. He gave one loud scream and tore off down the hill as if his time had come. He said later he thought about climbing one of those big cottonwood trees, but had no time to tarry. I switched off down toward the garden with my company, ran through a big patch of grass burs, and didn't feel a one of them. I was gaining on it then. By that time the dogs came to my rescue and bayed the polecat. I found a long-handled rake, and right there and then the murder took place. Capp came out and met me. I was still laughing. He said very dryly, "I don't know what you are laughing about. It wasn't a bit funny to me."

Mr. Jameson came by the next day and brought my mail and also hauled some water for me. I shall never forget his kindness. He hauled many,

many barrels of water for me, as well as doing many other kind acts. He had told me from the first that he would be a brother to me, and he certainly fulfilled his promise. Mrs. Jameson was like a sister. I had a good lot of mail, some letters from relatives, and others. One was from my Childress correspondent, Mr. D. P. He wanted me to allow him to come over and get acquainted with me. I did not care about this, so I did not grant him the privilege. I got by it somehow by saying that I was going away. Another letter was from Mr. F. P., the New Mexico man. It was some sentimental, I claim. He said he might visit Texas again some time in the near future, and that he longed to see the little white lady in the lonely little "chocy" again.[2]

We finally got everything arranged for our visit east. My team was fine. It stayed fat all the time, as they had little to do. They were a match team, both dark bays. They were rather good-sized and were fine travelers. One of them was a race horse. They were considered the best team in that part of the country. My husband was always a great lover of good horses, and he took much pride in those.

We were soon on the road to Young County, but we were not in a very great hurry. We visited quite a lot on the way, as we knew most everybody on the road. They always insisted on our staying over a few days with them. We camped out but little on this trip. We stopped with some friends in Benjamin,[3] the Weatherlys, and we visited with a number of friends in Seymour. We were eleven days on the road, only one hundred and fifty miles.

We finally arrived in Young County, Tonk Valley.[4] We found all the home folks O.K. and looking for us. We had tarried quite awhile on the way, but it always seemed the nearer we got, I could hardly wait to see my mother. My youngest brother, Lewis, and his family lived quite near them. He had been looking after them for several years, as they were growing old. The Old Soldier's Reunion was to be held again at the mouth of Clear Fork, four miles from my mother's home. They were all preparing to go to the reunion when we arrived, as it was only a day or two hence. We all got busy together and soon had everything in readiness. We hit the road in full tilt on the appointed day.

We had to cross the river, and it was up, coming down angry and red. It was barely fordable. There were hundreds of vehicles in a long train back toward Graham, everyone trying to beat the other before the crossing got too bad. Many of them stuck in the river, however. The women were very much frightened. Some of the boys had to carry their girlfriends out in their arms. One fell down, and they both went under but came up laughing and reached the bank all right. I think he did this, though, on purpose, for he was mischievous and could not resist the temptation.

We crossed all right and went on by Eliasville.[5] Just before we reached the grounds, we came to another creek booming full but not very wide. People were driving right into it. Some buggies and teams swam. One buggy turned over, and some children started floating off but were caught by parties on the other side in time. I heard some man call out loud and clear, "Going to the Reunion?" I don't think anything serious occurred on the whole trip. All reached the grounds safely, and [they were] jolly, bound for a good time.

This was an ideal place for this affair. It was a large grove of hundreds of very large pecan trees that made a dense shade, and the grounds were cleared off perfectly. This was in the bend of the creek and afforded fine fishing opportunities all around. There were many fish caught, but one especially attracted [the] most attention. This was a very large catfish four or five feet long, and while dressing it, they found a real gold watch in its stomach. People rushed in by the dozens to see the wonder, but pretty soon somebody discovered the watch was still running. This gave away the joke. However, one little real incident did happen. Reverend Black's[6] little boy found a twenty-dollar gold piece on the bank of the creek, just about where the big fish was caught. Possibly some of the parties who ribbed up this Jonah fish-and-watch fake may have lost this real cash in the operation, but no one claimed it. The preacher's boy came out first winner in the big fish tale after all.

The reunion went on in the same old way as usual, everybody having a good time, seemingly. I enjoyed this more than the last one. I met a number of old friends and was with Aunt Laura a good portion of the time. This was my Uncle Charles'[7] second wife. She and I could always have a good time together. She was younger than I.

The reunion was finally over, and we returned home without any trouble, as the river and creek had run down. We were tired out and did nothing but rest the next two or three days. Peaches and watermelons were fine, and also the gardens. Mother and I did quite a lot of preserving the next week. I made up ten gallons of peach preserves and sweet pickles to bring home. This was certainly a luxury in this old dry fruitless country at that time. Of course, we had the native wild plums, which were fine, but we grew so tired of them with no other varieties of fruit.

I spent the remainder of the summer with my mother. We went to the big meetings and had a good time in general. I also visited quite a lot with my uncle's family [that of Uncle Charles Benson] in Graham. Besides this I had some special calls by two different parties. They were both widowers, and one was an old friend. He was a good moral church-going man, a well-to-do farmer with a nice home. I was not in the market for matrimony, however, so I failed to be interested in either of those. I will call this one J. T. My reason for calling these parties by initials, or letters, is that there are a number of them still living, and they possibly would not appreciate my reference to them pertaining to matrimony. However, any of my old friends will recognize each party at once by description and location, and then, as we all know, a compliment is never lost on a woman. She appreciates every inch of it, so I humbly ask all of those worthy aspirants to my hand to kindly pardon my egotism.

I had several letters from my other two correspondents while on this visit, one of which I enjoyed very much. Mr. F. P.'s letters were always newsy and full of interest, with a good deal of common sense and philosophy.

The summer was about over and we were preparing to return home. After packing our preserves securely and arranging them in the hack, all was in readiness. We said goodbye to all the dear folks excepting my mother. She was always missing at that time. She would slip away to have a big cry unobserved. She had prepared lunch to take with us, but we went off and forgot it. My little cousin, Ollie Benson, who was twelve or thirteen, took the lunch and ran in pursuit of us, shouting and crying as loud as he could. We had gone about a quarter of a mile when I heard him. I got out and ran back to meet him, for I felt sure something very serious had happened. There was nothing wrong at all, and still he was crying as if his heart would break. I suppose it was at my going away. Now I had never thought he cared as much about me as this, but you never can tell what a boy of this age thinks. At any rate, it made me feel nearer and think more of him afterward than ever before. This was my uncle's only child by his first wife.

We journeyed on and made a good drive that day. We camped every night from there home. We went by way of Otta and took dinner with Mrs. Abbott. Mr. Dumont and Mr. McGaughey were there. We had been there but a few minutes when Mrs. Abbott called me to bring my gun and kill a hawk which was sitting on the corner of an outbuilding. I stepped to the door, pulled the trigger, and down it came. She said she owed me a chicken pie. I told her not then as I had to go in home that afternoon. A lady told me afterwards that Mr. Dumont said that liked to have plagued him to death, that he had been trying to kill that hawk for a month. We drove in home that afternoon and found everything O.K. We were glad to be at home once more. My, isn't it wonderful to have one little spot on this old earth to call your very own home. Be it ever so humble, this one word "home" has never received its due homage.

Fifteen

THE FIRST THING we had to do was to pen some of our milk cows again. The next problem was that we were out of bacon, and there was none at Teepee City. I solved this problem by going out on the river late each evening and killing a good lot of birds, doves and quails, to do through the next few days until the store supplies came in.

I had planned to make a move that fall over southeast on the prairie, where I had selected a place, a half section near the Ross headquarters. It was a good track of level land. I was over at Mrs. Carter's, and one of the boys, Mr. Summie James, went with me to select a building place. This was to be our permanent home in the future. I had a house built on it that fall. There was also a schoolhouse built adjoining my land later which made it more desirable. We were now arranging things in order to move. Mr. Carter came over from the ranch with his wagon and helped me move to our new home. I liked this location much better than the other. We were near more people, ranchmen, and settlers.[1]

Early the next morning after spending the night in our new home, I heard a disturbance among the chickens. On opening the door, there stood a coyote wolf not thirty feet away. My gun was sitting by the door, and in less than one minute, there was a dead wolf stretched out in the yard.

Paducah had just then begun to start up. There was one store kept by the Carroll brothers, Johnnie and Vent.[2] My, this had begun to assume the appearance of real civilization.

They often gave big dances around at the ranches. They were usually pretty swell affairs, as expense was no object. They were carried on in perfect order, as there was no whiskey in the country then. I attended most of these dances, as it was a treat to meet with the people. Everybody went. They always saw that we had a way to go. They would send a couple by in their buggy so that my little ones and I might drive behind, in order that we would get there safely. I never accepted company. That was understood. I preferred my little ones instead. Neither did I take part in the dancing at that time, much as they insisted on it. None but myself and God alone can ever know the comfort and wealth these two little children were to me in my loneliness. They were a part of my life—all I had on this earth to live for.

This was a prairie country. One could see for miles around. There was a bunch of antelope in sight most every day or two. This was too much temptation for me. I also tried to think it a necessity for fresh meat. We had been at this place but a few days when I saddled up my favorite horse, old Tod, strapped my Winchester with scabbard on the side of the saddle just as my husband used to do, took a skinning knife, and struck out in a long lope for those antelope. Buck Creek ran through this part of the prairie, and the antelope were only a few hundred yards on the other side in the flat, nearly one mile away. When I came to the creek, I rode up the bed of it until I was opposite the antelope. I tied my horse there, took my gun, and slipped out on the flat as near as I could before they discovered me. When the first one looked up, I plunked him one, and down he came. This was all I wanted at that time. The others ran off. This was a nice fat one, too. I went back, got the horse and skinning knife, and soon had the pelt off. I quartered the antelope, tied the hams and shoulders on the back saddle strings, and tied the other parts and the hide to the front saddle strings. I replaced the gun in the scabbard, mounted my good faithful horse, and went back home. We were now heeled for awhile for nice fresh meat.

This is only one trip of this kind out of many which I made. We were seldom out of fresh meat. Capp said he always climbed up on the house to watch me make my first shot success. He always knew just what I had before I came in.

The post office was at Otta, four miles away.[3] I often drove over in the buggy for my mail. One day I had just returned from a trip and was looking over my letters. This time they were all from Graham. Two of them I could not quite locate the writers of. On opening one of them, I found it was from Mr. J. T. He was one of the parties who called on me while I was at my mother's. It was straight business to the point, without any flourishes. He said that I was his choice of all women. The other letter was also from the other party whom I met while at my mother's, and of all the letters I have ever received, it was the most flourished and high-toned, as well as agonizing. It went on to describe his home as being most beautiful with imposing scenery. He asked me to share this home, but it all fell on a deaf ear. I did not answer either this or the other one. The other party wrote me once again, but I did not answer.

I was finishing up a fancy beaded buckskin vest and pair of gloves, an order of twenty dollars from a boy on the 8 ranch, Mr. Lon Caruth.[4] We

had one neighbor that I was not very well acquainted with until I moved
to this place. He was a man of good standing in the country and was a
widower. He had some stock, which he often herded around not far from
my home. He would often drop in and sit and talk with me awhile, and
this became more frequent as time went. One day he handed me his day-
book and said he had expressed some of his sentiments in this. He would
like me to read these, and he would like a reply. Well, I should say, I
thought him too dignified to express himself in such agonizing tones. He
said that I was more beautiful than the rose of Sharon and was the apple of
his eye, and on and on. However, I gave him credit as being rather an able
writer, most especially on this line of thought. I answered him, of course,
in the negative. I told him that I did not want to marry, and besides, I
thought it almost a crime to unite two families of children. He had some
children, two grown-up girls, of whom I learned to think a great deal as
time went on. We were quite chummy. One of them was very beautiful,
and the other was fine looking. He talked some afterwards, making other
propositions as to what our future might be, but I only said, "No." He
then told me he would leave this proposition open, and if I should ever
decide to accept him, all I had to do was to notify him. I thought this was
fair enough. I will call him Mr. J. W.

The Matadors were giving a big dance and supper at the Pane farm,
which was adjoining my old home on Tongue River. Two of the boys,
Charlie Bird[5] and Mr. Brisco, came over to invite me. Charlie was a special
friend of ours. I suppose one reason was on account of his name. It was
spelled the same as ours, and he always said he knew we were related. Yet
he and my husband had never tried to trace it back.

I agreed to go to the dance, but after they had gone, I debated a question long and seriously within myself. I had gone to all those dances and
sat back and looked on like a dummy, while all the others were having a
whizzing time. I made up my mind to either take a part in the dance, or
quit going, one or the other. No one knew of my decision, however.

When we arrived, the dance was well under way. It was a pretty swell
affair, and many nice people were there. I had been there but a short time
when Charlie Bird came around and sat down by me. We talked a little
until it came his time to dance. Only for politeness sake, of course, he
asked me to favor him in this dance. I first said, "No," but when I talked a
little more favorable, he began begging me in earnest. I said, "All right."
He got up and said, "Come on." Yet he did not believe that I meant it. So
out I went, and we were soon tripping the light fantastic. When this dance
was over, some of the boys came to Charlie and asked what in the world he

said to me that persuaded me to dance. He said he did not know unless it was his name that carried him through.

I danced with a number of the boys that night, and most all of them expressed their pleasure in seeing me take a part. The dance broke up about daylight. This was the custom. We all had breakfast and returned to our homes.[6]

The weather was cold. We made quick time. We drove in home and made up a good fire, and soon we were as cozy as you please. I was simply dead in the hull. I was sleepy, tired, and everything else. I think Capp and Baby were about the same, so we were soon huddled up on the bed sound asleep and dead to the world until about four o'clock that evening.

The next day Mr. James came by and brought my mail. A good lot of letters were from the home folks. There was also one from my Childress correspondent, Mr. D. P. He still insisted on making me a visit, but I had agreed in the first place to carry on a friendly correspondence just for [a] pastime only. Therefore, I was under no further obligations here. Another letter was from the Roswell man, Mr. F. P. He was thinking strongly of closing out his business and moving back to West Texas. If not this, he just had to make a visit back anyway. The other letter, the last one, was a new country heard from. This was from Mr. J. B., the number that wanted to drive my hack to Matador. He wished to know if I would correspond with him. In my reply I told him I would carry on a friendly correspondence. He thanked me very nicely in his next letter, but said he hoped it might develop into something better than mere friendship.

I was now making a large gyp rock vase, which I have mentioned in another part of this book.[7] It was a long, tedious, and hard job, and was the last piece of this kind of work that I have ever done.

Capp was still studying violin music. He had made very rapid progress. He had been practicing with Mr. Charlie Davidson,[8] a friend of ours who often played for the dances. He told me one day that Capp could play just nearly as good as he could to save his life, and that he would make a wonderful violinist some day.

This part of the country seemed rather a divide, though far apart. It was between the two rivers, Pease and Wichita breaks, and it was a trail by which wild game often passed from one breaks to the other. Sometimes large bunches of eight or ten loafer wolves would pass in a few hundred yards of our house. One day we were having a heavy snowstorm, and a bunch of about twenty antelope came up and lay down within fifty yards of the house. The snow was so dense that they did not notice the house. It was too cold to go out, so we let them go unmolested.

Our wood supply was getting low, and the boys did not know of it. As
soon as the cold spell was over and the weather pleasant again, the little
ones and I decided to haul a load of wood, which we had done a few times
before. Our team ranged up in the shinnery one-half mile from home.
Capp and I went after them, and we took the gun along. I shot an antelope
on the way, but I only crippled it, breaking both forelegs. Capp took in
after it like a greyhound. I went on after the horses. The antelope could go
pretty fast even that way, but Capp finally overtook it and was still scuf-
fling with it when I came on back with the team. I gave it another shot,
and we loaded it on one of the horses and took it in home. We dressed it in
a few minutes and had dinner.

Then we were off after our wood. We picked up a nice large load of
mesquite wood off the prairie. I killed a large eagle. On the way home, it
was getting rather late, and, oh, snakes, our wagon tire ran off and rolled
twenty feet away. Now, I had become equal to almost any occasion by this
time by way of necessity and self-confidence, so we took the tire, rolled it
on as I had seen my husband do, drove some wedges of wood under it,
and drove in home without further trouble.

We were lonely these days. The winter was not yet over, and we did not
see many folks. There was to be a big dance given at the McAdams Ranch.[9]
I had a special invitation, and arrangements had been made between two
of the boys that my two little ones and I would ride in a hack being driven
by one of these boys. The other boy came to consult me about it and insisted very much that I agree to the arrangement. He said he would like to
take the place himself, but he had other engagements which he must fill.
This boy I will call Mr. S. J. He was a nice boy and a favorite among the
people. He was paying his respects to one of the daughters of Mr. J. W., a
neighbor mentioned elsewhere. I agreed to go to the dance as they had
planned.

We were all to leave from Mr. J. W.'s home, but we had a general mix-up.
Mr. J. W. had arranged for me to go in the buggy with his other daughter,
not knowing I had other plans. Neither did I tell them. So when my hack
came, some of them told the boy I had other arrangements. He was as mad
as Tucker, so my man and hack went back under whip. I wanted to laugh
but didn't dare to, as the other boy, S. J., was mad too. They thought I had
framed this all up myself. I had not, but well knew I would have to make a
pretty smooth explanation to clear myself of the charge. That night at the
dance, I had a chance to talk to Mr. S. J. I pretended to be very much insulted too. I asked him why he sent my hack back. I could hardly keep my
face straight for wanting to laugh. He told me why. I explained everything,

and he was satisfied. He said that old man J. W. was at the bottom of every bit of it. Poor fellow, he had to bear all the blame. He went and brought the other fellow around, and we had a general straightening up.

When the dance was over the next morning, we all went back to Mr. J. W.'s. I asked Mr. S. J. in a very businesslike way if he would haul a load of freight for me up my way on his way home. He said he would be glad to. We were soon loaded in and on our way. When we arrived, he got out, went in and made us a fire, and sat and talked awhile. He and his girl had had a little spat that I happened to know of. I mentioned it in a joking way, rather holding up for the girl and putting him in the fault. After a few minutes of silence, he said in the most solemn way that she was not the woman his heart longed for. He rose up, walked up to me, and held out his hand for mine. I did not understand. However, I gave him my hand. He asked in the most earnest tones if I could not learn to love another man. I was so shocked and surprised that I could hardly make any reply at first. I had thought he was crazy about this other girl. He asked the same question again. I told him I hardly thought so, that I have never tried or even wanted to. He urged me to try to think of him in that way. At last I told him I would try. He and I were about the same age.[10] He was very well-to-do financially. He had a nice little stock of cattle, some land, and a home.

Spring was now at hand. At this time of year, we had many sandstorms. We had many more than in late years. It would sometimes blow twenty-four hours without ceasing, but never caused much inconvenience, as there was no farming to speak of at that time. There was only cattle raising.[11]

I was always considered somewhat of a flower fiend, and this special time a new mania had seized me. I was taking a little flower book, *Parks Floral Magazine,*[12] and just for an experiment, I put a little note in the exchange column of this book that I would exchange native cacti for others. I didn't know that anyone else cared for cacti but me. But as it happened, this was the time when everybody in the United States almost took a cactus craze, about 1892.[13] Well I simply was snowed under with letters answering my ad. They poured in, in every mail, more than a hundred letters in just a few days. There were also packages of cacti by the wholesale, the strangest looking things. I never dreamed of there being so many varieties of cacti. I was fascinated with them.

I had two nice long beds, one on each side of the walk, with some native cacti in them. I had received a nice large package of cacti from a lady in New York with three or four dozen varieties. They were beautiful, so I just walked out in the yard and set them out with the others. But what do you know? It came a big frost that night and froze every one of them dead as a mackerel. I was perfectly astonished. I did not think you could freeze an old cactus anywhere, but they had been grown in a hothouse up North where it was too cold to grow out in the open.

The first thing I did was to pot all the rest of the cacti that came in. Then I had a small flower pit dug on which I put a glass top. I answered all the letters by postal cards which I sent off in packs. Then the important thing came. I began learning the botanical names of all the cacti that came in. They were still coming, and I could not do any good exchanging without knowing the right names. Otherwise, I would get dozens of duplications of what I already had. Now this was a *study*. I enjoyed it though and was catching the cactus craze fast. They came in from every direction and every state in the union, each one requesting in exchange a collection of Texas cacti. Some from New York, Canada, and other places would request another fine specimen of that beautiful yellow-spined Jagger. Those are the kind we burn off of the prairie here to keep the stock from getting into.

I had letters of inquiry, also some catalogues of cacti from Erfurt, Germany. I always sent nice specimens, and I made many exchange friends, many of which wrote me extensively on flowers. One or two especially I enjoyed most. These were Mrs. Anderson of Long Island, New York, and Clifford Rannar, a boy twenty years old, also of Long Island. I made many exchanges of other flowers with them. They were friends of the Hobarts and McKinleys,[14] so I learned from another lady who knew them. I was getting up into the upper crust and did not know it.

I had now learned the botanical names of most of the cacti that came in, though not all of them. There are more than a thousand varieties. I have one catalogue of cacti that lists seven hundred. There are about twenty-five or thirty native varieties of Texas cacti, and perhaps there are more that I do not know of.

I was now fully in the swim. My collection numbered about three hundred varieties, and still they came. They had begun to slow up some, however. We wrote briefly on cacti and signed our names C. C.—Cactus Crank. I treasured my collection almost like gold nuggets. I had a perfect mania for cacti. As the strange specimens came in, they reminded me of the natives of each state and country from whence they came. One man, Mr. A. Blanc, a florist of New York, wrote me for several boxes of large-sized cacti. The pay accompanied the order. I soon collected them and shipped them by freight. They arrived safely.

The cactus craze did not wear off for several years. Every spring we would exchange a few packages. In fact the craze has not left me entirely. I still have a collection of about one hundred varieties.[15] I am about the only remaining Cactus Crank in Texas that I know of. I was so enthused over the above study that I almost lost interest in everything else for a while.

Sixteen

BUT BACK to where I left off. I had about forgotten my promise to the venerable Mr. S. J. Yes, I would think of him from now on as I promised, or at least occasionally. He did not call on me often. I did not understand. I thought him rather neglectful, though he was peculiar. I had many letters from my other correspondents, which I hardly took time to read or answer, except for one. I was more prompt with Mr. F. P.

Capp always read my mail. He was my only confidant. I knew it was safe. I think he got more kick out of my letters than I did. He would laugh sometimes until he almost fell over.

Mr. Dumont came by and had dinner with us. We always enjoyed having him. Capp and Baby thought more of him than anyone else that came. We had roasted antelope ribs for dinner. He made mention of this little incident years afterward. He said he thought to himself, "My God, if I only had this place. It just takes me to fill out the table."

We were to have our first school this year.[1] Miss Janie Roberts was to be our teacher, and she would board with us. So we were to have company. She was coming right soon, and we could hardly wait for her arrival. We had never seen her but knew we would like her, for she would be so much company for us. She came in on Saturday. We liked her fine.

School would begin on Monday. Capp and Baby were on their p's and q's.[2] Capp was then eleven years old, and Baby was six.[3] Capp had never been to school, but I had taught him some at home. None of the children except Larry Carter had ever been to school.[4] Miss Janie would laugh and tell me how they did. One boy would pick up the bucket and speak out loud and clear saying, "Come on, Tom (or Bill), and let's get a bucket of water." I was amused at Capp. They were all getting up some little recitations for Friday. He had gotten his about up and thought he could say it all right, but he became serious all at once and said, "But, Mama, what if she should call on me to say another one? What would I do?" He seemed to think he would have to say it whether he knew it or not. The school moved on very agreeably. Baby learned to read in a short time. She and Capp took great interest.

The next week we had an invitation to a dance and supper at Mr. Bailey's on Thursday evening. I had to go to the shinnery for the horses by myself, as Capp was in school. I could always walk good. I reached the shinnery soon. I could always catch Tod and ride him home bareback, but Old Steel Dust was a scapegoat.[5] I could never catch him, but he would follow on. We came by the tank to get water for them. When Steel Dust got a good drink, he deliberately turned around and started back for the shinnery. Now I could not round him in without a saddle. He went back about halfway and stopped and went to grazing on the high bald prairie. I was so mad that I could have killed him. I went in home fast as I could, saddled old Tod, and struck out in a long lope for old Steel Dust. When he saw us coming, he threw his tail in the air and made for the shinnery. Tod was an expert cutting horse as well as a racehorse. He took in the situation at once, laid his head straight out in front of him as he always did in cutting cattle, and made for old Steel Dust in a dead run. He cut him off from the shinnery in about two minutes. Around and around we went at racehorse gait, Steel Dust trying to get to the shinnery and Tod cutting him off on every corner. We made several rounds before Steel Dust gave it up and started in home. Mrs. Carr, our nearest neighbor, was watching us. The first time she saw me, she gave me a general rounding up. She said I was going to get killed. She claimed that she actually saw between me and the saddle on several of those short cuts we made.

Well, Miss Janie and the two little ones were at home when I came in, so we all got ready. We loaded into the buggy and were off to the dance. We had a nice time. We ate a fine supper, and we came home early the next morning. Miss Janie was delighted with the trip.

They were going to have a roundup of the cattle at the Ross Tank near my house, and I always made a very large cake or pie, and sometimes both, to carry down to the mess wagon in the buggy for their dinner. Sometimes the boys would be at dinner when I arrived and handed out the things. The way they would raise their hats in perfect respect appalled me. It made me feel how much they appreciated these things which were hard to get in camps. I always enjoyed doing this, for it was only a mark of appreciation on my part. These boys were ever faithful, generous, kind-hearted friends. They took care of my cattle by branding and seeing after them as if they were their own.

Two of the Matador boys on the trail with some cattle to market had a difficulty. One accused the other of mavericking one of my yearlings,[6] which was a mistake. He was furious over the accusation, and they had a terrible fight. I would rather have lost a yearling than have heard of this, for they were both my friends.

We were in need of another milk cow, so the next Saturday Capp and I saddled up the horses and went out to find one. The pasture reached down to [the] Wichita River, which was more than fifteen miles in length. We had poor luck. We did not find anything desirable and were out most all day.

I had never ridden horseback all day before, and I became weary before we reached home. When we arrived, I just slid down off the horse and almost crumpled down to the ground. I was simply shaken up all over and could hardly walk for a while. I did not get over it for several days. I made no complaint to anyone but the home folks. Now, Mrs. Murphy, one of my neighbors, often tried some of my crazy stunts. I had heard that she and her boy, Harve, had gone on the same round or trip that Capp and I had gone on. I wondered how she stood it, but would not have mentioned it to her at all. I thought if she stood it all right, she would never know what it did for me. I was at her house a few days afterward. She did not mention her trip until just as I was starting home, when all at once she broke out, "Mrs. Bird, do you know, me and Harve took that same trip you did, and I wish I may never stir if I could look around for a week!" She was Irish and witty too, and the way she spoke it, I thought I would die of laughter. I tried to hold in, however, until I got off. I laughed to myself all the way home. I knew she was giving me straight goods.

Our stock of fresh meat was about out, and I had begun to scan the horizon for antelope. I did not have to look long. A small straggling bunch was passing across from one prairie to another not far from the house. I got a good close shot but missed them clear. They ran off and stopped. I raised my sights to four hundred yards, and down I brought one. It was a large buck with big black horns like they have. I saddled the horse, mounted him, and drug this one in by the horn of the saddle and dressed it at home. I had a near neighbor now, Mr. Carr, about a quarter of a mile of me. He told me that anytime I killed an antelope he would haul it in and dress it for half the meat. Now this was picking for me. From now on all I had to do was to shoot them and show Mr. Carr where they were.

The summer was well on now. There was a summer school, and it would soon be over. All the children seemed to have done well and took good interest. Mine most especially seemed to have learned more by the time school closed than I thought it possible in so short a time. Miss Janie, the children, and I took our lunch and drove down to Mr. Dumont's place one Sunday to get mulberries. They were plentiful there. A family was living with him, Mr. Will Doolen. We drove down to the mulberry grove nearby and spread our dinner. Mr. Dumont had lunch with us. Mrs. Carter was going but failed to get off. After lunch we gathered a deal of mulberries, rested awhile in the good shade, then returned home with berries to last two or three days. Before leaving I discussed with Mr. Dumont the price and selling of my steers and he advised me the best he could about it. He said in after years that this was the most hopes he ever had for himself, when I would come to him for advice in selling my yearlings.

I drove over to the post office for the mail on Monday. I got a goodly lot of it too. I still received a few scattering letters from my flower-exchange friends, but the most attractive of all was a nice, large, red-backed bound book. It was *Stanley's Travels or Exploration in the Dark Continent of Africa.*[7] This book was a present by my Childress correspondent, Mr. D. P., and was a perfect surprise. I hated to accept it under the circumstances, but it was such a beauty and so desirable that I could not resist it. A letter accompanied this book. Another letter was from my New Mexico correspondent, Mr. F. P., which contained a goodly lot of interesting things aside from much "taffy," as I call it, and sentimentalities. I will spare my readers' patience of the latter. The third letter was from my Matador correspondent, Mr. J. B.

But the fourth was another country heard from. I was surprised on opening it, and I was rather flattered too. It was from a boy on the Pitchfork Ranch that we used to know when we were there, and of whom we thought a great deal. He was a fine, upright, good, moral, religious boy, and was fine-looking besides. He wished to know if I would correspond with him. Now I disliked to refuse this boy's request, for I would have enjoyed his correspondence. He wrote a nice hand and a good letter. He was educated. But since I had promised S. J. that I would try to think of him in that way, I had made up my mind not to take on any more correspondents. However, I had made but little progress in the above line of thought, so I refused this boy's correspondence on the plea that I had more than I could take care of already. I will call him Mr. J. S. Mr. S. J. called on me once in a while, but he seemed to feel himself pretty secure without any extra effort on his part unless it just happened to suit him. Had he known how little I worried, it might have been different.

We had never had any church in this country, so news was narrated around that there would be church the next Sunday at the home of Mr. Sul Carter. The sermon would be delivered by a preacher who was traveling through the country and who was then stopping with the Carters. He had come by way of the plains, stopping at different ranches on the way. There was quite a crowd assembled at the Carter home the next Sunday, and the preacher delivered a very interesting sermon. This was such an unusual affair that most of us donned some of our best apparel. Mr. S. J. was asked by one lady who was not there, "Who was the best looking woman at church?"

He said, "The widow, by far."

I hardly thought he would have passed this compliment on me, but I felt sure he thought I would not hear of it. But back to the preacher again. The news came out after him. It seemed he had stolen something from each and every place where he had stopped. One place he stole a horse, another a pair of slippers, another a gold ring and some money. But he had gone and they did not try to trace him. This is the record, therefore, of our first preacher in Cottle County.

Miss Janie and I made a trip to Childress, thirty-five miles away, to have her voucher cashed. We stopped at Judge Campbell's hotel.[8] We met Mr. W. Q. Richards, a ranchman from home, and also Mr. John Miller of the 3D Ranch.[9] They took us to a vaudeville that night, of which we enjoyed every bit. We returned home the next day, as Miss Janie had to hasten back to her school.

Capp had now advanced in his violin study until he could make good music for anyone to listen to. This made him a welcome visitor with all his playmates. Mrs. Gober and her son, Lev, often came over and spent the night with us. She was a sister of W. Q. Richards'. The boys would have a fine time. This was a custom of the western people to throw the children together as often as possible, in order that they be associated with their own kind and age and enjoy each other's company.

Our school was out now, and the teacher had returned home. We were left alone again. Mrs. Carter and I visited quite often, as they were always my best standbys. Capp did much prowling up and down the creek since school was out. Sometimes he would bring home strange water animals, such as enormous snapping turtles, or almost anything scary looking. He was out late one afternoon. It was almost dark, and I was very uneasy about him. Finally I saw him coming in. I thought he looked rather bulky, and he was coming slow. I paid no more attention until I stepped out in the yard when he was walking up, and, oh, horrors, he had a big bull snake as large as a medium-sized quart bottle wrapped around him a time or two. It was over his shoulders, and he was holding it by the neck with its head out in front striking and licking out its tongue with all its might. I threw up my hands and hollered at him to throw it down, but he only laughed. Now a bull snake is harmless, but a snake of any kind makes me shudder.

Not very long after this, he came home one day and wanted me to let him have the gun. He said there was a wildcat up in a big cottonwood tree down on the creek about a half mile. I told him it would be gone when he got back. He said no, it wouldn't, because it was asleep out on a limb. He

had tied his coat around the tree so it would not come down. I did not like
for him to have the gun, as he had never used it much, but I let him have it
this time. In about one hour, he came back dragging one of the largest
wildcats I had ever seen. He said it was still asleep when he went back.

They were preparing for a big dance at Matador. I received an invitation. This was to be the swellest affair there had ever been in the country.
It was an unusual occasion when Mr. H. H. Campbell, the foreman of the
Matador Cattle Company for the past eleven years, resigned his position
and turned over his management to the other owners.

This dance lasted about three days I think. They came from fifty and
sixty miles away. There were between two and three hundred people present, I think. The table was spread at all times with everything good to eat.
Sleeping quarters were arranged for the ladies at the Campbell home, and
everything went on beautifully.

Mrs. Campbell delivered a very able address to the friends, but most especially to the boys who had proven themselves so faithful through all the
years of their association in the interest of the Matador Company. This was
a most splendid talk and brotherly advice that she gave them regarding
their future and the advantages of the new country and land that lay before
them. Her closing words were pathetic, as is the breaking up and severing
of all relations with a large family. Her husband, Mr. Campbell, was supposed to have delivered this address, but through his special request, she
took his place.[10]

Everyone seemed to enjoy this affair immensely. After the jolly good-
bye that always belongs to the western people, all returned to their homes.

In a day or two after we came home, I had a very unexpected call. It was
from a gentleman living over near Childress. I had never seen or heard of
him before. He introduced himself. I will call his name Kirkland.[11] He was
a pretty fair-looking man, of very good appearance. He was about thirty-
five years old, I judged. He told me of his home over near Childress, and
that his ownership of property was very good. But what could be his business, I wondered? He went on to say that Miss Janie Roberts, our teacher,
lived neighbors to them, and she had told him about me. This was his
business: he was a widower and was very lonely. He was in search of a
companion, and he thought possibly I might look on him with favor. I
told him, "No, indeed!" I was not on the carpet any whatever. This was
some of Miss Janie's ribbing up just for pure mischief. I could have shook
her. He soon took his departure, though not altogether discouraged.

In about a couple of weeks we made a trip to Childress and came back
by the Roberts' home. They told me that very day this man had gone

down to call on me again. Now, I wanted to miss him, but there was only one road, so we were on the look out. We got a glimpse of him through the mesquite several hundred yards before we met. I speeded up the team in a high trot, and we passed him on the bend of the road like a streak of lightning. Mr. Richards was teasing me some time after this, and asked why I was driving so reckless over on the Childress road. I did not know how he found out about this.

We were now running short of fresh meat again. I spied two antelopes about a quarter of a mile from home, so I took my old reliable and made a sneak on them. I killed them both. Mr. Carr hauled them in, hung them up on the side of his barn by the road, and dressed them. He told me two men came by while he was dressing them and congratulated him on his good luck in killing two antelope at one time. He told them he did not kill them, but that I did it. One of them said, "What? A woman kill an antelope?"

The other man said, "Sure, I would rather any man in Cottle County would shoot at me than Mrs. Bird." He was someone that knew me, but I never learned who he was.

Seventeen

IT WAS SPRINGTIME now.[1] We had some new neighbors down on the river five miles away. It was Mr. Charlie Work's folks[2] from Dallas. We had Sunday School and singing at the schoolhouse now, which seemed quite easternlike. There were three of the Work children and my two. They visited quite a bit. Each bunch would spend a week with the other sometimes. I remember one week especially that my children spent with the others, which left me all alone. I did not think at first about this fact. All my near neighbors were also off on a visit east at that time. The Carters, Carrs, Canslers, and the Murphys were all gone, which left me all alone for one week, with not a soul nearer than five miles of me. I was not in the least afraid, but felt myself rather cut off from all connections. I was usually busy in the day, and I read late at night. One night about eleven o'clock I heard something at the well about ten steps away. I kept reading, but the noise kept up, working with the rope and bucket. My curiosity was aroused, and I just had to find out what it was. The night was dark, and I could not see, so I just stepped out around the corner of the house and fired off the gun. Almost at the report, here came a yearling sailing by me on twenty-one.[3] He liked to have run over me. I went back and finished reading my story and retired without further disturbance.

Another night I had a similar experience. Now, we had a hen that was very persistent on roosting on a ladder that was leaned up at the back of the house. A coyote came up and caught her and ran off a piece. I fired off the gun, and he dropped her. She came back and went onto the ladder again, so he came back in about twenty minutes and caught her again. I fired off the gun again, and he dropped her again. She hid out somewhere, and in a few minutes, he got her again. So bang went the gun again, and he dropped her. This time she made it back to the house and went under the floor to save herself after being caught three times that night.

I drove over to the post office the next day for the mail. Among the letters there was one of which I very much regretted having received. It was from an old man, but he was one of the noblest characters I have ever known. He was one of those few people who are the happiest when he is helping someone else. He never took any credit or reward for anything he did. He and Mr. Dumont were very close friends. He loved my children and was a friend to their father. But this letter! How could I answer it? He had asked me to share the remainder of his life and property, which I could not consider for one moment. In my reply I told him I did not want to marry. I said that I did not expect to marry at all, but I hoped he could still be my friend. In his reply he almost scolded me to even entertain a thought that he would not always be my friend. He also said I might think lightly of it, but this was the first time he had ever asked any lady to share his name. If he ever had an enemy, I never knew of it. He passed away several years ago. His name was Mr. F. E., I will call him.

The Paducahites were putting on another blowout, a dance and supper. Mrs. Cansler and I left our children with Mr. Cansler, donned our smartest evening attire, and drove up to the burg, looking as prim and smart as almost any two flappers you would meet. Of course, we knew everybody and met with hearty welcome and invitations on every side. Some of the Matador boys had come down for the occasion, and to my surprise, who should come around and ask me for the first dance but Mr. J. B., my Matador correspondent. I was rather pleased to meet him, as it suited me to have a brand-new one to rush for this occasion. Pretty soon here came Mrs. Cansler and her partner. Everybody was jolly, the music was fine, and the dance soon began. The whole affair passed off pleasantly and enjoyably. The next morning Mrs. Cansler and I drove in home ready for business just as if we had never been off on a lark. This was about the last good dance they had in Paducah by the old-timers.

We were becoming more settled and dignified as the country grew up.

We attended church regularly, and we tried to give our children all the advantages possible in the way of educational advancement.

There were some more business houses and a hotel in Paducah, and they were preparing to organize the town. Mr. Neff and Mr. Potts from Pottsboro came up.[4] They and Mr. Scott were the foremen in the business. They were laying off the lots. There was a drawing of lots. Each settler was given twelve lots, two business lots and ten residence lots. There were several dances during this proceeding, a big dinner, a dance, and a general blowout on the last.[5]

Just before all this took place, I had received a letter from my New Mexico correspondent, Mr. F. P. He was starting for Texas at once and would stop at Childress. He would visit me in Paducah right soon. I dropped a few hints around that a cousin from New Mexico was going to visit me, but I told my nearest neighbor, Mrs. Carr, the straight facts about it. They arranged for him to spend the nights with them while he stayed. Now, I must not deny that I had never given this man any encouragement before he came back to Texas, but there was no engagement between us. We had corresponded now about six years. In my last letter to him I said, "The greatest problem to solve is, what shall we think of each other when we meet? Will we seem as strangers, or will it seem that we have met before?" Again I told him in the same letter that he must not get it in his head that a wedding was to take place as soon as he arrived in Texas. Far from that! He must remember the greatest feat to accomplish was to make a woman marry when she did not want to or to keep her from it when she did.

He arrived in due time, two or three days before the big dinner and dance at Paducah. He seemed a little changed after six years of absence. Yet, after getting more used to him, he seemed more his old self again. In a day or two, Mr. S. J. met Mr. Carr. They were out looking for their horses. He asked if that man was my cousin. Mr. Carr laughed and said he guessed so. S. J. said he did not believe a bit of it.

The next day was the big blowout at Paducah. Mr. F. P. was wearing a beautiful ring. He said I might wear it if I wished. I put it on my forefinger, the engagement finger then. So he and I and the little ones drove up to Paducah the next day to see the sights. They were all at dinner when we arrived. They arranged a place for us. As it happened, Mr. S. J. was just on the opposite side of the table from us. I did not pretend to have noticed this, and was busily talking to my partner. The way I flashed that diamond ring was astonishing. The afternoon passed off very pleasantly. My partner was quite attentive and entertaining.

The dance began about four o'clock. I was sitting at the back of most of the crowd. Mr. F. P. had walked away for a few minutes, and no sooner had he done so than Mr. S. J. pulled through the crowd and asked me for that dance. He begged my pardon and said he did not blame me, but he wanted the next one. So the second dance came around, and he and I had no more than gotten on the floor when he asked me if I was going to marry that man soon. I told him I just could not tell exactly when. He said if I would only wait, he would be more attentive to me than he had ever been before. I asked him why he had been otherwise all these months. I told him that he had seemed to feel that he knew just where he could lay his finger down at anytime that might suit him best, but, alas, when he did, the flea was gone. I believed he cared for me all the time but only wanted to act independent and indifferent. He made many promises as to what he would do in the future.

He moved away from this country. He gave me a nice ring before he left. He also wrote me several times and said he never wanted to marry so bad in his life. I answered his letters, but I did not care for him anymore.

The dance lasted till morning and all returned home sleepy and tired, no doubt. I can speak for myself at least.

I received a letter the next day that capped the climax. It was from a bachelor living over near Otta. I had met him once. He popped the question right off the reel. He said he believed that with a little "energetic," he could build up my cattle to be worth a whole lot, and so on. I did not think this letter merited any secrecy, so F. P. and I had a big laugh over it.

I told him I guessed he would have to leave. Everybody thought I was strictly on the carpet, that the early bird got the worm. I said that he seemed to have dropped down in our midst like a bombshell. He enjoyed the joke but said he wished it was like they thought. He and Capp took little hunts out on the creek in the afternoon. Capp liked him and said as much to me. Now I had been in the habit of posting Capp to stay around close when I did not want to talk to certain parties that came sometimes. He thought this was one of them, so he said to me one day, "Mama, this is seventeen chances you have had that I know of. It looks like you would, well," he hesitated, as he did not know how to put it, "looks like you would propose to some of them." He did not know how it went, but he had read every letter I had ever gotten and was well posted on all facts.

Mr. F. P. was leaving the next day. Mr. Dumont had moved to Paducah and put in a store. He also had the post office. This office he held for more than twenty years, as long as he lived.

They had church once a month now in Paducah. Their pastor's name was Jameson.[6] Mr. Neff's family[7] had moved up from Pottsboro. I was so anxious to see them, for I had not seen them for fourteen years. We came up to church the next Sunday. It was a happy reunion of old-timers. The children had all grown up but the baby, and they were a good-looking bunch too, smart and intelligent. Two of them were teachers. We were together quite often, and I learned to think a great deal of the children. Miss Ola, their daughter, was going to teach our second school on Buck Creek. She would board with us. We were so glad to have her. She was just the dearest little body ever. She could not have been otherwise though and been the daughter of my dear old teacher, Mrs. Neff. She made herself one of us, and we were all as one family. She and I were perfect pals, confiding many secrets to each other. She took so much interest in my children and advanced them more than it seemed possible. Capp was getting to be fine on the violin, and she enjoyed his music so much. She gave him piano music later on, but having no instrument at home, we discontinued it. She said his violin music was his talent anyway. She and I both, I think, enjoyed this summer together immensely. She said as much herself. At the last of school, she gave a little entertainment. The children were all well drilled, and their recital was good. They had many different plays. The house was packed. People from town and all around came. They certainly applauded the whole program all the way through. Miss Ola had many compliments on this, as it was all her own getup. Capp received the medal. I was sorry when the school was out. We missed her so much. It was late summer now, and we were so lonely.

I was out in the yard one night, and I could hear something down in Mr. Carr's field about three hundred yards away. I could not imagine what it was. It sounded like a little lamb bleating. The next morning I was up just before good daylight. I took my gun and slipped off down there. I was determined to find out what it was. There was a small tank of water just inside the field. When I came in sight of this, two deer came bouncing out and stopped on the hill. I pulled down on them and killed one. This was the first and only deer I ever killed. Somehow I could never slip up in gunshot of them. They would always see me first. I went on up to Mr. Carr's and told them I came to get them to sit up with me that night. They looked serious and asked what was the matter. I told them I had killed a deer. They laughed. He said he would take care of it.

Mr. Jeff Short,[8] an acquaintance of the Neff's, had moved to Paducah and built him a residence there. He was going to teach the school there.

He wanted someone to live in his house, and he would board with them.
He and Miss Ola drove down to see me to see if I would not move to town
for the school that fall and take charge of the Short residence. After some
parleying I decided to do so. The move was soon made, and we were
settled in Paducah for the winter.

The courthouse was being built that fall.[9] There were many people here,
which made times much better. The cornerstone was laid later on. It was
quite a big occasion. There were a number of people from other towns.
There was a dinner, a speaking by the Masonic members, a march, and a
band playing.[10]

We had a good full school. Miss Ola was assistant in this. The children
took much interest.

Christmas came on, and they were preparing for a Christmas tree, which
proved quite a success. Not many children had ever seen one before. I
think it was the first Christmas tree in the Panhandle of Texas.

The school moved on quiet and successfully. They were now preparing
for the close of it.[11] They had a nice entertainment, and the children all
played well. Baby gave a reading of "Virginia Dare,"[12] for which she was
highly applauded. Many credits were given, Baker Harwell receiving the
medal. So the school was out, and we were ready to return home on Buck
Creek. Mr. Short's mother and the rest of the family were coming up soon
to live with him.

We moved the next week. After straightening up, there was nothing special that took place for some weeks. It was well up into the summer now.

The following incident that I will relate occurred on Friday the thirteenth, which has always made me a little shy of that date as being an un-
lucky one. The plum season was on now. There were acres and acres of
wild plums growing down on the river five miles away, and they were fine.
I had planned to put up a lot of them that week. Instead of waiting until
Saturday when the children could help me, I decided to go alone on Friday
afternoon to get the plums.

I cannot remember half the little hindrances that came up even before
I got started. But first, I began to harness up the team and discovered one
of the collars was gone. It was over at Mr. Carr's. I ran over and got it and
had them about harnessed when old Steel Dust turned the other way and
ran out on the prairie, clear of harness and everything. I caught him again
soon and had them harnessed up to the wagon. I had the tubs for the
plums in, and off I went in a high trot. My hat blew off, and I had to stop
and get it. On I went in spite of all obstacles. I crossed the branch and

discovered that I had dropped my whip. I ran back and got it, so I hit the road in earnest now. I had to pass by the schoolhouse. The children knew I was going.

I had not noticed a cloud that was coming up in the west until I was well on the way. Still I did not pay much attention to it, but it gathered fast. I drove on down on the sand bar of the river a quarter of a mile, where there were the most plums. The river was dry but wide. I unhitched the team and tied them out on the bank. By this time it was raining like forty.[13] I grabbed a light quilt that I had put in the wagon and threw it over me. Then I ran and sat down on a log under a hackberry tree. And right there I must say I never got such a drenching in all my life. There was not a dry thread on me.

The rain came down in torrents and wind with it. By the time it slacked up, the river was beginning to come down. There were some deep gullies between me and the bank. I threw off my wet quilt and made for the team. The wind and rain had frightened them until they had wound and twisted the harness until I liked to never got it untangled. I worked fast, got them loose, ran and hitched them to the wagon, and tried to drive out. The water was coming down in sloshes, and I could not tell where the deep parts were. There was a small knoll on the sand bar that reached up about level with the bank, so I drove the wagon up on this knoll. It was barely large enough but kept the wagon out of danger of being washed away.

Now the next thing was that I knew I must get out of here some way. The water was then half way up the knoll and still rising. I unharnessed the team, mounted old Tod boy-fashion, led old Steel Dust, and we made for the bank. We swam twice before we reached it, but we landed safely. Now I thought I was sitting pretty, but, behold, there were two or three small canyons leading down to the river between me and the road about a quarter of a mile above. They were booming full. But on I went. We had to swim two of these before we reached the high land, or road.

Now I bent my course for home and had gone but a little ways when I saw a boy coming horseback. His father, Mr. J. W. as mentioned in other parts of this book, was out on the prairie herding his stock. He had seen me when I left, so he sent his boy to see after me, which was pretty nice I thought. Now when the boy came in sight, I had to change my style of riding, as we all know it was a disgrace at that time for a lady to ride boy-fashion. So I slipped my foot over on the other side of my horse. The horse was so wet and slick that I could hardly stay on him. Just as the boy came up, my horse gave a little stumble, and I slid off just as pretty as you please.

After he got through laughing, he told me I could not get home because Buck Creek was up. I would have to go over to their house and spend the night. It was about three miles. He helped me on my horse, and I managed to stay with him until we reached their house.

The girls had a good joke on me, but they soon had me rigged out in some dry clothes. I really enjoyed the visit with them. I knew my children would go over and stay with Mrs. Carr until I came home. Mr. J. W. sent his boy to get my wagon. I rolled in home the next day about ten o'clock and did not take any plums either. I did take back rather a good lot of experience, however.

I had been out a day or two before this and stalked a large fat antelope. I had used a long-range gun that my husband used. It was a Marlin caliber .40.[14] Mr. Carr had just been out for a load of wood. He asked me why I did not go over that hill and get my other antelope. I told him I only fired one shot, but he said I killed two with this shot. The other one went just over the hill and died. I was sorry to have lost this one, but it was too late then.

Eighteen

TWO OR THREE WEEKS passed without any special event. Our school was out. Mr. Austin's folks had visited us. They were keeping the hotel at Matador now.[1] They exacted a promise that we would make them a long visit to Matador in the near future. So the time had now arrived, and we were preparing to go. But what would we do with our chickens? The coyotes would sure get them. After a little thought, I hit on a plan. I had plenty of water and food under the house. I dressed up a life-size dummy in my own clothes, painted the face somewhat vicious looking, set it up on the ladder at the back of the house, put one of Capp's hats on it, and put a long paper fly brush in the hand that the wind rattled all the time. This proved very effective. When we returned, not one chicken was gone, and besides, a hen had hatched out a bunch of little chickens. Mr. Dumont said he rode by the house while we were gone and took a big laugh at the lady on the ladder.

But on with our visit to Matador. The town seemed rather on a boom. It was building up fast, and the country was settling up. Now I must say, I think Mrs. Campbell's advice to the boys was being carried out. She told them as the settlers would move in, to invade their homes, to capture their daughters for wives and settle down. They were certainly following her advice. I think there was about half a dozen weddings during my two weeks' visit there. There was certainly a lively time. There were dances every few nights. I enjoyed the trip to Mr. Hugh White's wedding over at Whiteflat, twelve miles from Matador.[2] Two or three of the newlyweds were stopping at the Austin hotel [Southern Hotel]. I visited with the Campbells, the Moores, and the McDonalds[3] while there, and drove out into the country some. So I had an all-around good visit at Matador.

We returned home and found everything O.K. But it seems something common must always come up to make you drop your feathers when you are feeling so fine and important, and with us it was the absence of wood. Not one stick did we have to cook with, so the first thing we did was to harness the team to the wagon and drive out on the prairie to pick up a nice good load of wood. On our way home when we reached the creek and drove down the bed of it to the tank, an antelope jumped out. It had been to water and ran up and stopped on the bank within a few yards of us. I pulled out my old rifle and slew him right there. This filled another much-needed want just then. We loaded him onto the wagon and drove in home feeling we had killed two birds with one stone.

The next day was Saturday. I drove over for the mail. I had not had it for some time. I got quite a bunch of it. I got a letter from about all my correspondents. One was from Mr. D. P. at Childress, and he still insisted on calling on me. Now I was a little peeved at him. I learned from Mrs. Austin that he had showed some of my letters to a special friend or two of his. She said he felt so complimented over them. I had not cared so much for this correspondence anyway and was glad of an excuse to dispose of it. So I wrote and told him it was at an end. I told him the cause. Another letter was from Mr. J. B. of Matador, inquiring why I was so negligent in answering his letters. Another one was from a man who was distantly related to me by marriage, though no kin of course. He wanted to correspond. I received a letter later on from another man of about the same denomination as the above, with the same request. I replied to neither. The above two parties I will withhold the names or initials of, owing to the relationship.

They were preparing for a picnic at Paducah. Mr. F. P. came down from Childress for a couple of days for this, which was the third visit he had made us. We took in the picnic and had a very enjoyable day. He was talking of moving up into Oklahoma. He returned to Childress the next day.

I drove up to town in a day or two for the mail. In this lot was a letter from Mr. J. B., my Matador correspondent. This letter was somewhat out of the ordinary and was somewhat businesslike I claim. It was straight to the point with no foolishness mixed in. In other words, it was a first-class proposal of marriage. Now, this proposition did not exactly appeal to me, and I wrote him as much, saying I guessed our little romance was at an

end. Neither of us was ever under any obligation to the other more than as
a mere correspondent, and this seemed to have come to a close. We were
friends after this but nothing more.

A lady told me she overheard two boys talking in regard to me. One said
he thought I ought to marry some of them. He said that I was too independent, and that they had made me so. The other one said, "Well, she
does not have to unless she wants to. She makes her own living now."

This was the year we had such an awful drouth, and most of the cattle
had to be moved off the range. There was scarcely any grass at all. My
cattle were all that were on the range here. They lived mostly on sagebrush
that winter and lost pretty heavy too.[4]

In the fall when they were gathering the cattle, it began raining a slow
long rain that lasted ten days or more. The poor boys had an awful time
gathering the cattle in the rain and mud, and trying to cook in the rain. I
had made a large fine cake to send them. It was about fourteen inches
high, decorated in lace design, with ice trimming and fancy candy around
the center. The following words were written in raised ice piping, "Good
luck to the cowboy." It was some time before I had a chance to send it to
them. Mr. Carr was going over to the herd and said he would take it to
them. It was about five miles. I had a large tin bucket that just fit over this
cake with a lid on the bottom. I put this all in a flour sack and tied it hard
and fast. Mr. Carr tied it onto his saddle, and it reached them in perfect
shape. Mr. Carr said he never saw boys take on over anything so in his life.
They said they would sure hate for old F. P. to sit down to that. This was
my New Mexico correspondent.

This was Saturday.[5] We had planned to go up to town and spend the
night and Sunday with Mrs. Neff, and also to attend church. We called at
the post office to get the mail. When it was handed to me, to my surprise
one letter was from New Mexico and was heavily draped. Oh, who could it
be? It was possibly some one of the poor little children, I thought. We
went on over to Mrs. Neff's. I was so anxious and on such suspense that I
could hardly meet them cheerfully. As soon as I could, I went off into one
of the back rooms to open my mail. Of course, this letter was the first one,
and, oh, the shock and sad news it contained was too bad to be true. This
letter was from my brother-in-law, Willie Fite. My sister, my only sister,
Lucy, was dead. This was a blow that I was least prepared for and to which
I could hardly reconcile myself. I had always hoped we would be together
again and enjoy each other as we had in years gone by, but this hope was
no more and must go down with the many other heartbreaks and disappointments of this life.

I was buried in grief and sat motionless and stunned. Miss Ola came into the room and saw that something was wrong. She went and told her mother, and she came in and asked me what was the matter. I could not speak, but I handed her the letter. After reading a part of it, she tried to console me all she could. We stayed overnight with them but returned home the next morning.

My sister, Lucy, left a little babe only one week old. Lewis was his name. She named him for our father. It seems she should have lived to have known and enjoyed this child's success. By honest, upright, and fair dealing, he has made his mark in the commercial world. If he can have done her honors in this way, he has made her name illustrious. His home is in San Antonio, and he is one among the most shrewd and successful businessmen of that place. He takes an active part in the civic affairs of the community.[6]

Mr. Woods, an old man from Austin, taught a short school on Buck Creek that summer. It was now out, and we had planned a trip to Young County. We were off on this trip in two or three days. It seemed that I craved to see my mother and talk with her since sister's death. We arrived in Young County safely and found all well. It was a change from the dry country we had left. They had had plenty of rain, the fruit season was still in, and we enjoyed it so much.

Mr. F. P. had moved up in Oklahoma some time before this. I had several letters from him. Now, he was planning to visit one week before I returned home. I enjoyed his visit. We drove some, went to church, and visited with my uncle's folks in Graham and other places. I liked him, but somehow I could never make up my mind to marry him. We intended to marry sometime, but when, I could never decide. He never persuaded me but said he had no confidence in these long engagements, as they most always proved a failure. He said that he never would have left New Mexico had it not been for me. He said he thought he would never persuade any woman to marry him. He wanted her to care enough for him to make her own decision, and this was the way matters stood between us. When we were ready to return home, he accompanied us six miles out to the Graham road at Tackett Mountain.[7] Capp and Baby drove our buggy, and I rode with him in his. He seemed sad, I thought, and did not have much to say. I felt pretty much that way myself. It was here at Tackett Mountain that we parted, he going his way and me and mine the opposite direction. Something seemed to tell me this parting was final, though I did not want it so. It seems fate decides some things regardless of our wishes, for that was the last time I ever saw him, some thirty-four years ago. We corresponded more than a year after this, but I never called him back again. I had caused him enough disappointment already.

This was the year we had so many storms and cyclones in these parts. There had been several very serious ones, but one especially will be long remembered. One night a dark cloud gathered in the west, grew darker and darker, and we were uneasy. It looked very angry as it drew nearer. It was just dusk now. We had moved the flowers out of the pit. This pit was just six-by-three feet in size, and three–and–one-half feet deep with a glass top. We had used this for a stormhouse before, and were now preparing to do so again. We folded up some heavy quilts to fit the bottom, and some to cover with, and several pillows to put over our heads. We rolled all the quilts togethers, laid them across the kitchen door, and sat down on them to wait and watch the cloud. Poor Baby was so frightened, she said, "Mama, let's get in the pit right now and go to sleep. I would rather be blown away asleep than awake." But the cloud was so near now we did go to the pit. We lay down and covered up securely. Pretty soon the cyclone struck. It was one solid glare of lightning and the awfulest roaring and noise I ever heard. It went like thousands of tin cans and everything else going around and around. It was soon over, but we had not moved.

Then we heard someone call out, "Where are you?" It was Mr. Carr. He could see our house was gone, and he came to see what was done. He felt sure that we were all killed, but when we opened up the flower pit and stepped out dry and unhurt, he was astonished. He said he had never thought of us going in that little flower pit. There was not even one pane of glass broken out of the top of it. Our house was completely destroyed, and everything in it was strewn from there to the creek, near a quarter of a mile. The furniture and everything was broken into giblets. Of couse, I felt blue when I viewed the ruins of all this, but down in my heart I felt a thankfulness that both my children and myself had escaped safely and unharmed.

We stayed at Mrs. Carr's that night. The next morning Mr. and Mrs. Carter came over after us and what clothing, bedding, or anything else in that line that might not be destroyed entirely. Several of the Paducah people and others came down that morning. When they returned home, they made up a purse, which helped me out wonderfully.

We went home with Mr. Carter for a while. He and some of the neighbors decided they could fix me up a house of some kind of what lumber was left. Mr. Carter and one of his hands hitched up a couple of teams, carried two scrapers and went over to work. They scraped out a large basin about three feet deep and sixteen by twenty feet in size, squared it up with shovels, cut out an entrance, and this was the foundation. They built the rest of it up with lumber and floored it nicely, which made a very comfortable, desirable place to stay after the walls had been papered.

One afternoon I was preparing the dirt part of the walls for papering. I was filling in all the holes with mud and smoothing it over nicely. I had a good lot of it made up and my hands were a fright. Now, there was a man, a full-blooded German, living up in the Fairview settlement.[8] His name was Paul Phils. He was a widower and had some children. He had been out in his wagon on business of some kind, so in order to kill two birds with one stone, I suppose, he drove up and stopped. He said in a very businesslike way, as if he was out trying to buy a cow, that he thought while he was out he would just drive by and speak to me on a little matter he had been thinking of. He said that he was in need of a wife and thought I might marry him. I told him nothing doing, and to please drive on. I had a strong notion of stepping out and giving him a downright good snowballing with mud as he drove off, but I thought better and said mournfully, "Alas, another opportunity passed up!"

We stayed here until fall and then moved back to Paducah for the school and located there for good. Mr. Short's mother, brother, and little sister had moved up with him now. We lived close neighbors to them. His mother was one of the dearest, best women I have ever known. She and Mrs. Neff were my main neighbors, and dear Ola was my other little pal.

Mr. Dumont called occasionally. Sometimes the conversation would drift directly to ourselves, but I always changed the subject. I never allowed anything of this kind to come up between us. I needed his friendship always, but was content with only this.

I received an order from Mr. Jack Luckett of Matador[9] for a full-beaded buckskin suit. He furnished the material. It was heavily fringed, beaded, and had steel buttons. It was certainly a handsome suit.

I had a letter from Mr. F. P. He was doing a very good business, he said, but he longed to see the little white lady again. When we parted last, I suggested that we make each other a present of some kind as a keepsake to have, in case we were never more to each other than we were at that time. Therefore, I made him a very fine pair of gauntlet gloves. I put his initials on them, and sent them to him. He seemed very proud of them. Pretty soon he sent me a nice gold band ring with his initials inside. He said he wanted me to wear this as long as I lived. So far, I have been faithful to this request. I am still wearing this same ring today and have worn it all these years. It will not come off my finger now. It has not been off for several years, though it never gives me any trouble. He told me this ring was made of a pair of gold nugget cuff buttons and was from the mines of New Mexico. He had worn them several years.

Our school at Paducah was doing fine. My children were growing up now, and I felt so anxious about them. Baby was 8 and Capp was 14.[10] Yes, my boy had even begun to make eyes at the little girls. This made me feel slightly aged, but time and tide wait for no one.

We had just had an invitation to a wedding and dance. Mrs. Bailey's daughter, Nora, was to be married to Mr. Pat Murphy,[11] so a bunch of us, Miss Ola Neff, Mr. George Short, myself, and some others, rigged up and drove out. It was in the country. Everything was carried on nicely. Partners for a set were arranged on the floor, including the bridal pair. The officiating party came forward, faced the bridal party, and read the marriage ceremony. When all was over, the music began. This was a square dance, and all joined hands and promenaded, and the dance went on. This was a bit of western style. Pretty soon we were all invited out to a most splendid supper. The table fairly groaned with luscious good things to eat. Mrs. Bailey was a good hostess and could never be excelled on the preparation of a fine dinner. We returned home well repaid for our trip. I never took any part in the dancing anymore, and had not for some time. I had begun to feel myself more retired and dignified for so frivolous things.

Nineteen

THE LITTLE FOLKS had begun to come to the front now with their play parties and candy breakings.[1] We all went to church, singings, musicals, and little shows as most western people did. Mr. Dumont was generally in the crowd. Capp often tried to persuade me to go with him [Mr. Dumont] places, because it pleased him, he said. I never cared to go with anyone, though, so I did not care to change up at so late a date.

Baby came in with my mail one day. There were a number of letters from relatives and friends. One was from Mr. F. P. He had moved again to another town, Enid, Oklahoma. Another letter I did not recognize at first, but on opening it, I was very much surprised that it was from no other than Mr. J. S., formerly of the Pitchfork Ranch. He wished to correspond with me. It had been three or four years since he had written me asking the same above favor, but after I had written him, as I did, I heard soon after that he had married a little girl that we knew. She was a real good girl and very beautiful, but this turned out to be very sad indeed. She only lived about one year after their marriage. When she died, he was left all alone again. He and I exchanged several letters. He said he heard that Mr. Dumont and I were going to marry. I wrote him that I guessed it was someone drawing on their own imagination, as I knew nothing of it.

As time went on, it seemed to bring about many changes. While I could never make up my mind to marry anyone, yet, I expected to, at some future time or other, for I always had a horror and dread of being left in my declining years to live out my life alone.

I shall never forget one afternoon when I was ironing. Capp and I were talking, and the subject came up about our future, our past opportunities, and what would be the best for us to do. He and I always spoke of "us" either getting "married" or not getting "married," and I said in case "we do," maybe Mr. Dumont would suit us best after all. I had no more than said it till Capp said that was just what he thought. He and Baby always thought more of Mr. Dumont than anyone else, and this was a feather in his cap for me. He always petted and made over them and gave them anything they wanted. I always felt that in case I should ever marry, no matter if I worshiped the man, if he should prove unkind and cross with my children, I would soon grow to detest and dislike him. Mr. S. J. once told me I could either love or not love, just as my judgment might direct. I thought he guessed my combination pretty well, but on with mine and Capp's conversation. He said he would prefer Mr. Dumont to anyone else. He had been our main standby all these years, ever ready to render us any service we might need. To be honest, it seemed if I should marry some other man, I would still need Mr. Dumont, so this is the way matters stood. It had been some seven years before when he proposed to me, and I had refused him.[2] Now it seemed a proposal was about to come the other way.

After thinking a bit, I hit on a plan. I still had some letters from one of the parties who had given me a very pressing invitation to get married, so I wrote Mr. Dumont a note pretending I was considering this proposal. I asked his advice about it. I told him he had been a friend and advisor of long standing, and I felt sure he would recommend this party, as I thought it would be a very good chance for me. But I wanted his approval. This was Saturday afternoon, so I wrapped up these letters as mentioned in a nice little packet, enclosing the note to Mr. Dumont, went down to the store, and gave them to him. I suggested he wait till he went to his room that night to open it.

The next day was Sunday. I was looking for him, and I did not have to look long. He came up just as soon as etiquette would admit. He was carefully, though modestly, attired, and he looked real nice, I thought. He was never, to say, handsome, though he had unusually expressive, intelligent brown eyes, which made up for any other defects. He sat for some little time talking on general topics and seemed unable to lead out on what seemed to be on his mind principally. After a while, in a very common-place way, I broached the subject and said, "Well, what do you think of my plans?" He said he did not think very much of them. He thought I could do better. I said very innocently, "How is that?"

"By taking me," he answered.

"Oh," I said, "that is a new light on it." I pretended I thought he was just joshing. He did not mislead me very long, but put up one of the most earnest talks for Number One I had ever heard him make. He said that I must not marry this other man. If I did, his life would be wrecked. He had always thought of his future and mine in connection at some time or other. I finally told him I would call it off, as I did not care much for the other fellow anyway. I think he rather suspicioned it was a frame-up on my part, but he did not seem to care, though he teased me in after years and said I just everlastingly pressed him into a proposal, whether it suited him or not.

Now we talked some real business as to when the union between us should take place. I could not decide the exact date, but possibly about two months or more from that date would be good. Not much more was said about it. Time seemed to fly, and ere long, two months was drawing near. I did not feel anymore like I was going to get married than a spirit. Furthermore, I seemed to be drifting further away from it. Mr. Dumont called usually about once a week, but we talked mostly on ordinary topics. Occasionally he would say he hoped I would hurry and decide on the exact date.

Mr. F. P.'s letters came regularly, but I had dropped a hint in some of my last ones to him that our little romance might prove only a romance and nothing more, just as he had prophesied some years back. I had a reply to this without delay. His letter was so sad. It gave me the blues, and I did not get over it for some time, though I had decided not to marry him. However, it was hard to tell him so. After some delay I wrote him and told him all, that I had decided to marry another man. I told him who he was, and that it might be that the marriage would take place at an early date.

When I had finished this letter, my conscience smote me for the first time. I had always tried to deal fair and square with everyone I had corresponded with. It was not my wish to encourage or mislead anyone as to my regards for them, when I did not feel it. To do so, I always felt, was a crime almost unpardonable. I was honest and sincere with this party in the beginning and held out for a long, long time, but the above case seemed an exception. It was of such long standing and required more faithfulness and duration than the ordinary person usually possesses. However, I was the cause of this delay, and my reason for this was that I had never been associated with him sufficiently to be thoroughly acquainted with him. I could not consent to marry him under these conditions, so this was the way the matter stood.

I had letters from Mr. J. S., but they were mostly just a friendly correspondence. I think he still had an inkling of mine and Mr. Dumont's ideas, but, oh rats, I wasn't half ready to get married. I wanted to snide,[3] but how could I? Things were coming to a showdown. After some thinking, I settled on a plan. I was about out of material for glove making and had thought of ordering some from Dallas, which I had done before. Instead of this, I decided to make a trip to Dallas myself and lay in this material. I did not mention my plans to Mr. Dumont until I was about ready to start. The children were in school. I left Baby with Mrs. Neff and Capp with Mrs. Backus.

I was soon on my way but switched off at Henrietta,[4] took the mail hack over to Graham, and visited about two weeks with relatives there and in Tonk Valley. I went to Dallas from there. I had some acquaintances at Dallas. Mr. Charlie Work's folks had moved back there. My Uncle Charles had also given me the address of some parties there whom he wanted me to meet. They were spiritualists, and he was investigating that line of thought at that time. He gave me a letter of introduction to them.

I reached Dallas in due time. It was at night, and I put up at a hotel. The next morning I took the streetcar down on Harwood Street and met those people. Their name was McConnel. He was the president of the Spiritualist Association. They welcomed me in their home and treated me royally. He had been corresponding with my uncle, but they had never met. They took a great interest in me, it seemed. They drove with me, visited some of their relatives and friends. They also carried me to their séance. This was wonderful to me. I looked on in amazement, as I had never seen anything like it before. The forms, or spirits of which they claimed to be, came out in front of the cabinet in flowing white robes of gauzelike material. In low weak voices, they would call for different parties or relatives in the congregation who would go up and talk with them. One form came to Mr. McConnel. She was supposed to be one of his old sweethearts, he said. She had appeared to him before, so he brought her around and made me acquainted with her. I wanted to shake hands with her but felt a little creepy and did not have the nerve.

The next day Mrs. McConnel and I called on one of her friends. She was an old lady, a florist, and was a fortune teller. She was also a spiritualist. She told my fortune without any charges, and right here I must tip my hat to the old fortune teller. She told me about everything I ever knew, ever did, or ever thought of, besides a good lot of my future. She told me there was a marriage ahead for me, and that it was a truly wooed-and-won affair.

I was now ready to visit some with my other friends. It was my intention when I came to Dallas to apply for a position as sculptor at some marble yard or other, so Mr. McConnel drove me to a marble yard. I had my little rock book with me. Mr. McConnel showed this to the foreman, who complimented it very highly and said it was the finest piece of work that had ever been in Dallas, and that I ought to go to New York. He said he would give me a job, so I agreed to begin in a few days.

We drove on over to Mrs. Work's. I promised to go back and meet the McConnels at their church on Sunday. I visited with Mrs. Work about a week, [and] then met the McConnels at their church. This was the only spiritualist church I ever attended. It seemed very strange and different to anything I had ever seen or heard. They insisted that I should go back home with them and spend the night, which I did.

Somehow I was beginning to feel homesick. I had written Mr. Dumont while at Graham and had received a letter from him here at Dallas. He said he had gotten my letter, but, oh, Lord, how cold. I intended to have Capp and Baby come to Dallas and enter school there in case I accepted the position as mentioned. I went out on the town the next day alone and did a little shopping. By this time a fit of loneliness and homesickness came over me that seemed unbearable. I felt I had left all my friends and come down to this big town among strangers. Oh, I could not stay. I wanted to see my children, and I wanted to see Mr. Dumont. I felt lonely with them so far away. I had never realized I needed him so much. There was no question about it. I could not stay here. That afternoon I did some thinking. The next day I would hit the road for home, and the first thing on my arrival, I would just crack down and get married before I got out of the notion.

So I lost no time in making the Fort Worth and Denver train the next morning.[5] I arrived in Childress that night, met Mr. Dulaney at the depot, and went out and spent the night with them. They were Paducah folks too. I stayed over the next day and went out in town and bought my full wedding trousseau.[6] What do you know about that? Nerve unlimited, did you say? No one knew this but myself. I took the mail hack back to Paducah the next morning. Mr. Dulaney was mail carrier. I arrived in Paducah about five o'clock in the afternoon. Mr. Dumont very leisurely stepped out to the hack to get the mail bag, but his astonishment on meeting me was comical. We exchanged a few words, but it was mail time, and he had to rush back. I think he liked to have forgotten the mail bag.

It was now about one month since I had left home, and the goosechase I had made seemed uncalled for. Possibly my guardian angel may have had something to do with directing my wandering footsteps back homeward, for I felt footsore and homesick. We drove on up home, and my little shack never looked so good to me before. My children were there by this time, and the happy reunion took place. Again I realized in full that there is no place like home and the friends that surround it.

That night Mr. Dumont came up. All was as jolly as if the prodigal had returned. By and by the little ones went to sleep. Mr. Dumont moved a bit closer to me and said he hoped I had decided when our union should take place. He little thought I had my wedding trousseau in the house at that moment to marry him. I told him I might decide earlier than might suit him. He looked a little surprised and said a half day's notice was all he wanted. We talked on awhile about our general surroundings, and decided we would step off some time between Christmas and New Year's. When he took his leave that night, he seemed more cheerful and jolly than I had seen him in many days. The next day Capp, Baby, and myself had a little conference of our own. I put the question before them. Would we take Mr. Dumont into our little family, or would we not? I knew about what their decision would be, and sure enough they both agreed we would. It was all settled.

That night I went up to Mrs. Judge Campbell's and told her the secret. She was a dressmaker, and I wanted her to help me make my dress and outfit. She was carried away with the idea. She had always wanted me to marry Mr. Dumont. The next day we got busy and put in most of the week and finished everything complete.

Mr. Dumont was also deputy sheriff besides postmaster, dry goods merchant, and groceryman.[7] He had arranged for us to live in the lower story of the jail.[8] This apartment consisted of six nicely plastered rooms, and there was seldom anyone in jail overhead. This was a pleasant place to live. Mr. Dumont suggested I move before we married, in order to have plenty of room. The move was made and everything was straightened up.

Now, this was not all the wedding that was brewing. Miss Ola had up a very serious case. She and a young preacher of Pottsboro were going to get married soon. He was yet in school and was a fine young man. Also

Mr. Short was going to get married soon to Miss McFadden, who was visiting with relatives in Paducah, the Harwells. She was a fine musician, a beautiful girl, and so very jolly. She and Ola were good friends, and they were with me at the jail a good portion of the time. We were all interested in about the same cause just then. We worked together and had just a jolly good time. Either Ola or Mamie, the other girl, would play the guitar and sing while the others worked. It seems today I can almost hear one of those old tunes that Ola played and sang, "Wait for Me at Heaven's Gate, Sweet Belle Mahone." This was my favorite one.[9]

Thus the days went by. Christmas was drawing near. We had to arrange for the Christmas tree which was a great feature with us now. Everybody took interest in it. The tree must be gotten from the cedar breaks, and we must prepare the decorations. This was the next job, and we all got busy and soon had everything in readiness. This was the twenty-third of December. By the next afternoon, all was completed with presents on. The house was packed that night. The tree was beautiful, and everybody seemed to get a thrill out of it. Mr. Dumont and I took this in together. This was the first time he had ever escorted me any place. When this was all over, we got busy on another job of a different nature altogether. Mr. Dumont and I were to be married on Sunday the twenty-eighth of December. Some preparations had already been made. Several of my best old-time lady friends made two cakes each for me, two or three dressed turkeys, and everything else in accordance. This was a regular old-time wedding dinner with Mrs. Campbell directing. This was the twenty-seventh. I shall never forget it.

Something came up to throw a damper on all the splendors that the above preparations may have had for me. Late that afternoon Miss Ola came into my room with a letter for me from F. P. He had addressed it to her, enclosing a note to her, thinking perhaps I might be married when it arrived. And such a letter. I hope I may never receive one like it again, which I am not likely to do. Miss Ola said she felt like slaying me. She was very sympathetic and had always favored this party more than anyone else, but her mother, Mrs. Neff, told me Mr. Dumont was the one. Her judgment was always good. But this letter! While he did not censure me with anything whatever, he said I had removed everything from his life—everything, every hope that made life worthwhile. I had left him an aimless wanderer on the face of the earth. It was a long letter, and when I had finished it, I felt very sad indeed. This was the ending of an eight-year correspondence, and I have never heard from him again or had any trace of him whatever from that day until this. I have wondered many times whatever became of him, and if he is still living or has passed to that great beyond where we shall journey ere long.

I had no regrets for the step I was preparing to take. My mind was thoroughly made up, and I felt I was doing the right thing. I had no inclination to waver from it. It had now taken me just seven years to arrive at this decision, so of course it was final. The next day was the eventful one. Our marriage took place at the church, at the eleven o'clock service.[10] Ours was the first church wedding in Paducah. It was a bad day with snow and sleet on the ground, but the house was full. As we marched out at the door, Mr. Dumont deliberately invited the whole congregation over to dinner. Our house was only a few steps from the church, and I think more than half of them accepted the invitation. I was shocked when he did this, but as luck would have it, we had plenty for all and I was glad they came. I shall never forget the first words he said to me when we were in our room alone: "Ella, if you had married another man, my heart would have bursted." He said the reason he had always loved me above all other women was that I knew my power over him and was too loyal to abuse it.

Twenty

WELL, THE ROMANCE PART of this story is over, and now the everyday life of the Dumont family begins. What change! For the past nine years my two little children and I had lived all alone, but now we were located in this large house, with Mr. Dumont for the head of our family. Capp and Baby were delighted with the change, and I rather felt myself that it was an improvement on the old lonely life we had lived.

Baby was then eleven years old.[1] She enjoyed going up to the store and accompanying Mr. Dumont home at noon or in the evening. She made a playfellow of him and would often have him school hopping with her on the way home. He bought her a little gray horse or rather took him in on some debt I think. He was old and poor but rather cute. She was so proud of him that it was comical to see the antics she cut. She led him down home and was so overjoyed over him that she could hardly make me understand he was really hers. She said she had always wanted a horse, so this called for a little saddle, which was forthcoming. She took him out to the livery stable about a half dozen times a day and fed him up on oats and everything else that he would eat, which made him rather an expensive horse after all. Mr. Dumont gave her another little surprise. In some of his buying of goods, he took a little watch as premium and gave it to her. This completed her happiness. She came home and showed it to me and said,

"Mama, I believe he knows just what I want the most." She said she had wanted a watch so bad, but she knew good and well not to say anything about it.

Now, I suppose Mr. Dumont thought he was using some partiality. Capp was still using his father's old violin, but it had been broken up in the cyclone. I had taken all the pieces and glued them together so that he made very good music on it. Mr. Dumont told me he knew where he could buy a good violin that was practically new, and he was going to buy it for Capp. I consented, so Capp was also made happy too.[2] Everything moved on pleasantly, and the Dumont family was happy.

I had many beautiful flowers, roses and others, blooming in the windows. The large windows in the jail were equal to hothouses. The flowers were so fragrant that the rooms were perfumed all the time from them.

But now comes another change in the program. I had a rush call from Mrs. Campbell. Another wedding dress must be made. This dress was for Mamie, Mr. Short's fiancée. So I hastened on up to Mrs. Campbell's. We got busy and laid it on for the next few days. Finally this wedding trousseau was finished. I believe this was the next church wedding in Paducah.

It was now springtime and flowers must be planted out-of-doors. This was always an enjoyable occupation for me. I took much interest in the yard this year.[3] Flowers were blooming on every side. All four of those large windows had a solid wreath of morning glories all around them. The summer house was a solid mass of blooming vines with many beds of chrysanthemums, cannas, verbenas, pansies, and many other varieties.[4] Neither did I forget my cactus collection. The cacti always held a prominent place.

But back to where this flower planting began. It was barely finished when another call came from Mrs. Campbell. This call meant much to me, for it was for no other than my dear little friend, Ola Neff. Another wedding trousseau must be made without delay. I lent a willing hand to this until it was finished, but not with the lightheartedness as before, for this meant the separation from this cherished little friend. I had learned to love her dearly. As soon as they were married, they would return East where he could begin his lifework as a minister of the Gospel. This wedding took place at the church also, which was the third church wedding. They were leaving two or three days afterward. There was church service on the night before they left. I met her there, but did not dare to speak to her in the house for I knew I would break down. When church was over, we walked arm in arm without a word until we were out in the dark, [and] then we took our farewell of each other in the good old-time way. Had she been an own little sister, I could not have felt more grieved at parting with her.

There were several other weddings that year, but none in which I took so much interest.

Things were now changing up. The country was settling up fast and the town was also building up more with business houses, a Masonic hall, a printing office, etc. Farming was being done extensively. There were cotton raising, gardening, large orchards, etc. At times I seemed to stand and gaze on the progress of the country almost in wonderment. Only a little while ago it seemed there were nothing but buffalo. Then a space of time elapsed when there was nothing left but ourselves. Yet we remained. This was a time ever to be remembered. There were months and months that I did not see the face of even one woman. Next the cattle were being moved in, then the ranches, then a long space of time ere the farming and building of towns and schools began, and then the present. What a change, but this was a change I had longed to see, for I wanted my children to grow up with the advantages of a civilized country.

At this time Capp had begun to take great interest in the wireless or radio business. He worked and experimented with it almost continually, and as the years went by, he never lost interest in it. This should have been his life's career. He also kept up his violin music. He had gotten to be quite a violinist by this time. He played in public at times. Baby also took piano music and played the banjo. String music was the fad just then, and so the summer passed away.

It was well up into the fall and school work was the interest now. Baby and Maggie Culberson were schoolmates and great chums, and they continued to be so for several years until Maggie moved away. Then Lena Doolen was her next chum.[5] She always had a jolly time with all her little girl associates.

Christmas was near at hand now. Each year it was becoming more interesting, as there were so many more people in the country. However, our little bunch had all married, moved away, and retired from any active part in this line, leaving it up to the younger bunch. I was very busily engaged just now with some special work of embroidering. This was for a Christmas present which I will explain more about later. But on with the Christmas tree in all its splendor. It was more enjoyable to sit back and look on than to feel called on to take an active part. The rush was finally over, and all was calm again except the kid parties that came off. During Christmas week the pot flowers in all my windows were blooming good, and everything looked as if it were being decorated for some special occasion.

In order to avoid any misconception in the minds of my friends, I whispered to some of them a little secret. There was to be an addition to the

Dumont family right soon. New Year's came on[6] with the usual turkey dinner with a few special invited friends, and all the work was over and back to normal once more. The next two weeks passed off calm and peaceful, when on the morning of the seventeenth of January, there came to us the dearest little bright-eyed baby boy imaginable. He was received with open arms by all the family. Baby was simply in her glory when she learned that he was really ours to have and to keep. Many of the neighbors came in to see the new baby. They also admired the flowers in the windows very much. But now came the naming of the baby. We could not decide, so I left it all to Mr. Dumont. He decided on the name Leo after a special friend of his. But when Baby learned that his name was Dumont and not Bird, she cried and said he was no kin to her if his name was not Bird. So Mr. Dumont solved the problem. He said we would name him Leo Bird, and this made matters all right.

We were pretty well occupied the rest of the winter with the cares and the pleasures of the new baby. In the spring we bought a handsome little carriage for him with a red silk parasol and trimmed in lace. Baby's happiness was complete. She never tired of rolling the little one any[where] and everywhere over town. She was so proud of him.

The summer passed off without any special events, and the fall months came on with the school, the music lessons, etc. Capp continued his radio experiments, but never lost any time in school.[7] The younger bunch now had begun to grow up and had many little parties, or socials as they called them, on Friday and Saturday nights. Our dear little babe was now walking and toddling around everywhere. His father thought there was never such a baby in the world. Mrs. Minnie Neff often visited us while we lived in the jail, and she loved our baby so much. She was a sister of the other Neff, my teacher. She and I had been schoolmates and great friends. They had moved from Oklahoma down to Paducah after the other Neffs came. It was a treat to meet and be with her again after all these years.

There was much whooping cough in the town at that time, and our little baby took it. It lasted a long time, but he finally recovered from it. He was getting in good health again, but his lungs were yet weak from the cough.

It was a cold bad winter,[8] and regardless of all the tender care we took of our little babe, he took pneumonia and grew worse as time went on. We became very much alarmed at his condition and had two doctors with him. His fever was beyond control. We watched over him day and night with aching hearts, for it seemed there was but little hope for him. Oh, how could we give him up? He was such a beautiful child. His hair was a mass of yellow curls, and he had such a bright, intelligent face. Many of the kind and sympathetic neighbors came and sat with us day and night. Dear Minnie was also with us in this trial, but the life of our darling little babe was fast ebbing away.

This was Sunday morning, and at one o'clock that afternoon, he passed from our midst. He had lived with us only one short year and then was no more. Oh, how could we do without him, with everything to remind us, little garments, little shoes, and stockings here and there. Poor Baby and Capp were heartbroken. During his illness Capp would sit by his cradle and cry and look at his little worn shoes on the table, saying he would never wear them again. Mr. Dumont said he hoped we would never have another baby. It might be the same thing to go over again. He said the past year had been the happiest one of his life, but this was the greatest anguish his life had ever known. He said that if he should live a thousand years, he would never cease to regret this child's death.

Baby could not be consoled. One of her little girlfriends, Paula Harwell, came and spent a week with her which helped some to drive away her sorrow. Mrs. Richards came and insisted Baby and I go and spend a few days with her. I did not want to leave Mr. Dumont alone, but he insisted so hard that I should go. He said he would be at the store all during the day and I would be so lonely at home, so we went. They had lost their only little babe about the same age of ours a few months before, and they knew how to sympathize with us.[9]

She drove with us quite a bit while we were there. We called on Mr. and Mrs. J. M. Barron. They were ranchers at that time on Buck Creek. This was the first time I had ever met Mrs. Barron. They had three little boys, Elmo, Arbie, and Willie, the baby, not yet a year old. She looked so young and inexperienced for the hard western life that we lived here. She told me in after years how lonely she had been at that place and how very much she appreciated our visit.[10] Mr. Dumont came for us on Sunday. Capp stayed with some of his boyfriends mostly while we were gone.

Baby took up her music again and put more energy into it than ever before. Capp still worked at his wireless. I made three or four beaded vests that spring. I could not be idle, else I would worry all the time. So the long weary weeks passed by without anything special to mention.

We were now going to make another move. We bought the Campbell place, where we are now living. We have lived here for nearly thirty years. This was to be our permanent home, and I took much interest in it.[11]

Springtime was on now, and I planted many flowers. All summer the yard was a perfect bower of flowers. The porch and house were clad in beautiful vines. I also raised many chickens, white ducks, etc. That year I raised a fine garden and planted many fruit trees. I had bedded out a good lot of fine Elberta peach seed the fall before, so we planted them on this place. They came up and did fine. That fall we set the entire block with them, one hundred and eleven trees, mostly Elbertas. In three or four years we had the finest orchard in the country, with many trees that bore peaches measuring eleven and twelve inches around. We also set a number of shadetrees in the yard.

They built the new schoolhouse this year,[12] and it was not so far for Baby and Capp to walk. They were taking great interest in the school. Baby was also taking expression. Her teacher was Miss Elura Halley, a young lady from Round Rock, Texas. Her folks had moved to this country. She boarded with us. She was a lovable girl, and we became great friends and are until today, though she lives in faraway California.

Some other folks moved to Canyon City,[13] and from there to Corpus Christi. I hated so much to see them leave, but such is life—the best of friends must part. It was now well up into the fall, November. The youngsters were getting quite grown up by this time. There were basket suppers, literaries, plays, etc., which were quite the fad. Keeping company pretty regular was also becoming fashionable too.

Christmas was near at hand again. They always had to have a tree, or Christmas would not be. I helped with the decoration but did not attend. It all passed off nicely, and the young folks had a jolly time. During Christmas week there were parties, dancing, fruit suppers, etc.

New Year's was now over, and everything was calm once more. The children were getting down to the schoolwork again. Everything moved along quietly until near the middle of February. Right here I have a surprise for you. On the twelfth day of February, there came to us the cutest, sweetest, little brown-eyed boy that fancy could imagine.[14] His little brown hair lay in waves. My mother was with us at this time. In a few hours, they sent out a rush call for Baby and Capp to come home at once. Of course, they understood and were not long in getting here. They were the happiest kids I ever saw. The first thing Baby said when she came in and started to look at him was "Come here and see your Sitter," and Capp said, "And your Buddie, too." They had a tussle all the next week when they came in from school over who should look at him first.

He grew off nicely and soon became a bouncing little baby. I don't think a baby was ever more appreciated. Mr. Dumont thought he was a wonderful baby. Yet he could not forget our cherished little Leo, though as time grew on, he became more and more attached to this baby. This child was the image of Mr. Dumont. Little Leo looked more like Baby and me. He was a blond.

But the naming of this new baby was the problem that confronted us now. We could not decide on anything, so Grandma Clark, just across the street, sent word for us to name him Auguste for his father. We decided to do so. Then another thought came to me. We would give him my name too, my maiden name, Elgar. So his name was decided on, Auguste Elgar.

This child certainly did have a good time. Baby would roll him in his carriage to town every day, then to see her girlfriends, and almost everywhere she went she took him. I was never uneasy about him, for she was a perfect little mother to him.

Mrs. Barron had moved to town now.[15] We were together a great deal and became quite good friends. She also thought a great deal of Baby. So the time passed on with nothing special to mention.

We had some sad news from New Mexico. My Uncle Charles Benson, who had moved to Alamogordo, was dead. This was very sad news to me.[16]

We had some old-time friends with us for a few days, Miss Ola; her mother-in-law, Mrs. Crutchfield; and her mother, Mrs. Neff. They were attending a protracted meeting here. I enjoyed Miss Ola and her mother so much. The Neffs had moved to the country for a short time.

Capp and some other boys had gone to a picnic at Dickens City.[17] Capp always liked to take a part in the dance and did not want them to know he played the violin, but some of them gave it away. They soon had him on the job and would not turn him loose all day. They gave him thirty dollars for his day's work.[18] Mr. Dumont was in Matador a short time after that. A man told him Capp was the best violinist he ever heard in his life.

Fall was coming on now, and I was busy making Christmas goods. I made lace articles, painted pillows, pincushions, and other things besides. I did a lot of Celluloid work, painted glove boxes, handkerchief boxes, photo racks, picture frames, crepe paper flowers, and lamp shades. Goods of this kind sold very readily in the stores during the holidays. I also made a couple of fine beaded vests that fall for a ranchman, Mr. Collinson,[19] which were for himself and his son. With the price of this, I bought me a handsome full bacinet sewing machine. I was equipped now for any kind of fancy sewing, as it was for both leather and cloth.[20]

Our little babe was beginning to walk and talk some now, and we were all perfect geese over him. He sat by his father at the table in his high chair. He worshiped his father, who could hardly get off from him to go to town.

Capp and Baby were now stepping out with the grown ups, but Baby was only a child yet. I was having some serious fears about her just then.

She and a boy were getting up quite a case, of which I did not approve. Had it been all right otherwise, she was entirely too young. It may have terminated in a union between them had I not interfered. I begged, pled, and reasoned with her for some months before she gave it up, but when she grew older, she thanked me for what I did.

Capp was flying at the girls on every side. I thought he was going to marry before he was twenty in spite of all I could do. He had up several very serious cases before he was twenty-four or twenty-five, but he seemed to be out of one into another till I paid no more attention to him. Little did I think then that he would wait till he was forty years old to marry.

He became interested in his wireless or radio more than the girls. This should have been his life career, but the West does not afford any opportunities of this kind. For this reason many a talented child's ambition has been lost and wasted on the desert plains of the West. He had made a life study of this, read and experimented continually, and at that time he was considered as knowing more about wireless than any other man in Texas. Of course, it was in its infancy at that time compared with the present day. He still takes more interest in that line of study than anything else, though he has never profited very much by it.[21] His profession outside of this is jewelry repairing. He has worked at this almost from boyhood.

Baby was still taking music and expression regular. Miss Lura was with us a good portion of the time. The winter passed over with nothing to mention, but it was cold and disagreeable. Capp went out to the farm every day and fed the cattle through the winter.

Twenty-One

SPRING WAS ON, and the weather was more pleasant.[1] Flower planting and chicken raising were the next things on the docket. I bought a large two hundred–egg incubator that spring and raised many chickens, and also some white ducks. This was a seasonable year. My flowers did fine. The trumpet creepers climbed up over the gable of the house and bloomed in wild profusion. The moonvines, wisteria, and clematis were twined around every corner. The poppies, zinnias, gladiolus, cannas, and many other varieties here and there were a blaze of bloom most gorgeous to behold. This was real home for me, more than I had known in a long time. My little brown-eyed baby boy was ever toddling at my heels, jabbering about the pretty "frowers." The tubs of oleanders on the porch he called "Mama's anders." There was another admirer of the flowers. Baby, I think, enjoyed them more than anyone else. She made many beautiful bouquets, wore them, and gave them to her girlfriends and others.

Miss Lura was preparing to go to Austin. She was going to get married as soon as she arrived at that place. We hated to give her up, as she had endeared herself to us. It was hard to part with her, but these things must come about. She landed there safely, got married, and settled down in a home in Austin. We heard from her often, and she seemed quite happy.

Baby and Ora Winton were great pals. They had their boy company, and all had a jolly time together. Ora and Kelley, Baby, Tommy, and Mitchel were the team, as they called themselves. Kelley was the editor of the paper here.[2] Mitchel was a near neighbor of Tommy's down at his ranch twenty miles away. They always came to town and spent the weekend. All was jolly as long as they stayed.

Baby had many friends among the cowboys. She was always jolly and nice to everybody. Mr. Dumont said he was always glad when she came to the store in the afternoon when school was out. He said that she could come nearer having a pleasant word for everybody than any child he ever saw. Mrs. Barron remarked that so often there would be a bunch of young folks in some of the stores. All would be moping and having nothing to say, but let Baby happen in, and everything seemed to put on new life. In a few minutes everybody was laughing and was as jolly as could be. She inherited this gift from her father. There was never a person in the West, I am sure, that had more friends than he. Often when he went back east to Seymour and other towns, there was always a bunch of men around him as long as he stayed, laughing at his jokes and having a big time. He was gifted with a wonderful amount of ready wit and a hearty laugh and a handshake that everybody seemed to enjoy.

Baby and Ora were together a good portion of the time and would often spend two or three nights with each other in succession. I was busy most all the time. I was now operating six incubators and was fully in the poultry business and enjoying it. It took much interest for a time and was also quite successful for a time. This kept me busy through the summer. In the fall I did much artwork, painting and making Christmas goods, etc. This netted me about two hundred dollars each season. I had bought Baby's piano sometime before this and was paying for it with my art goods. I had it almost clear at this time.

Baby and Mrs. Barron were good friends and were together a great deal. Mrs. Barron was going to visit relatives at Thornton, Texas,[3] and Baby went with her. She enjoyed the trip very much, and most especially the beautiful flowers in that country. She sent Tommy a large bouquet while there. After they returned, she visited a month with Mrs. W. Q. Richards at Quanah. Ora was also with her there most of the time. She had a very pleasant and enjoyable visit. Many of the girls visited with them, inviting them to their house and parties.[4] When she came home, I was preparing for a visit to my mother in Young County. I insisted she stay and keep house while I was gone, which she consented to do.

Elgar and I were soon off and arrived there safely. We found all well. This was the first time I had visited them since I married.[5] I went to the reunion again, but I did not enjoy it so much as before. It seemed that the old acquaintances were dropping off and moving away until there were but few left. I did not visit much this time, but I spent most of the time with my mother and brother's folks. Neither could I make a very long visit because we were going to send Baby off to school at Austin that fall, and I had to prepare her for this.

Baby was very anxious to go. Miss Lura lived there, too. She would get to see her again. She could hardly wait to get off. We sent her to St. Mary's Academy.[6] I knew she would be well taken care of there, and I could feel easy about her. She and Miss Lura both wanted her to stay at Miss Lura's, but the sisters insisted she stay in the school. It would be much to her advantage, so she was willing to do so. But poor child, she had never been away from home so far before, and she did not realize that she would be lonely and homesick. Miss Lura took her over to the school and stayed with her awhile, [and] then left her and returned home. She said she would visit her often, but her husband was sick and she did not get back to see her for a week or ten days.

Baby wrote me soon as she arrived there. She liked everything very well but said she felt just about as big as a pinhead with so many strange people. The next letter we had from her, she was homesick and blue and said Miss Lura had just been to see her for the first time. She said she went and put her arms around Miss Lura's neck and just bawled. Baby said she was never so glad to see anybody in her life. In her schoolwork, she was specializing in three studies: music, art, and expression. She also did some fancy handwork, pyrography,[7] and others. The next letter we had was, oh, so blue. She said when she sat down to write, she broke into a cry. She said there were also some others around her doing the same thing—writing home and crying. However, she said, "Mama, don't think I'm going to give it up. I will stay if it kills me!" From then on the Sisters, and also some of the girls, seemed to take special interest in her, and she became more acquainted. Later she met a little girl by the name of Laura Gray from Blanco

County where Baby's father's relatives lived, fifty miles from there. The girl knew all of them, and Baby learned that her grandfather, Rev. Joseph Bird, had performed the marriage ceremony for this same girl's father and mother. As time went on, they became great pals. They went by the name of "The Chums." She did not grieve so much about home anymore, but we certainly did miss her.

Christmas came on and Baby went out and spent the holidays with Miss Lura. She wrote us about having such a fine time. She was invited out to the masquerade parties and others, and she was going most all of the time.

She did well in her schoolwork. She worked very hard the rest of the term and made fine progress. She wrote us many letters. The most she grieved about was Elgar. She said if anything should happen to him, she would never get over it. He was four years old then.[8] He wrote her many letters every week, or thought he was writing. He would give them to his father to mail. One day he said, "Daddy, did you mail Sitter's letter?" He said, "Yes, yes, sure." He looked at his daddy a little suspicious and said, "I speck you never." So he ran his hand down in his daddy's pocket, and out he brought the whole bunch of letters he had given him at different times to mail. He didn't say a word but gave his daddy one of the most distrustful looks imaginable. I felt sorry for Daddy. He was not expecting the kid to catch up with him so completely.

The weeks and months were dragging by slowly, yet the time was nearing when Baby would be at home and with us again. We had planned she would visit her father's relatives in Blanco County before she came home, as it was only fifty miles from Austin. She would also visit some of my relatives at Belton.[9]

I made her a beautiful commencement dress and a blue satin dress. This dress was a dream. It was shirred, tucked, and elaborately trimmed with wide cream silk lace and banding. I also made another suit, a black tucked skirt of silk gauzelike grenadine. It had a shirred waist of pink satin trimmed with cream appliqué and flowing sleeves. I made plenty of underwear to match all. Baby was always very appreciative, and the way she wrote me about these things, I felt fully repaid for all my trouble. She was perfectly delighted with everything I sent. She thought they were so beautiful and thanked me over and over again. Mrs. Barron often helped me with her clothes. She loved Baby and enjoyed helping her in every way.

The school was out now, and Baby was visiting our relatives in Bell County. She enjoyed the short visit with them, [and] then went to Round Mountain, Blanco County, to visit her father's relatives. There one of her uncles met her at Marble Falls[10] and said he came near not owning her, as she was the first white-headed Bird he had ever seen. Baby was a perfect blond. She made them quite a little visit. She had never seen any of them before but enjoyed it, and most especially her Grandfather Bird at Johnson City. He was County Judge at that place then. He was with his second wife, and she was lovely to Baby.[11] He drove with Baby and made her visit a very pleasant one. She only stayed a week or so, as she was so anxious to get home again.

We could hardly wait. It seemed ages since she had gone away. But she was now making her way homeward, and everything was in readiness for her arrival. Her little room was arranged so cute and nice. I was expecting her at any moment. I felt rather tired and lay down on the bed to wait for her coming. I dropped off to sleep and must have slept thirty minutes. When I awoke, there were two large inky black paper boxes sitting on the porch heavily packed. When I looked at them, a cold shudder ran over my body. It seemed some bad omen awaited me. I rose up, bathed my face, and tried to shake off this feeling. Baby was coming on the mail hack, and some of the girls had gone in buggies to meet her. Of course, she was with them, and the mail hack had brought her boxes on home ahead of them. So after awhile, they all came rolling in, and the happy reunion took place. What a jolly crowd it was. Baby was so rejoiced to see Elgar that she could hardly turn him loose. She had been gone nine months. Everything was quiet now that the company had gone. Ora spent the night with Baby. Mr. and Mrs. Barron came over and sat till bed time. Baby entertained the crowd. She had so much to tell and talk about. She liked the school fine and wanted to go back the next fall. She brought home some beautiful paintings and works of art she had done.

The next day Baby and the girls took a drive with several buggies and had lunch out. They had a good time in general. Tommy and Mitchel came up on Saturday. In a few days she and Capp had an invitation to a big supper and ball at the McAdams ranch, so she and her brother went. They had a good time, but the weather was awfully warm and they felt tired and more like resting when they came home.

We did little for the next few days. Mrs. Barron's sister, Mrs. Cage, was visiting her.[12] Baby was with them quite often. She had been at home now about two weeks. She was over at Mrs. Barron's, and they had made up for a horseback ride that afternoon. There were only two horses up, so Baby and Miss Fannie, as they called Mrs. Cage, saddled those horses and rode down below town a short distance to get another horse for Mrs. Barron. She came over to tell me the arrangements. We were standing in the door when they came in sight, driving the bunch of horses on up the street leisurely. Baby was not yet in sight, but all at once we saw Miss Fannie stop, slide down off her horse, and run. I said, "Oh, I know something has happened to Baby." Mrs. Barron and I both ran. She went on ahead, for it seemed I could not make any time. I saw people running from every direction. The doctor was there when I reached the scene. The first thing that met my eyes was poor Baby being held up half sitting, reeling back and forth unconscious. The blood was streaming down from her forehead. I heard the doctor say, "This is a fatal wound." They brought her home on a sheet.

My grief was beyond control. Something told me that was her death. There was no hope for recovery. I don't know how I ever got home, but I remember Mrs. Barron and Hunter Goodwin on each side of me.[13] It seemed more like I was on the march to her funeral. She had slightly regained consciousness by the time they reached home with her, and she remained that way till late in the night. All her girlfriends were there. Miss Fannie said the first thing she noticed, Baby was leaning down. She thought she was fixing her slipper, but she kept going over till she fell from her horse. Her head struck first on the hard street road. This cut a gash over one of her eyes and nearly all her front teeth were broken. Pieces were chipped off them, completely ruining them. The doctor thought it might have been a sunstroke that caused her to fall.

As the night wore on, it was about ten or eleven o'clock when Baby seemed to have regained consciousness. All at once she said, "Oh, I know what happened to me." She said the awfulest pain struck her head all at once, and that was the last she remembered. We were so rejoiced that she had come to herself and knew everything, but, oh, that wound on her forehead! And her teeth were ruined! She had such beautiful teeth, too. She was still suffering some with her head. The girls all remained with us through the night. The next morning she was resting fairly well, but she was weak and pale. Some of them stayed through the day. The doctor gave her medicine to ease her head, but her recovery was very slow. We had to keep up the medicine all the time to ease her head. These dear girlfriends were so faithful to come day and night to help us. I shall never forget them.

We had to sit up with her more than two weeks. She finally began to gain a little strength but was in bed more than three weeks before she was able to be up. Then she gained very fast and was beginning to be her old self again, jolly and full of life. She was always the life of our home. She never suffered any now, except occasionally her teeth would ache. We used medicine to relieve them. With this exception, she seemed now fully recovered. The wound on her forehead healed up without leaving a scar.

She, Ora, and the girls were together as of old, all having a jolly time. This was Saturday afternoon. Baby was in the kitchen baking a cake. Tommy and Mitchel came to town. Tommy and Kelley always sent each other after the other one's girl when they wanted them to come to town, so Kelley came up after Baby and Tommy went after Ora. When they came back, Baby said she and Tommy were going down to Ora's that night. Kelley would also be there.

Baby and I ate supper together alone that night. This supper is one memorable one never to be forgotten. I think of it almost sacredly as that of the Lord's Supper or Last Supper. As I looked at her across the table, it seemed I felt more proud of her than ever before. In one respect, I felt she had been given back to me almost from the dead. When supper was over, she went into the front room, sat down, and played some on the piano. I can't remember the tunes, but the music seemed more beautiful than I had ever heard her make. Tommy came in pretty soon, and they left for Ora's.

During the summer months, we always slept out in the summer house under the trees. Baby's little bed was by the side under the shade, and Capp's was over on the other side. Both were about thirty feet from the house. It was fine sleeping quarters. We had retired, and it was about ten o'clock when I heard Baby and Tommy coming in. I heard her laugh before they reached the house. She always laughed loud and clear. They came on and stopped and talked a few moments at the porch. Both were jolly and laughing when he left. She went into her room, prepared to retire, put away her clothes nicely as she always did, came out, and went to bed. About four o'clock the next morning she awoke me and said her teeth were aching. We got up, went into the house, and doctored her teeth till they were easy. She said I might bring in her little mattress and spread it down in front of the dresser, which I did. I sat by her awhile, and she seemed easy. I asked her if she wanted me to stay in with her. She said there was no use, so I went on out to bed again. This was the first time I had ever slept away from her since she was hurt.

The next day was Sunday, and we slept late, till six o'clock. Mr. Dumont got up, went into the house to get some matches, and tipped across the floor to keep from waking Baby. Elgar and I got up and went into the house. I had made Elgar a little gown the day before and trimmed it in red embroidery. He said he was going to show "Sitter" his new gown. I stopped at the head of her bed. She was lying on her side and seemed to be asleep. I looked at her a moment. She looked so pale. I bent over her and felt of her face, and, oh, God in Heaven's name, how could I say it? She was dead!

The next hour was the bitterest my life had ever known. I had drunk the cup of gall to the dregs. I seemed to have lived ages in this short space of time. I seemed to have been carried back over my past life of the years and years I had lived with my two little children all alone with no one to comfort me but them, and now the tie was broken. Oh God, would she not return to us again? We were all sitting and kneeling around her bed almost prostrate with grief. Capp was heartbroken over the death of his only sister. Mr. Dumont said there was one thing he could thank God for and that was that he had never spoken a harsh word to that child in his life. This was the truth. Poor little Elgar, when we noticed him, he had crouched down behind a table in front of a window. He was still in his little gown, looking so mournful.

When Ora and her mother came in, her mother fell on her knees inside the door. Ora was weeping aloud. I called to her to come near and help me mourn, for who but Ora could feel more deeply the loss of this dear girl-friend she had loved. She and Baby had been chums from early childhood. Mrs. Barron was another cherished friend of hers. In sickness or in trouble, she was ever ready to help and console. She was the first one to our aid when this awful trial fell upon us. While weeping herself, she strove to console us. The first burst of grief seemed to have left me in a frame of mind more calm and rigid. I sat through the day thinking, thinking this dear child on whom I had built so much hope for her future success and happiness—could it be she was no more? I had even thought of her tender care when the hand of time had marked me in my tottering old age.

Through the hours I sat by and looked at her dear little form, for soon even this privilege would be denied me. A smile was on her face from the first and seemed to grow as time went on. The dear friends had prepared and dressed her so beautifully that she looked like a little bride. She wore the beautiful pale blue satin dress I had made and sent her during the commencement of the school. She had never worn it till then. The day was drawing near to a close. I heard a commotion at the door. The casket was being brought in. This was the last bitter stroke, and all consciousness left me for a while. Soon was the procession to the cemetery at twilight. Six of her girlfriends were robed in white. The pallbearers, resembling a band of angels, marched behind the vehicle with her remains.[14] All was over, and now the future must be met with all reverence. I asked God to help me.

The next issues of the *Paducah Times* contained an article about Baby written by Mrs. J. M. Barron, the sheriff's wife at that time, and city marshall of today:

Another Bright Star in Heaven, Bessie Bird is dead. The dear Girl who has electrified her many friends with her sweet spirit is gone. The gentle lips that have whispered so many words of hope and encouragement to the sick and distressed have been closed, and her warm heart, overflowing with kindness and love, has ceased to pulsate. . . . Bessie was a sweet pure girl in the nineteenth year of her age, and throughout her broad acquaintance, she was always known to be on the sunny side of life. She was successful in all her undertakings and took no credit for herself, but accorded it all to others. . . .

She was my friend. She shared my joys and sorrows. If she knew anyone was in trouble, she would lend a willing ear, a helping hand, and a kindly word that never failed to bring relief. . . . She was gracious because she reverenced her Father, she was good because she loved her Mother, and she was womanly because she was true to her friends. She was a truthful girl, pure in heart. She has seen her God there in her work for him.

Bessie, farewell, for a short time only, for you will greet us on the other shore in the same happy way there spiritualized in which you greeted us here.

One Who Loved Her,
Mrs. J. M. Barron

The following is an article written by the editor of the *Paducah Times*, Oran Kelley:

In Memoriam

Oh ye whose cheek the tear of pity stains,
Draw near with pious reverence and attend.
Cold lies the precious darling's dear remains,
The tender daughter and the generous friend.

The pitying heart that felt for human woe,
The dauntless heart that feared no human pride,
The friend of all—to vice alone a foe,
For even her failings leaned to virtue's side.

It is with feelings of deepest grief that we today chronicle the death of one of Paducah's fairest and most lovable young ladies, Miss Bessie Bird. Death at any age is sad indeed, but it seems that the bitterest tears of grief are shed when we are forced to mourn the death of one called away in the bloom of youth.

Miss Bessie Bird died at an early hour Sunday morning, August 21st, 1904, at the family residence in Paducah and was laid to rest in the City Cemetery Sunday evening. She sustained serious injuries by a fall from a horse several weeks ago, which is supposed to be the cause of her death. Her sudden taking away has caused profound sadness throughout the entire town and community where she has lived from infancy and where she was so well-known and dearly loved. . . . Her short life clearly exemplified the beauty of service. Every day, every hour of her life, was spent in doing kind deeds for the sake of kindness, in doing good for the sake of goodness, and the world is brighter and better by her having lived in it.

Times extends sincerest sympathy to the Father, Mother, and Brothers who are left to mourn the loss of the only sister.

For weeks the world seemed dark and empty. I sat by the hour in perfect idleness. I had no heart for anything but to mourn. I realized though that I must arouse myself from this and try to take up life anew. I began work at any[thing] and everything, first in the house, but mostly with the flowers in the yard. I did not allow myself to be idle at all. My little boy, Elgar, was a source of comfort and consolation to me. It seemed I could not have lived without him. Many are the times at night after he had gone to sleep that I would go to his bed and love and kiss him over and over. This seemed to console me more than anything else.

Twenty-Two

AT THAT TIME quite a number of the people were becoming interested in a lead mine over in Dickens County in Croton Breaks, which was reported to have been found during buffalo time by some of the hunters. It could never be located again, so they all seemed to think I might be able to find it. They insisted that we take a trip over there and try to locate it. I told them I felt sure there was nothing to it, and that it was a false alarm. We had been over in that country quite a bit in early days, and I had never heard anything about a lead mine. However, we went, for a trip like that suited me just then. I felt as if I wanted to go far into the wilds, even beyond the haunts of man where nothing would lend to carry me back to the heartbreaks which I had recently undergone. We took a camping outfit and a large closed hack. We were out several days, but without success, as I felt sure would be the case. But the trip did me good. I roamed over the hills and country alone for hours each day, recognizing many places that I had been in years gone by, when my life knew not a care. After driving over much of the country, we returned home, and we all felt benefited by the trip.

I took up my work again and continued busy all the time. I took more interest in my home for the sake of the dear ones that were left me. Only one sad thing remained in sight as a reminder of the past. This was the stand table by the window which was draped in a black scarf, and which held many letters of condolence that came in daily until they numbered nearly one hundred. There was one other change too—at the time of Baby's death, I assumed a black costume, and from that day till this, twenty-four years, I have never worn anything but black. A few times of late I have tried to wear a light touch of color, but I never feel right until I have discarded it.[1]

I saw Ora pretty often. She visited me. I needed her so much at that time, as she was next to Baby to me. She said she saw Tommy most every-time he came to town. He would often go up to her house. She said he told her once that Baby was as pure as the driven snow, and that if anyone ever went to Heaven, he knew she did.

The winter passed over with nothing special to mention. Springtime came on with the usual busy time with my flowers, garden, and chickens.[2] Mr. and Mrs. Neff had returned from California for a visit with their young married daughter, Mrs. Mayers, and they visited with us while here. Mrs. Neff was like a dear relative in our home. My baby, little Elgar, was so much company to me. He was always laughing and so happy. Mrs. Neff said, "Ella, he is a perfect little sunbeam." Mrs. Neff was soon to return to California. Miss Lura was also moving to California. She came up from Austin and joined Mrs. Neff here. They made the trip together. Her husband had gone on before. I hated so much to see them leave, for they were some of my dearest friends.

That fall Mrs. Barron and I went to the Dallas fair. While there, I saw some very beautiful statuary made in plaster of Paris. This was more attractive to me than anything I had seen on the trip. I bought several pieces of it and brought them home. Since I could not develop or profit anything by my carving in rock, I had wanted to learn plaster casting. This would satisfy to some extent my longing for sculpture. After studying these pieces, I ordered some books that treated on this work. After a little practice, I had no trouble in learning the work. I soon learned to make my own moulds and could make anything in the line of plaster casting. This was very fascinating and interesting to me. As time went on, it grew more and more so. I learned to do the work more perfectly and satisfactorily. I did much of this work, and every year was a great addition to my line of Christmas goods. I could now compete with anyone in the East, in the line of plaster casting, bronzing, and decorating same. Each fall from year to year I do quite a bit of this work. I have more than one hundred designs on hand at present. However, I shall not do quite so much of it in the future, and perhaps none later on, for it is rather hard work for a lady, and most especially at my age.

The next winter also passed off in the usual way, with nothing special to mention. I always had good return from my holiday goods.

The next spring and summer my poultry business did fine, and netted me quite a little income. This was the year Capp put in the first telephone in Paducah.[3] It was only two boxes and one line from home to the post office. He made the entire system himself. He whittled out the boxes and the tiniest little switchboard, the smallest that is made I suppose. This sufficed for a year or so, and then a large telephone system was installed.

Just at this time something unusual was about to take place. We had an invitation to a wedding, and who should it be but Tommy and Ora. They were going to get married. This was a union I had long hoped might take place at some time or other. Tommy was a noble boy and deserved a good girl such as we all knew Ora to be. She had confided a bit of this to me one afternoon when we were at the cemetery.

That fall two of my nieces, Pearl Fessenden and Oma White, both age fourteen, came to stay with us and go to school.[4] These girls were a great deal of company for me, and were also a lot of help, as they were quite handy and smart. Our home seemed more cheerful after they came. They were so jolly and full of life. They stayed through the school and returned home for the summer at Graham, Texas. They liked the school so well that they could hardly wait to come back in the fall.

They did well in school. My brother Lewis and my mother's family moved to Cottle County that fall,[5] so the girls still stayed on with us. I felt so rejoiced to have my mother so near me then, as she had never been before. These were the first relatives that had ever lived near me since my first marriage, besides my own family.

The girls had been with us two years and were getting to be quite grown up young ladies. My stepfather died very suddenly with paralysis the second year after moving to this country. He was very old. My mother came and lived with us then.

The railroad was being built from Quanah to Paducah that fall. It was about completed and that train was to come in November ninth.[6] Everybody was going to meet it. The band was going to play and have a regular jubilee. The girls and I were going, but they failed to get off from school so this left me to go alone. I harnessed the horse to the buggy. He was perfectly gentle but rather mean. When I got in the buggy, both of the lines had dropped. He ran away, threw me out of the buggy, and crushed my ankle, tearing my foot just half off. This sad accident occurred not very far from where Baby was hurt. Several of the neighbors saw me and ran to my assistance.

I was carried to the house. Two doctors attended my wound. First they thought they would have to amputate my foot, but they decided to try to save it if possible. After binding it in a plaster cast, I was stretched out on a bed to suffer the agonies of a broken leg. It was weeks and weeks before it began to heal. I was in bed just six months before I was able to sit up and bear any weight on my foot. Gradually I became able to use crutches, and I went on these crutches six years. Had it not been for the girls, I don't know what we would have done. They kept the house, did all the work, and one of them made a regular hand in the post office all the time up till they both married and left us.

I had gone out of the poultry business sometime before I was crippled. I had grown tired of it and sold my incubators. I was crippled though never idle. I sewed for the girls, did much fancy and art work, such as plaster casting, painting, and decorating. I could sit down and do all this.

Elgar had grown to be quite a lad by this time.[7] He confided in his father, and they were perfect pals. His father never struck him a blow in his life, and he never punished him otherwise than to talk positive with him. He controlled him perfectly through kindness. Elgar did well in school, always making good grades.

There was to be another wedding right soon. This was to be in our home. My niece, Pearl Fessenden, and Albert Swint got married. I hated for Pearl to leave me, but she was getting a good man, and I could not object.[8]

The next two years passed over of which my memory does not record anything special to mention more than the ordinary routine of our general home affairs.

We had only one girl with us now, Oma. She was in the office most of the time. My crippled foot was getting better now. I did not use the crutches all of the time, and could do most anything I wanted to do. I did much work in my studio. In plaster casting I made many large statues and busts besides many smaller pieces. I also made flower decorations, many dozen pots of flowers that sold more readily than anything I made. I could not supply the demand for those at that time. I enjoyed the work and never grew tired of it, most especially the plaster of Paris.

Mr. Dumont had now kept the post office in Paducah twenty-one years.[9] He also served two terms as county treasurer during this time. He had been in the post office work at Otta some ten years before this. His health had always been good, but I could tell it was failing some now, though he never complained. He was always pleasant and lighthearted in the home. Mr. Dumont was a great reader and always kept up with the foreign news especially. The World War had begun brewing at this time, and he was very much interested in it.

Another little change was about to take place in our home. Oma, my other niece, and Mr. Melvin Woodley were going to get married. We were very lonely when Oma left us, but she was also getting a good man.[10] These things naturally must come about, so we had as well reconcile ourselves to them. But Mr. Dumont said we would try to get another one of Brother Lewis's girls to come and live with us. So Lizzie came next. My poor old mother was now very old and childish, though I felt thankful her health was good.

Mr. Dumont had slight attacks of bronchial trouble, but not often. I felt uneasy about him, but he never seemed to think it amounted to anything. Still he stayed in the office, but as time went on, they grew more frequent. The first bad spell he had was at the Masonic Hall. It was a kind of sinking spell, and he was brought home and was not able to be up for nearly a week. From this time on, we were all very uneasy about him, though he went to the office regularly as soon as he was able. He seemed to gain strength and was better for a while.

Mr. McGaughey, Mr. Dumont's partner of earlier days,[11] had been living at Matador for several years. He was postmaster there for a while, but had moved with the Campbell family out to their ranch. He had made his home with them for several years. His health was also failing, and his condition had become very serious. We went and stayed a few days. He was able to be up part of the time, but his illness was incurable. When we left him, we had but little or no hopes of ever seeing him again.

Mr. Dumont still had slight sinking spells, and his health seemed more on the decline. Elgar was now fifteen years old. He idolized his father and was a great comfort to him. He often drove for him out to the farms and ranch to see after things.[12] It had now been about four months since we visited Mr. McGaughey. We heard from him, and he was about the same. A short time after this, Mr. Dumont had another bad attack. He was never well again but would get up almost every day and go to the office for an hour to show the other man, Mr. Stradley,[13] something more about the office. Mr. Stradley was taking charge of it.

Mr. Dumont was growing weaker all the time, and he was not able to be up at all now. With aching hearts and saddest of feeling, we noted each day that he was slowly but surely passing away from us. Oh, how could we do without him? How lonely it would be. How we would miss him. But the hand of fate is relentless and spares no one. We were facing another most grievous and bitter disappointment. I felt so sorry for poor little Elgar. He could not be reconciled at all. His father had been seriously ill now about ten days. We had three doctors with him, but no hopes. The end was drawing near. I tried to meet it with all the courage I could sum up, but it was hard to give him up.

He and I had been married twenty years. We had always had harmony in our home. We had never had a quarrel, not one. No one ever heard a cross word between us for the reason that there were none. This may seem a little unbelievable. He talked to us a good deal after he realized he could not live. I asked him in the presence of some of the friends if we had ever had a quarrel, and he said, "No." He made a beautiful talk to us all, such as few people can make when death is calling them from this earth. He charged Elgar to take good care of Mama and always deal fair and square with everyone.

He even tried to console us in our grief when death was so near him. He lingered on through the night until the next day, when he passed away at one o'clock.[14] When all was over, poor little Elgar was heartbroken over the loss of his father. It seemed both my boys were destined to be fatherless. Mr. Dumont was laid to rest by the Masonic Order.

There were only three of us left now. I said to Capp, "Oh, son, what would we do if we did not have Elgar left us? There would only be you and me left alone." Again Elgar was a consolation to me.

One afternoon a fire broke out at the school building. As I saw the smoke boiling up and people rushing to it, my heart seemed to sink within me. Elgar was there. I was yet on crutches and could only go very slowly, but I did not hesitate one moment. Before I hardly knew it, I was on my way up to the school building just as fast as those crutches would take me. However, I only went a part of the way, as the fire was soon put out. Little damage was done. Mrs. Barron asked me why I tried to go up there like that. I told her I did not know, but that I realized in full if anything should happen to Elgar, I could not live one hour afterward.

Twenty-Three

THE WORLD WAR was now in full blast. Mr. Dumont made mention that he would liked to have lived to see how the war came out. After the elapse of twenty years, I was now left again to assume the management of my own affairs. But how changed, oh, how changed! It seemed that I had lived an ordinary lifetime in this space of twenty years. We still had our number, but it was not the same as when we were left before. Baby was gone and Elgar was left in her place to console us. Had it not been for him, life would have been almost unbearable for Capp and me all alone.

We were fixing to build a new home at the time of Mr. Dumont's death, but when this occurred, I postponed it for one year. I had made out the plan for the house throughout. The next year I went on with it.[1] I built the home all complete and furnished it. This was a task off my hands. There was much to do out at the place, such as farms to rent, cattle to see after, etc. Having had some experience in this before my last marriage, however, it was not hard for me to do this. Capp could help me whenever necessary.

Elgar hauled many bales of hay from the place for our own use and also to sell. He did the milking and attended to the stock at home. My crippled foot had gotten much better the past two years before this, and now I did not use the crutches anymore. I scarcely limp at all at the present time. I still worked steady at my plaster of Paris statues in the fall. I enjoyed this work, and it netted me an income that we would not have had otherwise.

As the war was now on, times were getting very hard. People were economizing and saving every penny to help our poor boys that had gone overseas. Capp worked steady at his jewelry repairing, but business of all kinds was dull. Elgar worked a short time on the W. Q. Richards ranch that summer after school was out. He had always wanted to run cattle, but this, I think, satisfied him with the business. He never cared anymore about it. That fall he went to T.C.U. at Fort Worth. He liked the school, but it was rather hard on him. He stayed till the war was over and sometime after. He came home and stayed through the summer, [and] then the next fall he went to Tyler Business College for eight months. He did fine in this school. He took a stenographic and business course and brought back a diploma. He went to work for Carroll Motor Company that summer and stayed with them nearly two years.[2]

At this time I had switched off on another class of work, but only for a short time. I was making some hair watchchains for Capp and Elgar, weaving them of my own hair. They were double strands, four braids to the chains. They make beautiful chains, and these were keepsakes for my two boys.[3] [A passage is omitted here that describes a 1920 trip to New Mexico.][4]

Sometime after this, Lizzie went to live with her preacher brother, Ercell White, at Amarillo. While there she decided to take nursing. She entered training at Baylor Hospital at Dallas. She worked very hard and made good grades all the way through. She stayed out the full three years and got her diploma, besides winning the Duchess-ship.

The fall and winter passed off with nothing special to mention. Another very sad thing must come to us. My poor old mother was taken suddenly ill and died within a few hours.[5] She did not live more than twenty-four hours after she was taken ill. Her death was a shock very unexpected, as her physical condition had always been so good. She was eighty-six years old. It was hard to give her up. She had been the kindest and best mother in the world. These calls had come to me so often it seemed they would never cease, but I feel thankful that my two boys are left me. I trust they will be spared to me for the remainder of my life.

My younger boy, Elgar, was now quite grown up. He was twenty-one years old and was stepping out among the ladies.[6] I will say promiscuously, and he had been for some time. I felt a little anxious about him as he was yet young, and I wanted him to remain with me for a while longer. I did not discourage him, however, in any way, for sometimes we make a mistake in this. I did not have to think over this matter very long. One morning as he was standing in front of the mirror combing his hair, he told me in a very commonplace way, as if he was just going on a drive, that he was going to get married. Imagine my surprise! I could not say a word. I felt choked, and soon the tears began racing down my face. How could I give him up? There were so few of us left already. He said, "But Mama, we will stay here with you." Of course, this consoled me some. Yet, I knew this was not always a success, but I made up my mind there and then that I would be so good to them that they would be contented with me for a while at least.

I had known Oma Irons from babyhood, but I had never been associated with her during her growing up to speak of. This was the girl Elgar was to marry. She was a good-looking girl, a perfect blond. She was on the same type of my own dear little Bess that had gone away from us so long ago. I knew I could love her, and she would be so much company for me, too. From then on I tried to be reconciled to Elgar's marriage, even though he was young. After thinking it over, I was really anxious for Oma to come and be one of us in our home. They were married at the home of one of her girlfriends, Mrs. Ellis.[7] That afternoon when Elgar brought her home, I met them at the door and put my arms around them both. The thought came to me, oh, maybe this is my own little fair-haired girl who has come back to live with us again.

This was springtime. It was Easter Sunday. My decorations in the house were large Easter lilies. Out in the yard the large clumps of bridal wreaths on each side of the steps were in full bloom. The next week Oma and I did some flower planting, made flowerbeds, etc. It seemed good to have someone else to share my interest in the flowers and the household in general.

So the days and weeks went by. Elgar still worked with the Carroll Motor Company. Some two or three months had elapsed when something very unexpected occurred—Capp got married.[8] He had gone with this girl some, Oma Smith was her name, but I least suspected he had any intentions of getting married. He had said many times long ago that he never expected to marry, as he preferred living an old bachelor. But the world is full of surprises, and we might as well be prepared for them. After taking a short trip east, they returned home and settled down to housekeeping to themselves.

Elgar was not working for the Carroll Motor Company now, but had gone into business for himself. He and another man, Mr. Stewart, were partners in a garage and were agents for the Star car.[9] They did a fine business for a time, but it grew more dull later on, as there was much competition.

So the months went by with no changes to speak of, and the next year Capp and his wife had decided to move to California. They had a fine little boy baby now.[10] He was a cute baby. I could hardly bear to think of Capp's going so far away from me, but they were now ready to start on their long journey. They came by home to say good-bye, and they were gone. I spent the day crying. After this I began to take on new life and new hopes. I did some planning. I would visit California myself. I had always wanted to, so I would go the next summer. I had many very dear friends in Los Angeles that had moved from this country, and they had been urging me to visit them ever since they had gone on.

Elgar still worked hard at his business and was doing very well. I heard from Capp and wife often. They liked California fine. Capp worked at the jewelry business. I had always corresponded with some of the friends ever since they had moved there. Now I had mentioned my intention of visiting California, and they were writing me to come. I already had the date set when I was to start, and this was June 1st, so it was some little time yet.

Springtime was on now.[11] I had much to do to get ready for my trip, such as flower planting, sewing, etc. At last all was finished, and the time had arrived for my departure. Elgar took me to Childress, and I took the train there. How I hated to leave Elgar and go so far away, but I was coming back to him. This was all that consoled me. I tried to keep down the tears when I said good-bye to him, but they came with a doubleheader after I had gotten on the train. Elmo Barron met me at the train at Amarillo. I got off and spent the night there, and he helped me on the Pullman next morning. Then I was headed straight for Los Angeles. [Details of the author's trip are omitted here.][12]

I took the train at Los Angeles at eleven o'clock on the evening of September 5. I arrived in Salt Lake City early in the morning, had breakfast there, and took the train for Denver, Colorado. I have a niece living at this place, and I had promised to visit her on my way home. This niece was my only sister's only girl and is the nearest woman relative I have living. I had not seen her since she was a wee little girl. Of course, neither of us had any idea how the other one looked, although she said she believed she would know me. I felt the same by her. I had her pictured out as the image of her mother, but in this I was not quite right. Yet after being with her awhile, I could see some resemblance of her mother and some of her father. However, I was not disappointed in her in the least. I found her to be a wonderful little body, and I learned to love her even in the short week that I spent with her. In her I saw many kind and gentle traits of her mother. We drove around some and I saw quite a bit of Denver. While there we went to their church a couple of times. I enjoyed my visit with her very much. She was a great lover of flowers and gave me quite a lot to bring home. I was also favorably impressed with her husband. He seemed so kind and nice to her, and he was also nice to me while I was in their home.

After one week's visit with these relatives I was ready to continue my journey homeward. I had begun to feel anxious to see the homefolks and could hardly wait till I got home. I believe I failed to mention that Capp and wife were also returning to Texas. They started the day before I did and came the southern route. I took the Fort Worth and Denver in the morning and arrived in Quanah about 2 o'clock in the afternoon. I came out to Paducah that afternoon.[13] I was so rejoiced to see my boy Elgar again. I met him at the garage, and he brought me up home. It seemed so good to be home again after being away so long.

This long visit had been wonderful to me. I had enjoyed every moment of it. It will go down as one of the most prominent and enjoyable features in my life's history. As I returned to my home to the loved ones that surrounded it, however, the same old thought came to me: after all, there is no place on this earth like home.

I busied myself for the next few weeks with the many things that I had left undone when I went on my visit. It was well up into the fall now, and I was getting busy with my Christmas display, which was mostly plaster casting and decorating same. I had brought some new models from Los Angeles and was using those first. Finally everything was finished and complete. The Christmas was over, and I had made very good sales. Everything was now off my hands, and I felt free and at leisure. This was the time that I usually took my layoff or vacation, during the two cold winter months, but unlike most others, I usually took it around the fire and most comfortable places in the house.

Springtime was coming on. It was March, and I had begun looking about my flowers. Elgar had turned his part of the garage business over to his partner to run. Elgar had been appointed postmaster at Paducah,[14] so he could attend to both.

Everything was now moving on very smooth and quietly, when one day a young and very aristocratic gentleman made his appearance at our home. He seemed of much note and distinction, and he also seemed to exact much of our attention. I judged that he had traveled from some distance, as about the first thing he did was make a strong demand for refreshments. He was quite handsome. We further learned that he was of French descent. He was one-fourth French Canadian. I thought he slightly resembled Elgar, and what do you know about it? He actually called Elgar "Daddy," Oma "Mother," and he insisted on calling me "Grandmother." I understood him perfectly. His name was J. Verne Dumont. He was born March 26, 1925, and he weighed eight pounds. This was the dearest little babe that had come into our home in many years. He was a perfect little cupid, and we were all crazy about him. After tussling through a pretty tough three-month period, he grew off nicely and was soon the cutest baby in all the land.

We took a trip to New Mexico that summer in July, mostly through the mountains from Cloudcroft down to Hope. We saw all the relatives and enjoyed a little visit with each family of them. The vegetables and fruits are always so fine in the mountains that one can never fail to enjoy a trip there. The vegetables grow so very large and fine that they have to get seed of the dwarf kinds, as they are more saleable. When we left Hope, we bent our course homeward and arrived on the second day. We found all O.K., and we felt better by the trip. We could not make a very long visit on account of Elgar and the post office. Everything was quiet again with nothing of interest to mention, and it remained so for the next two or three months.

I believe that I have failed to mention that Capp and his wife had another baby. His name is Thomas Telsa.[15] He was an exceptionally fine-looking baby, and today he looks to have the material in him for a smart man. You never can tell though. Capp lives several blocks from me in the north part of town, but I do not see him as often as I would like.

I was now busy with my holiday goods, as it was nearly Christmas time. This was all the same old thing over, as well as the remainder of the winter, so will pass it on.

It was now springtime, and flowers were to be planted again. When I returned from California, I had planned to build an apartment house. I saw so many nice ones out there that this spring I built one. It has five apartments in it. This gives me more employment to see after it, but having only nice, first-class tenants, it does not give very much trouble. It is quite near me too.[16]

Twenty-Four

SPRINGTIME WAS ON and at this time another change was taking place in our home. Elgar and Oma were moving to themselves. It almost broke my heart for them to leave me alone. Elgar hated to leave me, but it is only natural for young people, most especially the girl, to want a home to themselves. Neither is it right to interfere if you only know their wishes. They would live in the apartment house until ready to build them a new home.[1] This was some consolation to have them near me, but, oh, to be left all alone in this large house of nine rooms with no one to look for at mealtime and no one to come home at night. To sit all alone with no one to speak to seemed unbearable. I shall never forget the first night of this trial. After trying to read, I became so blinded with tears that I could not see. I rose up, strode across the room nearly tearing my hair, and almost fell to the floor. Oh, how cruel is nature. Besides death, it seems the hardest trial comes to us in our declining years when the last child is leaving us to go out from the shelter of the old home to battle with the world for himself. But this is nature, and we must make the best of it we can. It is for the child's own interest and good that they go out and build them up a home of their own.

I became more reconciled to my situation and decided that I could stand almost anything. I was more content than I ever thought possible. I did much artwork, such as painting, flower making, and other fancy work. I took my meals with a couple of my roomers who came later and who had charge of my kitchen, a young lady by the name of Byers and her adopted brother, Mr. Johnson. They were linotypists at the printing office. I learned to think a great deal of this girl. She was a fine girl and was so much company to me. We became quite pals, regardless of the extreme difference in our ages. We had many pleasant drives together, and I enjoyed her so much.

While Miss Byers and Mr. Johnson were with me, we took our lunch one afternoon and drove down south of town about eight miles. The object of this trip was to search for the place where my old Buck Creek home used to stand. I doubted very much if I could locate the exact spot where the house stood, as everything had been moved away. Strange to say, I had never visited this place since my two children, Capp and Bessie, and I had left there and moved to Paducah. For many years it had all been fenced in by parties who bought the land, and some of it had been put into cultivation.

We drove through a gate into a small pasture which was about one section in area. I first thought we would find it was in some field, but not so. After observing the surrounding country, I noted a small rise of the land out near the center of the pasture which looked familiar. This was about one-quarter of [a] mile from the old Ross tank on Buck Creek, which is now in ruins and can hardly be distinguished from any other part of the creek. From these bearings we had but little trouble in locating the place. There was nothing to show for it except a small depression in the ground where the old half dugout was made after the cyclone had blown my house away, the spot where we spent the last summer. As we neared this spot, I cannot describe the feeling I had. It seemed a multitude of revelations and past memories rushed one after another through my mind. Aside from the many lonely hours I had spent here, there were many thrilling incidents that took place. They would be worthwhile to mention if I could only recall the half of them.

While standing here I pointed out to my companions many spots where I had killed antelope, deer, and wolves. We searched for the old well but failed to find any trace of it. After walking around over the grounds, I pointed out where the walk used to be, on either side of which grew many cacti of rare specimens, which were of about three hundred varieties from most every state in the union. I told them the cactus mounds on either side of the walk were covered with cacti and beautiful specimens of fancy gyp rock. Some bits were still there, and many other small fragments still remained that recalled to memory things long forgotten.

While viewing these old ruins, a slight sadness seemed to have crept over me, which required some effort to shake off. Why feel sad? Some talk of the good old times, and on this I feel myself some authority. Of course, we were content and satisfied. At the same time, we suffered many more hardships and privations than at the present day.

It was near sundown and quite pleasant. Mr. Johnson and Miss Byers had quite a jolly little romp around on the green grass over the prairie. We then spread our good lunch on the grass beside the old dugout and partook of it to our entire satisfaction. We then proceeded to take some pictures of the place, ourselves, and the car. We had a pleasant drive home, feeling well paid for our trip.

For some time Miss Byers and I had been planning a trip out twelve miles beyond Matador to Mr. Harry Campbell's ranch.[2] His mother now makes her home with him. He is her only child. Judge Campbell, her husband, passed away several years ago. I wanted to see Mrs. Campbell again as it had been twelve years since I last saw her. The next week Miss Byers, Mrs. Barron, and I drove over to the Campbell Ranch, which is located out at the caprock, just at the foot of the plains. This is a splendid piece of property of several sections, well stocked with fine cattle, large lakes, springs, and a running stream through it. Farther down on the creek the home is built, which nestles back in a cove of timber, densely shaded all around. It looks very picturesque. This home, though built some years ago, is very convenient and modern throughout with large spacious rooms. It has much concrete paving and porches.

As we drove through Matador, it happened we met Mrs. Harry Campbell there. She had just purchased a new car and was driving out home that afternoon, so we joined her there. It was agreed we would see if Mrs. Henry Campbell would recognize me. At first she did not, as her vision had slightly failed from some trouble from her eyes. Soon, however, she knew me and seemed her same dear interesting self as of old. I could see but little change in her appearance, if any. She was always an interesting person to converse with and is still so.[3] We had but a short time to stay, as it was late in the afternoon when we arrived there. We enjoyed the little visit with them immensely, though. Mrs. Harry Campbell, being an ideal hostess, made it quite interesting for the other two ladies in showing them out and around the place. After the good-byes and promises to see them again soon, we bent our course homeward, arriving safely just at dusk.

The time was near at hand now when Miss Byers was to leave us. She left for Colorado Springs the next week. I was so sorry when she left, but her health failed slightly. She had to move to a different climate. Mr. Johnson also left for other parts. Mr. and Mrs. Turney were with us at that time and took Miss Byers' place. I boarded with them. They were real nice and good to me, and they remained with me quite awhile. This made it very easy and pleasant for me with but little to do. I had all the time to work at anything I chose.

Shortly after this we had an unexpected visitor in Paducah from Corpus Christi. It was Mrs. Sul Carter, a friend of old.[4] She was visiting her daughter, Mrs. Eblen, and other friends of this place. It was a treat to see and be with her once more. [A passage is omitted here that describes a 1927 trip to New Mexico.][5]

That fall and winter passed over about the same old humdrum way with nothing special to mention. The Turneys had gone east some time before this, his health having failed. The publisher of the Post, Mr. Carlock,[6] had a message from Mr. Johnson. He would return to his old position with them as linotypist and wished to secure the same place in my home that he and Miss Byers held. They arrived in due time. He was married and brought with him the nicest and best kind of a little wife. He was a fine, good boy, and they made a cute couple. They were so agreeable and congenial, and they were lovely to me.

My little grandbaby, J. Verne, was now past two years old. He could talk and make many trips over to see "Mama," as he called me. He was already a source of company and pleasure to me. This summer Elgar built a nice little modern stucco home, on the English style.[7] This is very close to me, not more than a dozen steps away.

Some two or three months later another very unusual occurrence took place in this new home. It was nothing more or less than the arrival of another eight-pound bouncing baby boy.[8] A finer baby you seldom ever see.

Some four months has elapsed since my last writing. During this time another dark cloud has swept over our homes. Little Phillip is no more. The darling little babe, Phillip Eugene, whom we all idolized, has been removed from our midst.[9] He was in his eighth month, and had grown into one of the most beautiful angellike babes I have ever seen. He was so good and so lovable, and he always had a sweet smile for everyone. His look was so pure and so angelic, as if he was not born for this world. I often feared that he would not be spared to us.

Some two weeks before little Phillip was taken ill, I had a dream that was a most troubled one. I thought I was drawing water from the cistern of which the curb is quite low. At first it seemed that it was J. Verne, the other baby. He came up close, and I motioned him back fearing he might fall in. But he came closer. I kept pressing him back, but he seemed intent on looking in. Before I was aware of it, he toppled and fell over into the cistern. I screamed and shouted for help, but no one came. I rushed out a few steps, still screaming for help. When I returned, I beheld him lying down in the bottom of a very deep well with only a small bit of water in it. It was not J. Verne, but little Phillip. I could see him so plainly in his little white dress lying so still that I felt sure his little life had been crushed out by the fall.

But soon to my great joy, I discovered he was yet living and was moving. Yes, he was moving up the side of the well, and was slowly making his way upward by little steps in the crevices of the rock. I was still shouting for help, for men to come and rescue him. I began climbing downward myself to a little bench in the side of the well, in an effort to reach him. There were many women there by this time. They were dressed up all around it seemed, and they were trying to assist all they could. I could see little Phillip coming upward almost halfway. He had reached a little jot in the side of the well, and it seemed he was just hanging in a balance there, as if between life and death. This was only for a short time, however, for the little footing gave way and again he was hurled to the bottom of that treacherous well. My last hope was shattered, and I seemed to have lost consciousness for a time. Next, it seemed there were some men there, and I saw little Phillip lying on the ground near the well. I saw him slightly move once or twice, and then all was over. At this I awoke.

It was daylight, and I was so tired and worn that I was almost unable to rise. Imagine my great joy to find it was only a dream, and little Phillip was still in the flesh, hearty and well with the sweet little winning smile that always greeted me and the dear little hands that were always stretched out to me. Now I am not, to say, a believer in dreams, but I have had others similar to this that seemed a presentiment.

Little J. Verne and I are real pals. He is a world of company and comfort to me. He makes many trips everyday over to see "Mama." There is no music sweeter to my ear than the patter of his dear little feet coming up the steps calling for me, and then the pressure of the dear little arms around my neck declaring his love for "Mama."

AFTERWORD

ELLA BIRD DUMONT completed her memoirs in 1928. Living in her handsome two-story home in Paducah, she spent the last fifteen years of her life trying to find a publisher that would agree to pay royalties. She was usually seen at work in her flower garden. Occasionally she went into the local schools to talk to students of Texas history. Lottie Gibson, who lives in Paducah, described in a 1987 interview these visits in the mid-1930s: "Unlike what one would expect of a frontier woman, Mrs. Dumont was rather fragile in appearance, with extremely pretty skin. She spoke in a soft, low voice. If the students had remained in their seats, they could not have heard her. I let them sit around the desk on the floor and listen to her fascinating stories of her life." Grace Jones Piper, a student of Lottie Gibson's in the 1930s, vividly remembers Dumont's entertaining narratives.

During the last few years of her life, Dumont had diabetes. As a result, Capp Bird moved in with his mother to care for her. On Saturday, April 10, 1943, at the age of eighty-one, Ella Bird Dumont died. She is buried in Garden of Memories Cemetery in Paducah beside her husband, Auguste Dumont; her daughter, Bessie Bird; and her infant son, Leo Bird Dumont. Pallbearers at her funeral were old friends: Bud Barron, Charlie Bird, Collie Briggs, Jim Gibson, Jack Parnell, and J. W. Woodley. On the family monument, flanked by evergreen shrubs, the following inscriptions appear:

Ella Bird Dumont	Auguste Dumont
1861–1943	1845–1915
A Frontier Woman	A Man Who Loved
Buffalo Hunter	His Friends and
A West Texas Pioneer	Had Many
	A West Texas Pioneer

Above the inscription for Ella Dumont appears the symbol of the Order of the Eastern Star.

A large monument of special significance stands at the main entrance of the Paducah cemetery. A metal plaque reads: "In Loving Memory and Grateful Appreciation of Outstanding Service, We Honor: Ella Bird Dumont [and] Addie A. Barron. Project Sponsored by Sorosis Club, Texas Federation of Women's Clubs. Dedicated 1951; Erected by Public Donation."

Capp Bird continued to live in Paducah until his death of a stroke in a Lubbock, Texas, hospital on November 6, 1957, at the age of seventy-six. His oldest son, C. J. "Junior" Bird died somewhere in New Mexico in the 1970s. A county official notified the Dumont family, but no record exists of the exact time or place. According to Oma Dumont in 1963, Junior Bird had one daughter, Jamie Carol. Should the daughter be living today, she would be approximately thirty-three years of age. The second son of Capp, Thomas Telsa ("Tommy") Bird, preceded his father and his brother in death. He died of a gunshot wound on January 20, 1946.

Elgar Dumont, or "Frenchie" as everyone in Paducah knew him, served as postmaster until 1932, when he resigned after a second term in order to farm and ranch the Dumont land. Late in the 1930s, he accepted a position with Production Credit Association, making loans to farmers and ranchers. In 1951, he resigned this position and began farming and ranching once again. Frenchie Dumont died of heart failure on October 7, 1958, at the age of fifty-eight. Oma Dumont, Frenchie's widow, continued to live in the stucco home that her husband had built for them in 1927. She died in 1980 at the age of seventy-eight.

J. Verne Dumont began a career as rural mail carrier in Cottle County in February 1955, a job he performed for over thirty-two years, retiring on May 30, 1987. Following his father's death, J. Verne also assumed responsibilities for the family farming and ranching operation. On January 8, 1956, he married Mrs. Oline Bockleman of Turkey, Texas, who had one daughter, Gail, and one son, Randell. Today Gail Bockleman Hulen lives in Paris, Texas, and Randell Bockleman farms the land of Auguste and Ella Dumont, four and one-half miles southwest of Paducah.

In 1953, Ella Dumont's two-story house was torn down, and in 1961, J. Verne built a new home on the site. J. Verne Dumont is the only known living progeny of Ella Bird Dumont. He lives today with his wife on the same ground where his grandmother lived for forty-five years.

NOTES

Chapter One

1. Arrie Ella Elgar was born July 3, 1861, at Guntown, in northeastern Mississippi, north of Tupelo and south of Corinth. Oma Dumont, interview with editor, Paducah, Tex., April 12, 1963. Today Guntown is on U.S. Highway 45.

2. Corinth is on the Tennessee border in northeastern Mississippi.

3. *Camp fever* was a popular name for typhus. *Dorland's Illustrated Medical Dictionary*, 25th ed., s.v. "fever."

4. "The Dying Californian" was based on a letter containing the words of a traveler who died on his passage to California. This trip, whether around Cape Horn or through the Isthmus of Panama, was dangerous, travelers being especially susceptible to disease. Several versions of "The Dying Californian" exist. A version presented by the Missouri Folk-Lore Society consists of seven eight-line stanzas, the first of which appears in the author's text with only a few insignificant differences. "Ballads and Songs Collected by the Missouri Folk-Lore Society: 'The Dying Californian,'" pp. 350–351.

5. Following a period of great missionary activity among Protestant churches during the first part of the nineteenth century, a feeling of antimissionism began to emerge among Baptists in the early 1820s, mainly on the frontier. The missionary Baptist faction fostered organization of societies for the promotion of the spiritual and social welfare of mankind, societies that were directed by officers and field secretaries. Missionaries of this faction, often from the East, were usually well educated academically and theologically, and they were paid for their services. Antimission Baptists, in contrast, claimed that missionary societies were contrary to Scripture—the church was the only organization authorized by Scripture. In addition, complete independence of a congregation was necessary instead of the centralization of authority of the missionary group. The antimissionists lived where there were few educational facilities and cultural influences; hence, the educated Easterners sharply contrasted with the farmer-preachers of the frontier. Finally, these frontier simple folk accused their paid counterparts of doing work only for the money and not for God. Generally speaking, the antimission Baptists "taught that God in his own time and way would bring his elect to repentence and redemp-

tion, and that therefore any effort on the part of man to assist God in his redemptive work was not only presumptuous, but wicked." William Warren Sweet, *Religion on the American Frontier: The Baptists 1783–1830,* pp. 58, 62, 66–67, 72.

6. The handmade hammer crafted by the author's grandfather is in the Panhandle-Plains Historical Museum in Canyon, Texas. The handle is now broken off. Also included in the collection, donated by both the author and her daughter-in-law Oma (Elgar Dumont's wife), are the following: (*a*) a lemon squeezer; (*b*) a knife sharpener used to sharpen buffalo hunters' knives; (*c*) a vest worn by Lewis Steptoe Elgar, the father of the author and her sister, Lucy, when he was a schoolboy (the vest was made by his sister, Martha Elgar); (*d*) a white baby dress that was worn by Elgar ("Frenchie") Dumont, the author's son; (*e*) a black shawl with fringe, which belonged to the author; (*f*) a baby toilet set, including a brush and powder box with a puff, which belonged to the Dumont family; (*g*) a sofa pillow made by the author in 1885. Ella Bird Dumont Collection, Panhandle-Plains Historical Museum, Canyon, Tex.

7. Elizabeth Benson Elgar, the author's mother, was born in Alabama. She joined the Eastern Star at the age of eighteen. Clarence R. Wharton, *Texas under Many Flags,* vol. 4, p. 137. The author, like her mother, also was a member of Eastern Star in later years in Paducah, Texas.

8. Lucy Elgar was the name of the author's sister.

9. *Congestive chill* is "pernicious malaria with gastrointestinal congestion and diarrhea, preceded by a chill." *Dorland's Illustrated Medical Dictionary,* 25th ed., s.v. "chill." Matthews states, "No one knew then [in 1867] that mosquitoes caused malaria; we thought we had eaten too many watermelons and half ripe peaches. . . . Mother made tea from a plant, a wild Canterbury bell, called 'balmony' by the pioneers. The tea was boiled down with sugar to a thick syrup and fed to us. It was a rather bitter dose, but we took it with a very good grace for the sake of the sugar." Sallie Reynolds Matthews, *Interwoven: A Pioneer Chronicle,* pp. 44–45.

10. The grandmother was the author's maternal grandmother, Mrs. Benson. According to Exley, who consulted the 1860 Eighth Census of the United States in Itawamba County, Mississippi, the grandmother's first name was Lucretia. Jo Ella Powell Exley, *Texas Tears and Texas Sunshine: Voices of Frontier Women,* p. 209.

11. Charles Benson was the author's maternal uncle.

12. The author states later in the text that the family migrated to Texas, arriving in Johnson County in November 1867. If indeed the family had joined the author's grandmother at the end of the Civil War (1865), as the author states previously, they could have lived with the grandmother for only two years, not three.

13. The famous Mackenzie Trail was the route followed by R. S. Mackenzie in the Panhandle and South Plains of Texas and in western New Mexico. Carl Coke Rister, *The Southwestern Frontier, 1865–1881,* p. 159. The author may be referring to another trail with the same or a similar name somewhere between Mississippi and Texas, or she may be confusing another trail with the famous Mackenzie Trail.

14. Helena, Arkansas, lies on the border between Arkansas and Mississippi on

the bank of the Mississippi River, not the Red River. The wagon train would have crossed the Red River later in southwestern Arkansas or northwestern Louisiana, near the Texas border.

15. Burleson County, Texas, is approximately eighty miles northeast of Austin. The county seat is Caldwell. *Texas Almanac and State Industrial Guide, 1986–87,* pp. 250–251.

16. The author's Aunt Julia must have been a sister to Elizabeth Benson Elgar White and to Martha, George, and Charles Benson. The diary spoken of in the text no longer exists.

17. The author probably means Kaufman, Texas, in Kaufman County, approximately thirty miles southeast of Dallas. According to the *Texas Almanac,* the Grand Prairie is "near the eastern edge of the North Central Plains . . . extending south from the Red River in an irregular band through Cooke, Montague, Wise, Denton, Tarrant, Parker, Hood, Johnson, Bosque, Coryell, and some adjacent counties. It is a limestone-based area, usually treeless except along the numerous streams, and adapted primarily to livestock raising and staple crop growing." *Texas Almanac, 1986–87,* p. 61.

18. Johnson County is directly south of Tarrant County and the city of Fort Worth. The county seat is Cleburne. Ibid., pp. 311–312.

Chapter Two

1. According to Price and Rathjen, "By early in the eighteenth century the historic complex of Native Americans was firmly established in the southern Plains. The Comanches were the largest and dominant tribe, hence the term *Comancheria,* which denotes an area approximately 400 miles wide and 600 miles long under Comanche dominion. [The northern border penetrated Colorado and Kansas, the western border included eastern New Mexico, the eastern border stretched from Kansas across the middle of Oklahoma down to Austin, Texas, and the southern border stretched roughly from Austin westward to the Pecos River.] The Kiowa Apaches, closely identified with the Kiowas, shared the southern Plains with the Comanches and Kiowas. Although they were a much smaller tribe than the Comanches, the Kiowas were no less formidable in hunting and warfare and they, with their Kiowa Apache associates, became firmly entrenched, along with the Comanches, in the area called *Comancheria.*" B. Byron Price and Frederick W. Rathjen, *The Golden Spread,* p. 18. At the time of the narrative, the author's family lived on the eastern border of Comancheria.

2. The area fifteen miles southeast of Weatherford is across the county line from Johnson County into Parker County. *Texas Almanac, 1986–87,* pp. 311–312, 338–339.

3. *Tea cakes* are cookies usually served with tea, coffee, or punch. The following recipe belonged to Margaret Nichols Patton (1877–1973), who was born in Kendall County, Texas: *Recipe:* 1 cup butter, 2 cups sugar, 4 eggs beaten, 4 cups flour, 1

teaspoon salt, 6 teaspoons baking powder, and 1 teaspoon vanilla. First, cream the butter and add the sugar. Then add the beaten eggs. Sift the dry ingredients and add them to the butter mixture. Blend all well with the vanilla. Roll out the dough very thinly on a floured surface, and cut out the cookies with a biscuit cutter. Bake at 375° for about ten minutes or until golden brown. Mrs. Patton's granddaughter, Louise Patton Smyres, contributed the recipe. Mrs. Smyres states that after the tea cakes had cooled, her grandmother put them into a cloth flour sack and hung it on a nail in the kitchen. Louise Patton Smyres, telephone interview with Donna Gene Reardon, October 14, 1986.

4. Either the author mistakes her age as seven, or a year had passed since her arrival in Texas. The Christmas that the author speaks of may have been either 1867 or 1868.

5. Paducah, Texas, the future home of the author, is the county seat of Cottle County, on U.S. Highways 62, 70, and 83.

6. Of Lewis White's family of twelve children, today Bertha White Flowers and Theola White Beauchamp still live in Paducah.

7. Martha Benson was the author's maternal aunt.

8. The Caddo and Waco tribes (the latter a subtribe of the Wichitas) lived in the region. Visiting tribes were the Shawnees, Iron Eyes, Tehuacanas, Tonkawas, Kickapoos, Bidais, and Anadarcoes, with an occasional roving band of the most hostile Comanches. *A Memorial and Biographical History of Johnson and Hill Counties, Texas,* p. 65. Indian treaties with the U.S. government were hard to enforce because the government made little preparation for the tribes on the lands to which they were assigned. The decreasing game supply could not keep the tribes alive. As a result, Newcomb says, "the winter of 1867–68 saw as many depredations in Texas and Indian Territory as ever. But by the summer of 1868 the beginning of the end was in sight. If the Indians went on the reservation there was not sufficient food for them; if they remained away they were attacked by troops." William W. Newcomb, *The Indians of Texas,* p. 361. Eventually the Indians were to come to "defeat and submergence in a white world." Ibid., p. 362.

9. Veal's Station was twelve miles north of the present site of Weatherford in Parker County. William G. Veal, later to become a captain in the Confederate Army, arrived there in 1852, opening a store and establishing a pioneer school, which was called "Parsons College." The community became known as Veal's Station. The school building remains today, and in 1936 a state historical marker was erected at the site. Walter Prescott Webb, ed., *The Handbook of Texas,* vol. 2, pp. 834–835.

10. Alvarado is in Johnson County, twenty-four miles southeast of Fort Worth, on Interstate 35W. *Texas Almanac, 1986–87,* p. 312.

11. The Hickman and Barnes leagues of land lay east of the crosstimbers in Johnson County. This improved and cultivated land stretched from the interior of Tarrant County (to the north) southward through Johnson and Hill counties. It was six hundred square miles or 384,000 acres. Farms ranged from 50 to 1,100 acres

each. A. J. Byrd, *History and Description of Johnson County and Its Principal Towns,* pp. 83–84.

12. Ben Bickerstaff and Jo Thompson terrorized the citizens of Alvarado in late 1868 and early 1869. Bickerstaff was charged with robbing E. M. Heath, the deputy tax assessor and collector of Johnson County. In addition, Bickerstaff was charged with robbing blacks and interrupting farming interests by running blacks off the farms where they were employed. Bickerstaff threatened the lives of many of the best citizens of the town, including those on the grand jury, if they spoke out against him. Jo Thompson had lived in Alvarado for two years or longer, during which time he opened a whiskey business, in spite of a law against it. *A Memorial and Biographical History,* pp. 111–113. When he was forced to close, he threatened to "burn the town to ashes and send every man to hell!" Ibid., p. 113. Both men were shot down in the streets of Alvarado on April 5, 1869, when they rode into town to pick up a barrel of flour. Ibid., p. 113.

13. A Major Purdum, a prominent citizen of Alvarado, was known to oppose the course of Ben Bickerstaff. Ibid., p. 112.

14. The railroad did not come to Fort Worth until seven years later, July 19, 1876. Oliver Knight, *Fort Worth: Outpost on the Trinity,* p. 85. The author reports later in the narrative that her mother had moved west to Young County by 1873; therefore, it is not likely that she saw the first train enter Fort Worth.

15. Parker County is directly west of Tarrant County. Today the county seat is Weatherford on Interstate 20. *Texas Almanac, 1986–87,* pp. 338–339.

16. This is the same uncle, Charles Benson, who had come for Elizabeth White (the author's mother) and her three children, Lucy and Ella Elgar and Thomas White, in Memphis at the end of the Civil War.

17. The Kiowas and Comanches "shared each other's hunting territories and often raided together." Newcomb, *The Indians of Texas,* p. 195. Wayne Gard reports in *Rawhide Texas* that these two tribes often "indulged in savage massacres" (p. 36). On May 17, 1871, a band of about 150 Kiowas and Comanches, led by four Kiowa chiefs, were raiding in northern Texas. In the flat of Salt Creek, near the present town of Graham in southeastern Young County, the raiders attacked a ten-wagon corn train: "The warriors destroyed the wagons, killing the wagonmaster and six teamsters. They left the victims stripped, scalped, and otherwise mutilated. They beheaded some and scooped out their brains. From others they slashed fingers, toes, and private parts and stuffed them into their mouths. They gashed bowels and placed live coals in the exposed abdomens. They tied one scalped man between two wagons and roasted him to a crisp." Gard, *Rawhide Texas,* p. 36. Frank H. Mayer and Charles B. Roth report in *The Buffalo Harvest* the account of Bob McRae, a buffalo hunter during the great slaughter of the 1870s, of a similar atrocity that he had witnessed. McRae once "came upon the body of a teamster, who had been stripped, scalped while alive, his privates cut off and stuck into his mouth and fastened there with a sinew cord. Fat pine splinters had been stuck into his flesh from ankles to chin until he resembled a hedgehog. These were ignited at his

feet, causing an upward slow flame which literally roasted him alive. His body had been fastened to a dead tree trunk with his own chains" (pp. 44–46). It was after this incident that McRae invented the poison vial, "a device made by sticking a .40 caliber shell inside a .45 caliber" (p. 46). Inside the .40-caliber shell was a very thin glass tube containing hydrocyanic acid. According to McRae, it was "sure medicine against scalping and torture," since the Indians would not bother a corpse (p. 46).

18. Young County is northwest of Parker County. Today, the county seat is Graham on U.S. Highway 380. *Texas Almanac, 1986–87*, pp. 375–376. The move that the author speaks of would have been approximately fifty miles from Parker County.

19. The author turned twelve in 1873, not fourteen.

20. The author refers to land appropriated for an Indian reservation for the Tonkawas and other small tribes in 1854. The Texas legislature authorized the U.S. government to set up two reservations—one on the Clear Fork of the Brazos (along the present boundary of Haskell and Throckmorton counties) and a second in southeastern Young County. The former reservation was for Comanches and the latter for several destitute tribes: Delawares, Shawnees, Tonkawas, Wichitas (subtribes Wacos, Tawakonis, and Kichais), and Caddoes. Because these reservations were unsuccessful in restraining the tribes, however, by 1858 and 1859 fighting and bloodshed were worse than ever. As a result, on July 31, 1859, the Indians from both reservations began a trip northward to Indian Territory on the Washita River in west-central Oklahoma. The Texas reservation lands, consequently, reverted to the state of Texas. In 1874 the Young County reserve was opened to settlers for preemption. By November, a number of people had settled along the Brazos. Old-timers referred to the first preemptors as those living on "the Nine Mile Square," because the former reservation covered nine square miles. Newcomb, *The Indians of Texas*, pp. 354, 356–358; Muriel H. Wright, *A Guide to the Indian Tribes of Oklahoma*, pp. 32, 250–251; Carrie J. Crouch, *A History of Young County, Texas*, pp. 56, 91.

Chapter Three

1. Because the land formerly reserved for the Indians was opened for settlers in 1874, and because Crouch says in *A History of Young County* (p. 56) that by November of that year a number of preemptors had settled along the Brazos River, the year of the first school must have been 1875. The author turned fourteen in July of that year. It was over two years later, in September 1877, that the author married and left Young County; therefore, the three terms of schooling that she refers to must have been between early 1875 and mid-1877. Mrs. M. H. Neff, the author's first teacher in Young County, was a member of the same family of Neffs that moved to Cottle County during the organization of Paducah in 1891 and 1892 (see chapter 17).

2. The quail trap that the author devised was probably a tunnel underground large enough for quail to pass through. At the far end of the tunnel lay a pen to catch the birds. Grain was scattered along the inside of the tunnel to entice the

birds along until they entered the pen, where they were trapped. In contrast, a turkey pen would have had a "trigger" that would fall when hit by the bird, causing a trap door to fall behind. Jim Bob Bigham, interview, Paducah, Tex., October 11, 1986.

3. Tom Bird signed his marriage license as James T. Bird in Young County, Texas, September 9, 1877. La Fonda Taack (District and County Clerk of Young County), letter to editor, July 16, 1986. His full name was James Thomas Bird.

4. Blanco County, of which Johnson City is the county seat, is about fifty miles directly west of Austin. *Texas Almanac, 1986–87,* p. 245. Contemporary Texans speak of the area as a part of Central Texas, although the author, with her limited knowledge of geography, calls it "southern" Texas.

5. The only early record that exists concerning J. T. Bird's activities before the Ranger company was organized shows that he acted as a substitute for J. C. Davidson, who was absent from Company A of the Minute Men stationed at Round Mountain in Blanco County. Bird served under Lieutenant James Ingram from June 18 to June 24 in 1872. *Texas Ranger Muster Rolls,* Company A, Minute Men, 1872–1874.

6. In August 1873, a band of marauding Indians murdered Thomas Phelps and his wife while the couple was fishing on Cyprus Creek near their home in Blanco County. A few days later, a group of six men rode out from the settlement of Round Mountain to track down the savages. The men were Thomas Bird; Joe Bird (Thomas's brother); John O. Biggs; Stanton Jolly; and two brothers, George and Dan Roberts. Four others joined them on the way: Captain James Ingram, William Ingram, Frank Waldrip, and "Cam" Davidson. After following the trail for about fifteen miles, the men found the Indians sheltered at Deer Creek, a shallow ravine protected by a scrub growth of Spanish oak on each side. When the Indians opened fire, two men were hit and had to be taken out of range. Rufe Perry (who would become Captain Rufe Perry of Ranger Company D in 1874) learned of the fight and sped with his men to the scene of the battle. The Indians had fled, leaving blood spots of their dead and wounded on the ground. Other parties who had seen the Indians come in had counted twenty-seven warriors. One group reported finding the graves of four braves who had died as a result of the fight. State Senator H. C. King introduced a bill in the Texas legislature suggesting that each of the ten men who participated be awarded a gun. As a result, each man received a repeating Winchester of the current 1873 model. Captain Dan W. Roberts, *Rangers and Sovereignty,* pp. 19–27. According to Charles Edward Chapel in *Guns of the Old West,* the Model 73 "made the name of Winchester" (p. 248). Its beginnings were in 1857 when Oliver F. Winchester and others reorganized the bankrupt Volcanic Repeating Arms Company and named it the New Haven Arms Company. Sixteen years later, after successful developments in rifle production, the Winchester 73 was introduced. It was reported to have killed more Indians and more game—and more U.S. soldiers after the Indians discovered it—than any other type of rifle. Chapel said that "it was fast, reliable, and strongly constructed, and adapted for short-range shooting and mobile warfare" and that just as the word "Colt" came to mean

revolver in the Old West, "Winchester" meant rifle (p. 248). It was the most widely used shoulder arm in the post–Civil War era. Chapel, *Guns of the Old West*, pp. 247–248. Mr. Bird's rifle is now part of the collections of the Panhandle-Plains Historical Museum in Canyon, Texas. The written description in the museum's library reads as follows: "Winchester Center Fire Rifle, Model 1873; Serial Number 3518; brass floor plate; overall length, 43″; barrel length, 24 1/2″; round barrel; .44 caliber." A silver inlaid shield on the stock is engraved as follows: "Awarded to J. T. Bird by the XIII Legislature, 1873." To the right of the shield is a silver inlaid "J. T.," followed by a silver bird, representing his usual signature—according to the library's written description and history of the rifle. Markings on the rifle read: "Winchester Repeating Arms, New Haven, Connecticut, King's Improvement, Patented March 29, 1866." A description placed beside the rifle states that the firearm was donated on June 25, 1934. Speaking of the rifle in a recent article, Rattenbury of the Panhandle-Plains Historical Museum says, "The piece exhibits the wear and patina typical of long field use, an appearance attractive and evocative to many students and collectors of historic, frontier period arms. . . . It [the rifle] remains a tangible and well-documented link to the Texas frontier of a century ago." Richard Rattenbury, "A Winchester for All Seasons," pp. 12, 14.

7. The name J. T. Bird appears on the muster rolls of Ranger Company D of the Frontier Battalion from May 25, 1874, to September 14, 1874, during which time he received a total of $148. The name appears again on the rolls of Company D from March 1, 1876, to August 31, 1876, during which time he received a total pay of $193.33. Company D was camped near Menardville (now Menard) from June 1875 through the winter of 1876, though the company had been in both Menard and Mason counties since its organization in 1874. Captain C. R. "Rufe" Perry commanded the group for the first six months, after which Captain Dan W. Roberts took command. Captain Roberts identifies the camp location as four miles east of town, whereas Mrs. Roberts says it was in a pecan grove about two miles below Menardville. Texas Ranger Muster Rolls, Company D, Frontier Battalion, 1874–1876; Roberts, *Rangers and Sovereignty*, pp. 61, 84; Mrs. D. W. Roberts, *A Woman's Reminiscences of Six Years in Camp with the Texas Rangers*, pp. 14, 16.

Among the men of Company D under Captain Roberts was James B. Gillett, author of *Six Years with the Texas Rangers* (published in another edition under the title *The Texas Ranger: A Story of the Southwestern Frontier*). Gillett tells of scouting for Indians with Tom Bird in Kimble County when the men encountered a female black bear and two cubs, one male and one female. After killing the mother, the Rangers tied up the fighting cubs and took them as pets. Gillett tells, "They were kept chained in camp for nearly two years and grew to be great pets. The male especially gave great amusement to all of our company. The female was not so tractable. She showed such a savage disposition, indeed, that later she had to be killed. Her brother was kept with us until Tom Bird quit the ranger service, taking his pet bear with him." J. B. Gillett, *The Texas Ranger: A Story of the Southwestern Frontier*, p. 34. The author never refers to her husband's having a pet bear after he resigned from the ranger service. In another source, "'Slick' Clements Was a Good Marksman," Gillett refers to Tom Bird's marksmanship: speaking of the best shot in Company D, W. T. "Slick" Clements, Gillett states, "The nearest approach we had to [Clements] as a shot in the company was [*sic*] Ed Sieker, Tom Bird and Jim White" (p. 17).

8. No record exists of J. T. Bird having belonged to another Ranger company prior to his coming to Young County.

9. Joseph Bird was born in North Carolina on July 15, 1821. Prior to coming to Blanco County, Texas, he and his family lived in Arkansas where James Thomas Bird was born in 1848. Eleven other children were born to Joseph Bird and his wife, the former Eliza L. Dorriss. There were six boys and six girls. In 1854 the family came to what is now Round Mountain, Texas. Mr. Bird was a prominent livestock raiser and a well-known Baptist minister. He was elected county judge of Blanco County on November 4, 1890, when he was almost seventy years of age, and he was chosen again for a second term on November 8, 1892. John S. Moursand, *Blanco County Families for 100 Years,* pp. 19–21. Wharton records that Joseph Bird served in the Confederate Army as captain of a company in the regiment commanded by General J. D. Harrison during the Civil War. Wharton, *Texas under Many Flags,* pp. 275–276.

10. If J. T. Bird was born in 1848 and if the family moved to Blanco County in 1854, then J. T. would have been only five or six.

11. A *deadfall* is "a trap, especially for large game, in which a weight falls on and crushes the prey." *The Random House Dictionary of the English Language,* s.v. "deadfall."

12. A *sacque* is "a loose-fitting dress." Ibid., s.v. "sacque."

13. In 1877 Lieutenant G. W. Campbell commanded Company B of the Texas Rangers (not Company A, as the author states), which first was camped on Elm Creek, near the current site of Throckmorton in Throckmorton County. Shortly afterward, the company moved to Camp Sibley on a creek by that name, near its junction with the Clear Fork of the Brazos River, about ten miles northeast of Fort Griffin. The Rangers moved into this area because open warfare had developed between two vigilante groups in the settlement. Carl Coke Rister, *Fort Griffin on the Texas Frontier,* p. 157. Muster Rolls show that J. T. Bird served under Lieutenant Campbell in Company B from March 13 to November 30, 1877, for which he was paid $345.33. Texas Ranger Muster Rolls, Companies B and D, Frontier Battalion, 1874–1877. Today, Fort Griffin State Park sits on the county line between Throckmorton and Shackelford counties. This is approximately one hundred miles northwest of Johnson and Parker counties, where the author's wagon train had first stopped to settle in 1867, and forty miles west-southwest of Young County, to which her family had migrated in 1873.

14. The community of Bunger is now on Texas Farm Road 1287 south of Graham in Young County.

15. Gard says that on the frontier religion came to the early settlers in two ways.

One was the circuit preacher who traveled great distances, enduring many dangers and hardships. The other was the "potent institution of backwoods Protestantism, the camp meeting. Usually held in the late summer or fall, the camp meeting was a big social event for rural families and was attended by evangelistic fervor. . . . The camp meeting outdid even the political rally in excitement. . . . An ordinary camp meeting might last only Thursday through Sunday, but a big one continued through two weekends." Gard, *Rawhide Texas*, pp. 124–129. Matthews describes the event: "In the summer there were camp meetings where we would join the neighbors in a camp of several days, with revival services held under a large arbor of green brush. Several families would pitch their tents together, and cook and eat together. All this was one big picnic to the children and was thoroughly enjoyed. We took plea-sure in it all, especially the shouting and singing. . . . There would be visiting among the campers between the religious services, although sunrise prayer meet-ing, services at nine and eleven o'clock in the morning, at three in the afternoon, vespers at sundown and services at 'early candlelight' were calculated to keep people rather well employed." Matthews, *Interwoven*, p. 68.

16. The community of South Bend exists today south of Graham in Young County on Texas 67 and the Clear Fork of the Brazos River. *Texas Almanac, 1986–87*, p. 376. Drilling for commercial oil began on nearby Fish Creek in 1887. Oil exploration was slow, however, until the 1920s when the South Bend and Bunger fields were developed in southern Young County. Crouch, *A History of Young County*, pp. 159–162.

17. Records of the Young County Clerk's office reveal that James T. Bird and Ella (spelled "Ellah" on the documents) Elgar were married by G. W. Black on September 9, 1877, not October 10, 1876. W. T. Ditto signed the certificate as county clerk. What is interesting and inexplicable about the records is that the couple's marriage license is dated a month later, October 9, 1877. It too is signed by Ditto. Taack, letter, July 16, 1986.

Chapter Four

1. Graham, Texas, the county seat of Young County, is named for two broth-ers, Edwin S. and Gustavus A. Graham, who came to the area from Kentucky in 1871, purchasing 125,000 acres in the county. The Graham brothers called their town "The Gem City of the West." Crouch, *A History of Young County*, pp. 55–56. Gard states, "In 1874, Graham won over old Fort Belknap to become the seat of Young County. Graham had appealed to the frontier cowmen by laying out one of the biggest courthouse squares in all Texas." Gard, *Rawhide Texas*, p. 172.

2. In nautical jargon, a *gudgeon* is "a socket attached to the stern frame of a vessel, for holding the pintle of a rudder" (*Random House Dictionary*, s.v. "gudgeon"). Like the expression "from stem to stern," meaning from the front of a ship to the back, "from stem to gudgeon" designates the same expanse but sub-

stitutes a specific mechanical part of the stern. As a metaphor for the condition of Tom Bird's underclothing, the phrase suggests that these garments were torn from one end to the other.

3. Tom Bird's song was apparently an adaptation of the second verse of the popular "There Is a Tavern in the Town":

> "Adieu, adieu, kind friends, adieu, adieu, adieu,
> I can no longer stay with you.
> I'll hang my harp on a weeping-willow tree,
> And may the world go well with thee."

The Oxford Dictionary of Quotations, p. 10.

4. Any bachelor wearing the badge of a Texas Ranger was rated as a top matrimonial catch. Leading Texas families often encouraged Rangers to court their daughters, and they sometimes gave big tracts of land as dowries. Harold Preece, *Lone Star Man,* p. 67.

5. The author was sixteen at the time of her marriage in 1877, not fifteen as she states in the text.

6. The marriage certificate on file with the county clerk in Young County is signed by G. W. Black, M.G. (M.G. probably stands for Minister of the Gospel.)

7. *Jaconet* is a lightweight cotton fabric, sometimes finished as cambric, lawn, organdy, or voile, used in making clothing and bandages. *Random House Dictionary,* s.v. "jaconet."

8. Fort Belknap was established in west-central Young County on the left bank of the Brazos River in the early summer of 1851 by General William Goldsmith Belknap. At that time, "Fort Belknap was the frontier's westernmost line of civilization." Barbara A. Neal Ledbetter, *Fort Belknap: A Frontier Saga,* p. 39. Occupied until 1867 (the year that the author's wagon train arrived in Johnson County, Texas), the fort was evacuated by the troops who moved southwestward to Camp Wilson, which later came to be known as Fort Griffin. While in operation, Fort Belknap provided protection for early settlers and travelers. In 1961 the former fort was designated a Registered National Historic Landmark by the U.S. Department of the Interior National Park Service. Fort Belknap is just outside Newcastle. Crouch, *A History of Young County,* pp. 16–17; Ledbetter, *Fort Belknap,* pp. 15, 39.

9. Major John B. Jones was appointed to command the newly organized Frontier Battalion on May 2, 1874. Six companies of seventy-five men each—lettered A to F—made up the battalion. These companies served the frontier until about 1881, the year that Major Jones died. Walter Prescott Webb, *The Texas Rangers,* pp. 307, 309, 425. Muster rolls for Company B in 1877 show a high strength of thirty-five men on May 31. At the time of J. T. Bird's discharge on November 30, twenty-nine men were left. By February 1878, only twenty-one remained. Texas Ranger Muster Rolls, Companies B and D.

10. Article 4413(11) of Vernon's Texas Civil Statutes, which lists requirements and

authorizations for the Texas Rangers, makes no mention of a marital restriction. *Vernon's Annotated Revised Civil Statutes of the State of Texas,* vol. 12A, pp. 197–198. The rule allowing men to stay only six months after marriage may have originated with Company B and Lieutenant Campbell. The date of J. T. Bird's discharge was November 30, 1877.

11. By 1876 hunting parties were swarming in the buffalo country northwest, west, and southwest of Fort Griffin. Prices were ranging from $.75 to $2.50 per hide. Around Colorado City, approximately 110 miles southwest of Fort Griffin, hides sold for $1.00 to buyers making the rounds of the camps, but the same hides brought $1.50 if hauled to Fort Griffin. A deluge of hides eventually pushed the price down to $1.25 each, but the two hundred thousand sold at Fort Griffin in 1876–1877 brought the hunters a quarter of a million dollars. Fort Griffin, in addition to being a camp for Texas Rangers and a marketing center for buffalo hides, had also become a center for outfitting hunting parties. To take the hunters' money, the town was filled with saloons, gambling houses, dance halls, and bagnios (brothels). Wayne Gard, *The Great Buffalo Hunt,* pp. 218–233. Martin Hornecker reports the response of two adventurous men from Illinois who described the tough frontier town as follows: "'We thought Fort Worth, when we first saw it, was the worst city in the United States, but its wildness was no comparison to that of Fort Griffin.'" Martin Hornecker, *Buffalo Hunting on the Texas Plains in 1877,* pp. 3, 12. The western fort had one redeeming feature, however—a school that taught reading, writing, Greek, mathematics, and grammar. Frederick W. Rathjen, *The Texas Panhandle Frontier,* p. 168. Among the more successful outfits at work in the buffalo area in 1876 was one headed by noted marksman Charles Hart. His men moved into the area of the Salt Fork of the Brazos River and into the Pease River country, where they took 3,361 hides in three months. Gard, *The Great Buffalo Hunt,* p. 223. The Salt Fork of the Brazos River, at its closest point, was approximately seventy-five miles west-northwest of Fort Griffin. The three branches of the Pease— the South, the Middle, and the North Pease rivers—varied in distance from 100 to 125 miles northwest of Fort Griffin. This area was to become the buffalo-hunting country and the eventual home of Tom and Ella Bird. It is likely that they were influenced to go there by the success of such hunters as Charles Hart.

Chapter Five

1. Actually, Tom and Ella Bird were headed for the northwestern area of the North Central Plains, country just south of what is commonly referred to as the Panhandle of Texas and just east of the High Plains of Texas. The buffalo area where the Birds settled is rolling country, occasionally rugged, unlike the flatter land of the Panhandle and the Texas High Plains.

2. According to Lee Burke in "I. Wilson Knives," the I. Wilson skinning knife was the product of John Wilson's cutlery shop founded in Sheffield, England, in 1750. The use of *I* for *J* as an initial was a practice that continued in general use

through the first several decades of the 1800s in England. Wilson's trademark was a cluster of four whiskered circles representing peppercorns and a small vertical diamond. Wilson claimed that a knife with this mark "cuts as keen as pepper and carries an edge like a diamond" (p. 39). Wilson also produced butcher knives and sticking knives. During the period of the great American buffalo harvest of the 1870s, the Wilson brand was preferred by the best of hunters. Eventually, in the 1930s, the Wilson business, name, and trademark was absorbed by Joseph Elliot and Sons. The Wilson name and trademark are still used today in Sheffield. The Wilson knife, which was humble in appearance and the essence of simplicity in design, was called by name, a distinction rarely extended to tools on the frontier. Lee Burke, "I. Wilson Knives," pp. 38–42. The Bowie knife was widely used throughout the South and Southwest. Reportedly given to James Bowie by his brother Rezin, the knife was "on proportions of a short butcher knife, . . . forged from the best steel procurable. It was differentiated from other knives by having more curve on the blade near the point, by having a heavier handle, often of horn, and by having handle, blade, and guard all so well-balanced that the knife could be cast a maximum distance with the most deadly effect. . . . It was both economical and practical for skinning, cutting up meat, eating, fighting duels, stabbing enemies, hammering, and performing other services." Walter Prescott Webb, ed., *The Handbook of Texas*, vol. 1, p. 198. A *steel* was a pistol. *A Dictionary of Americanisms on Historical Principles*, s.v. "steel." The Sharps .45 buffalo gun evolved as follows: Christian Sharps patented his first breech-loading rifle in Washington, D. C., in 1848. The Sharps Rifle Manufacturing Company was incorporated on October 8, 1851. Frank Sellers, *Sharps Firearms*, pp. 3, 10. Early in the 1870s the Sharps Rifle Company began production of large-bore rifles that fired cartridges of large powder capacity. Ranging from .40- to .50-caliber, Sharps rifles were designed especially for big, tough game, and were, therefore, ideal for killing buffalo. Rathjen, *The Texas Panhandle Frontier*, p. 170.

3. The term *breaks*, referring to the land, means a succession of sharp interruptions of the terrain, or broken country. *A Dictionary of Americanisms*, s.v. "break." The breaks of the South Wichita River follow its course from its beginnings in eastern Dickens County, through King and Knox counties to the Knox and Baylor county lines where it unites with the North Wichita. From there the larger Wichita River flows into Lake Kemp in northern Baylor County.

4. The actual year was 1877, confirmed by the marriage license of Tom and Ella Bird dated September 9, 1877, not 1876 as the author mistakenly states. The couple went into buffalo country soon after their marriage and J. T. Bird's discharge from the Texas Rangers on November 30, 1877.

5. Ernest Lee reports in "A Woman on the Buffalo Range" that King County surveyors' field notes indicate that "a pre-emption survey of 160 acres was patented to J. T. Bird on March 6, 1885. This survey is described as 'on Bird's Creek, a tributary to the south fork of the Wichita, and nine and one-half miles north fifty degrees east of the center of the county.' This survey appears on the land office map in

the name of J. T. Bird and is located in the southeast corner of the Masterson Ranch. This fully substantiates Mrs. Dumont's statement that they later 'filed a claim' for land upon which the camp was located and would seem to refute her statement that they pitched this camp 'where Dickens County joins Cottle.' The Cottle-Dickens common corner is 25 miles northwest of the head of Bird's Creek" (p. 147). The ruins of the original settlement of Tom and Ella Bird and of Alec Jones and his family remain today on the Masterson Ranch located 8 miles east of Guthrie in King County and 14.5 miles north from U.S. Highway 82 and Texas 114. The Birds' headquarters are 3.5 miles east of the home of the Masterson Ranch foreman, Ralph Mote. After the Birds and the Joneses left the area of their original settlement, John Farrar established the JF Ranch. Alma Gibson Long and Tom Long, interview with editor, Paducah, Tex., March 20, 1987. The JF Ranch became the property of R. B. Masterson and son in 1898. J. W. Williams, *The Big Ranch Country*, p. 136. Today the Masterson Ranch is often called the JY Ranch because of the $\mathcal{Y}$ brand originated by Frank Collinson and sold to R. B. Masterson around the turn of the century when Collinson became Masterson's partner. Frank Collinson, *Life in the Saddle*, ed. Mary Whatley Clarke, p. 222. Bird Creek, as the name appears on official state maps, is now dammed to form a watering tank for cattle. It eventually empties into Ox Yoke Creek, which in turn drains into the South Wichita River. Texas, Texas Water Development Board, Ox Yoke Creek Quadrangle Map, King County, 1981.

6. Buffalo tepees of the Indians were made of dressed hides sewn together, and they were supported inside by twenty or thirty poles. These living quarters could be taken down and packed in a few minutes' time, which was handy for tribes following a buffalo migration. E. Douglas Branch, *The Hunting of the Buffalo*, p. 27. Barsness says that buffalo hides provided such warmth that men sometimes crawled into buffalo carcasses to escape a blizzard. Occasionally a man awoke the next morning to find the carcass frozen stiff and himself a prisoner inside. Larry Barsness, *Heads, Hides and Horns: The Compleat Buffalo Book*, p. 6.

7. A china, or chinaberry, tree is native to the West Indies, Mexico, and the southern United States. *Random House Dictionary*, s.v. "chinaberry." The Texas variety, known as the Texas Umbrella because of its dense mound shape, grows twenty-five to thirty feet tall. Its berries are poisonous. James Underwood Crockett, *Trees*, p. 128.

8. Haines explains, "A large cow in good condition would produce about 500 pounds of meat, and a very large bull, 900 pounds. This included back fat, tongue, and heart. The liver, kidneys, lungs, paunch, small intestines and sweetbreads were all saved, but were not classed as meat, for they would not be preserved by drying but had to be eaten within a short time. . . . When a large kill was made . . . most of [the offal] was left untouched . . . for the handling of just the meat took all the time and energy of the butchering crew." Francis Haines, *The Buffalo*, p. 26.

9. The algerita, or agarita, berry is more commonly known as the Texas Barberry. The acrid berry ripens on the tall evergreen shrub in May and June. It is

excellent for jellies and wines, and the wood and roots furnish a yellow dye that
was used by Indians and pioneers. Eula Whitehouse, *Texas Flowers in Natural Colors*, p. 30. The Spanish *agrio* means "sour."

10. Gyp rock is formed by deposits of the mineral gypsum, which is very soluble
by water. Certain areas of Cottle County produce water commonly known to residents as "gyp water." Speaking of Cottle County, Brune says that "some springs
containing water that is high in sulfate content trickle from Blaine gypsum, White-
horse sandstone, and other Permian formations. . . . The spring water is generally
of a calcium sulfate type, slightly saline, very hard, and alkaline. The sulfate content
(from gypsum) often causes diarrhea in humans and may be so high that livestock
will not drink the water." Gunnar Brune, *Springs of Texas*, vol. 1, p. 135.

11. According to Rathjen in *The Texas Panhandle Frontier*, Anglo-American hide
hunters took advantage of the buffalo's inability to comprehend danger by employ-
ing the still hunt. The hunter took a concealed position and killed the buffalo as
they came into range. The still hunt produced what the hunters called "a stand,"
that is, "a number of buffalo grazing within a restricted area" (p. 171). This allowed
the hunter to approach the stand and conceal himself without alarming the grazing
buffalo. The hunter carefully selected his targets, first killing any animals who
showed signs of alarm. Rathjen recorded the evaluation of naturalist William T.
Hornaday, who said that the buffalo was "'a stupid brute,'" who "'would very
often stand quietly and see two or three score, or even a hundred, of his relatives
and companions shot down before his eyes, with no feeling other than one of stupid wonder and curiosity. Neither the noise nor smoke of the still-hunter's rifle, the
falling, struggling, nor the final death of his companions conveyed to his mind the
idea of a danger to be fled from, and so the herd stood still and allowed the still-
hunter to slaughter its members at will'" (p. 149). The well-known expression "He
sure had him buffaloed" comes from the ease with which the hunters bluffed the
animal. Barsness, *Heads, Hides and Horns*, p. 10.

12. The time was May or June of 1878.

13. Seymour is the county seat of Baylor County, fifty miles southwest of Wichita
Falls on U.S. Highways 82 and 277. *Texas Almanac, 1986–87*, p. 242. Seymour was
approximately fifty miles east of the hunters' camp on Bird Creek.

14. A *square* is the town block upon which the county courthouse is built.

15. The current community of Round Timbers is approximately seventeen miles
southeast of Seymour in Baylor County on Texas Farm Road 1285. *Texas Almanac,
1986–87*, p. 242.

16. Bob and Ellen Buse Cunningham. (See beginning of chapter 4 in the author's text.)

17. The year was now 1878, not 1877.

18. Ledbetter verifies that Fort Belknap, during the 1870s, was in shambles:
"War, Indians, and economics had destroyed the once thriving village and post on
the left bank of the Brazos." Barbara A. Neal Ledbetter, "Fort Belknap 1880–
1890," p. 13. By 1880 approximately 150 people lived on the townsite until it was

plowed under to make corn and cotton fields at a time when the landowners decided to plot a new town to be called Fort Belknap, Texas. As a result, several primitive businesses sprang up. By early 1881, "there lived in the new village . . . a minister, a saddlemaker, a druggist, a blacksmith, two farmers, two stockraisers, and four general store merchants." Ledbetter, "Fort Belknap 1880–1890," p. 16; Barbara A. Neal Ledbetter, letter to editor, December 22, 1986.

19. C. A. ("Chess") Tackitt, Baylor County's (and Seymour's) first sheriff, served from the county's organization in 1879 through 1881. Sarah Ann Britton, *The Early History of Baylor County*, p. 76.

20. James E. Martin, a thirty-six-year–old New Hampshire native, ran a general store that housed the U.S. Post Office in 1881. Ledbetter tells that on Thursday evening, June 9, Martin closed the store and went home for supper. Just as he finished eating, he heard a knock at the door. Three brothers, Pete, Nick, and Middleton (Dee) McDonald asked Martin to open the store so that they could buy groceries. Martin complied, because this was no unusual request. Early the next morning, June 10, Alice Martin, the storekeeper's twenty-year-old wife, awoke to find that her husband had not returned home. Upon searching the store, she found that about $75 and a great deal of clothing had been taken. Neighbors followed tracks northwest toward the river crossing until they came upon Martin's body. He was buried on June 11 in the Belknap cemetery. A posse of men led by Dr. William Benoit, a former Fourth Cavalryman with Colonel R. S. Mackenzie, followed the trail of the McDonald brothers, capturing them one hundred miles south of Fort Belknap in Brown County. The thieves-murderers were taken back to Young County where they were indicted on September 20 for robbery and murder. Three months later, on January 1, 1882, the prisoners escaped from the Young County jail in Graham, killing a sheriff's deputy and taking another deputy as hostage. Hearing shots from the jail, several Graham citizens quickly armed themselves and ran to see what the problem was. After a shoot-out, the McDonald brothers lay dead. Although the hostage had been shot through the mouth, he lived. Ledbetter, "Fort Belknap, 1880–1890," pp. 16–19. The author speaks of the Martin incident as being in 1878, though Ledbetter says it was in 1881, three years later. Tom and Ella Bird made numerous trips through Fort Belknap on visits to the author's family, so the author probably confuses the actual date and the specific trip to Young County.

21. Fort Belknap is in Young County. The author means merely that they traveled the remainder of the distance from Belknap to her family's home.

22. Reports of the buffalo slaughter shocked people in the East. Some protested on sentimental grounds; others objected to the waste of meat. Many feared that the herd might be completely wiped out. Various attempts were made at legislation in Washington to stop the slaughter. In 1876 several members of the House from Texas took part in the debate, some speaking for the bill and some speaking against it. The bill to halt the killing passed by a vote of 104 to 36 and was sent on to the Senate—from which it never emerged. Gard, *The Great Buffalo Hunt*, pp. 206, 213–214. In *Fort Belknap* Ledbetter states, "In three years, 1872–73–74, an

estimated 3,700,000 buffalo were slaughtered. Of that number, Indians killed only 150,000; the rest were killed by white hunters mostly for hides" (p. 212). Rathjen describes the effect: "During the 1877–78 season, the hunters took more than 100,000 hides. . . . Before the year of 1878 was very old, a herd of fifty buffalo was a rarity." Rathjen, *The Texas Panhandle Frontier,* p. 174.

23. "'The buffalo is our money,'" said Chief Kicking Bird of the Kiowa tribe, as reported by Gard in *The Great Buffalo Hunt.* "'It is our only resource with which to buy what we need and do not receive from the government. The robes we can prepare and trade. We love them just as the white man does his money. Just as it makes a white man's heart feel to have his money carried away, so it makes us feel to see others killing and stealing our buffaloes, which are our cattle given to us by the Great Father above to provide us meat to eat and means to get things to wear'" (p. 155). In defense of the Indians, Matthews states in *Interwoven:* "While the pioneers of this country suffered greatly in many ways . . . I do not think the Indians were by any means altogether to blame. The white people came to America as Christians. . . . And they did treat the Indians kindly in the beginning. . . . But this did not continue for long, and as the settling of the country by white people went on, we know there were many who cheated and exploited the Indians in every way possible, and in some instances treated them with ruthless cruelty" (pp. 37–38). Such a statement from a cattlewoman is rare, because most ranchers looked favorably upon the extinction of the buffalo and the subjugation of the Indians. Representing this latter view, General Phil Sheridan, who was in command of the military department of the Southwest, went to Austin to speak against legislation to protect the buffalo: "'[The hunters] have done in the last two years, and will do in the next year, more to settle the vexed Indian question than the entire regular Army has done in the last thirty years. They are destroying the Indians' commissary; and it is a well-known fact that an army losing its base of supplies is placed at a great disadvantage. Send them powder and lead, if you will; but, for the sake of lasting peace, let them kill, skin, and sell until the buffaloes are exterminated. Then your prairies can be covered with speckled cattle and the festive cowboy, who follows the hunter as a second forerunner of an advanced civilization.'" As quoted by Gard in *The Great Buffalo Hunt,* p. 215. According to Frank H. Mayer, who was a buffalo hunter from 1872 to 1878, "Army officers in charge of plains operations encouraged the slaughter of buffalo in every possible way. Part of this encouragement was of a practical nature that we runners [hunters] appreciated. It consisted of ammunition, free ammunition, all you could use, all you wanted, more than you needed. All you had to do to get it was apply at any frontier army post and say you were short of ammunition, and plenty would be given you. I received thousands of rounds this way." Mayer and Roth, *The Buffalo Harvest,* p. 29. Price and Rathjen assess the situation as follows: "By 1872 European and American tanneries had learned techniques of tanning buffalo hides that produced leather of unique traits, making it highly desirable for certain uses, such as the belting which manufacturing plants of the time used for conveying energy from power

source to machine. This relationship between industry and the frontier is indicative of a much broader phenomenon that spelled the doom of Native American culture. Industry created a demand for a commodity, in this case buffalo hides, important to the Indian life-style, and industry produced the means to acquire the commodity—large-caliber rifles, metallic cartridges, and railroads. The result was an uneven contest between the numerically superior whites equipped with industrial tools and backed by the demands of an industrial society and the relatively limited population of Native Americans who, in a technological sense, were still stone age people. The surprise is not that the Native Americans were overwhelmed, but that they resisted as effectively as they did." Price and Rathjen, *The Golden Spread,* pp. 45–46.

24. Fort Worth was approximately 200 miles east-southeast from their camp. After this bustling little city received the railroad in 1876, bales of odorous hides were stacked in tiers, sometimes tens of thousands on a single platform. In 1877 a newspaper reporter noted the arrival of a train of ten wagons from the West carrying from 2,500 to 3,000 hides. Later in 1877 another observer noted sixty thousand baled hides piled on a platform along the Texas and Pacific tracks. Gard, *The Great Buffalo Hunt,* pp. 217, 233.

25. Newcomb says that the Medicine Lodge Treaty set aside 2,968,893 acres for the Comanches, Kiowas, and Kiowa Apaches between the Red and Washita Rivers in southwestern Oklahoma. Newcomb, *The Indians of Texas,* p. 362. The reservation was a beautiful country of wide, rolling plains, richly grassed and well watered, extending northward from the Red River into Oklahoma. Each year, during the early fall and winter, however, the buffalo all drifted down from the plains of Oklahoma and Kansas into Texas. The Indians, therefore, often rode south to hunt. Zoe A. Tilghman, *Quanah, The Eagle of the Comanches,* p. 1035. In addition, hunters had become so numerous in Kansas by 1873 that the buffalo were almost gone. Gard, *The Great Buffalo Hunt,* p. 131. The Comanches that the author speaks of were probably in the area to hunt at least for one, if not both, of the reasons above.

26. Cottle County is directly north of King County where the Birds were camped.

27. Samuel Colt of Hartford, Connecticut, is credited with inventing the revolver, later called the "six-shooter." John W. Oliver, *History of American Technology,* pp. 169–170. The Colt Model 1872, the Colt .45, was also called "the Peacemaker" and "the Frontier Model." The .45-caliber pistol was a six-shot with a 7.5-inch barrel. It was 12.5 inches long, and it weighed 2 pounds 5 ounces. The manufacture of the .45 began in 1871, and the U.S. Army Ordnance Department placed the first order for it—8,000 revolvers to be issued to the U.S. Cavalry in 1873. Chapel, *Guns of the Old West,* pp. 232–33.

28. By 1878, the year in the narrative, Quanah Parker had become "Chief of the Comanches," by appointment from General R. S. Mackenzie and U.S. Indian agent P. B. Hunt. The latter divided the Comanches into thirty-three bands for issuing rations, Quanah's band registering ninety-three members. The chief was

noted for cooperating fully with authorities on the Fort Sill reservation. In *Quanah Parker and His People,* Neeley states, "Quanah's integrity and force of character, along with great intelligence, thrust him into the role of primary chief for a widely divergent people." Bill Neeley, *Quanah Parker and His People,* pp. 132–133. Quanah claimed that he was born about 1850 (ibid., p. 47), so he would have been less than thirty years of age at the time of the author's narrative. When Quanah Parker was the guest of Burk Burnett and Dan Waggoner in Fort Worth at the stock show in the late 1870s, he wore a buckskin tunic, leggins, moccasins, and a red breechcloth. Thrown about his shoulders, he wore a Mexican blanket, and he had bright feathers in his hair. The chief did wear a suit of white man's clothes in later years, but he always kept his long braids of hair. Tilghman, *Quanah,* pp. 129, 133. From the activities cited and the description given in the author's narrative, the chief of the roving party of Indians was probably not Quanah Parker.

Chapter Six

1. The time was winter, 1878–1879.

2. The South Pease, Middle Pease, and North Pease rivers flow through western Cottle County and join in the northeastern corner of that county, flowing on across Foard and Wilbarger counties into the Red River.

3. In later years, the author's son Capp Bird used the mattress until his death, November 6, 1957. Afterward, it was stored and eventually lost. Oma Dumont, interview, April 12, 1963.

4. The peak of the buffalo hunting period was during the winter of 1876–1877 when an estimated fifteen hundred hunters and skinners were out on the ranges. One man took 4,900 hides on a hunt near Big Spring from the fall of 1877 to May 1878. Two others took 6,300 hides the same winter. By the winter of 1877–1878, however, the Mooar brothers, who were famous hunters, saw that the hunting business was about to play out. Gard, *The Great Buffalo Hunt,* pp. 218, 251. The time that the author speaks of was 1879.

5. The term *shinnery* comes from the French *cheniere,* which means a live oak forest or grove. *A Dictionary of Americanisms,* s.v. "shinnery." On the frontier, *shinnery* referred to a dense growth of small live oak, commonly called scrub oak, growing in sandy soil.

6. Gard says that to remove the hide from the carcass, usually a rope was noosed around the buffalo's neck, and a horse pulled the hide away. If no horse was available, the skinners kicked the hide under the carcass and flopped the animal over and off the hide. Gard, *The Great Buffalo Hunt,* p. 126. Speaking of a need to use caution, Mayer explains, "Careful skinning is one reason why I always commanded top prices for my hides," Mayer and Roth, *The Buffalo Harvest,* p. 47.

7. According to the chronology of this narrative, the year was 1879.

8. Adams says a "loafer" is a gray wolf, usually called a "lobo." Ramon Adams, *Western Words: A Dictionary of the Range, Cow Camp, and Trail,* p. 92. *A Dictionary*

of Americanisms cites a source that suggested "loafers" was a corruption of the Mexican word "lobo" (s.v. "loafer"). The predatory lobo male might have reached "a length of six feet from its nose to the tip of its tail, a height of two-and-one-half feet at its shoulders, and a weight of 130 pounds." James I. Fenton, "The Lobo Wolf: Beast of Waste and Desolation," p. 57. Although the lobo wolf was powerful, swift, and quite intelligent, the concerted efforts of stockmen finally resulted in its extinction. Ibid. Collinson says that the lobo could "kill anything from a rabbit to a grown steer," and though it is now extinct in Texas, it is found in the Sierra Madre of Mexico. Collinson, *Life in the Saddle,* p. 172.

9. The surcingle is the band that passes under the horse's stomach. The rocking bolster is the transverse bar above the axle of a wagon on which the bed of the wagon rests. The swivel supports the bed of the wagon and enables it to turn under the rocking bolster. The clevis pin connects the tongue of the wagon to the rocking bolster. The hames are linked pieces of metal that fit tightly around the leather collar passing over the horse's head and resting on his shoulders; they are fastened at top and bottom by hame straps. The martingales are attachments that pass between the horse's forelegs, with one end fastened to the saddle girth and the other to the bridle; their purpose is to keep the horse from throwing his head. The thimble skein is a conical sheath for the spindle of the axle. The singletree is a swinging bar to which the traces (straps leading from the collar back to the wagon) are attached. The hounds are sidebars attached to the tongue and the forecarriage of the wagon, which offer additional rigidity. The tugs are parts of the traces nearest the collar. They are attached to the collar which give pulling support. *A Dictionary of Americanisms,* s.v. "singletree" and "thimble"; *Encyclopedia Britannica,* 14th ed., s.v. "saddlery and harness."

10. The year was 1880.

11. The Narrows is a high natural ridge between the South Wichita and Brazos rivers, approximately ten miles east of the town of Benjamin in Knox County. From the settlement on Bird Creek to Young County, travel through The Narrows prevented the Birds from having to take their wagon across any riverbed. The Indians knew about The Narrows and often tried to ambush travelers using this passageway. Alma Gibson Long and Tom Long, letter to editor, Paducah, Tex., December 17, 1986; J. Verne Dumont, interview with editor, Paducah, Tex., October 11, 1986.

Chapter Seven

1. Eugene, Alonzo, and Hiram Millett, who founded the Millett Ranch in 1874, were the sons of Samuel and Clementine Bartlett Millett, pioneer settlers in Guadalupe County, Texas. Floyd Benjamin Streeter, "The Millett Cattle Ranch in Baylor County, Texas," p. 65. The ranch stretched from the Wichita River to the Clear Fork of the Brazos, west as far as Knox County, and east to near where Olney now is in northern Young County. In 1881, it was sold to the Continental Land and

Cattle County. Britton, *Early History,* pp. 61–62. Because of the rugged country and hostile Indians, the *Fort Griffin Echo* of June 21, 1879, described the Millett Ranch as "'one of the toughest spots this side of hell.'" As quoted in Rister, *Fort Griffin,* p. 143. As for the Bedford Ranch, Britton states that the H. B. Bedford family was one of the first to settle in Baylor County. Bedford was a wealthy cattle-man and a Christian minister. Britton, *Early History,* pp. 134–135. To the west of Baylor County, Benjamin, in Knox County, was named for Benjamin Bedford, whose father, Hilary G. Bedford (relation to H. B. Bedford is unknown), divided a section of land and sold the sites to people interested in locating a town between the South Wichita and Brazos Rivers. Webb, *The Handbook of Texas,* 1:147. Amy Haley, district and county clerk of Baylor County, states in a letter of November 10, 1986, that there is no record of the Oxford Ranch.

2. According to Collinson, what killed the buffalo herds so rapidly was that there were no calves to replace the slaughtered cows. Even the little calves' hides were worth something, and Collinson believed it was better to kill them than to leave them "to starve to death or be killed by the wolves and coyotes. . . . These little calves were lying by the dead cows. We had to keep driving them away while killing the cows. After the mothers were skinned and the hides were in the wagon, the calves followed. They could smell the hides and would follow them to the hide yard. They were gone the next morning—gone back to where they had sucked the last time, either to starve to death or to be killed by the wolves." Collinson, *Life in the Saddle,* pp. 56–57.

3. The Double Mountain Fork of the Brazos River runs across southern Kent County, through parts of Fischer, Stonewall, and Haskell counties, and finally empties into the Salt Fork of the Brazos in northeastern Stonewall County. The trip that the hunters made was anywhere from thirty-five miles (Croton area) to about fifty miles (Double Mountain Fork of the Brazos River) west and south of their settlement.

4. According to Whitlock, Yellowhouse Canyon "received its name—*Casas Amarillas* (Yellow Houses)—from a flattop yellow bluff about a hundred feet high with caves in its side. When seen from a distance, it resembled flat houses with windows." V. H. Whitlock (Ol' Waddy), *Cowboy Life on the Llano Estacado,* pp. 7–8. Also known as Yellowhouse Draw, the canyon begins about fifty miles northwest of the present site of Lubbock and extends into Garza County to the southeast, where it widens into a broad valley. The incident that the author refers to here must have been approximately three years after the Battle of Yellowhouse Canyon in 1877. As for the famous battle, on March 4, 1877, forty-four hunters left from Camp Reynolds, which was approximately 100 miles southeast of Yellowhouse Canyon, in southern Stonewall County, about fifteen miles south of present Asper-mont. The expedition sought the Comanches who had murdered Marshall Sewell, a buffalo hunter, on February 1. The hunters finally found a large Indian encamp-ment in Yellowhouse Canyon on March 17. The battle, which was indecisive, oc-curred on March 18, with neither side sustaining casualties. Since the Comanches

retreated, however, the hunters considered themselves victorious. The following morning, they began their return to Camp Reynolds, arriving on March 27. William C. Griggs, "The Battle of Yellowhouse Canyon in 1877," pp. 37–50. In *Life in the Saddle,* Collinson, who was a participant in the battle, says many versions of it were hardly recognizable to him, "so highly were they polished and so heroically pictured were the hunters" (p. 101). There were, he states, two casualties—Spotted Jack, the hunters' guide, and one of the hunters—plus numerous men sustaining injuries. He acknowledges that if any Indians were killed or injured, the hunters saw no evidence of it. Collinson attributes their failure to lack of proper leadership and to too much drinking the previous night. As a result, he says, "we got licked and well licked" (p. 106).

5. The hunting party was camped in southeastern Dickens County, about sixty miles east of Yellowhouse Canyon. The year was 1880.

6. The Red Lake pasture was part of the Matador Ranch in northeastern Dickens County, approximately five miles east and twelve miles north of Dickens. This area came to be called Red Lake because of the color of the lake's water, a result of having red claylike soil in a small lake (tank). Verlon Bigham, interview, Lubbock, Tex., October 11, 1986.

7. Auguste Dumont emigrated from his Quebec, Canada, birthplace, Sorel, which is northeast of Montreal on Lake St. Peter. He arrived in Whitehall, New York, on the Vermont border, on November 1, 1861, when he was fifteen years of age. Wharton, *Texas under Many Flags,* p. 139. (This was the year that the author was born.) Dumont received his naturalization papers thirty-eight years later in Cottle County on May 27, 1899. Cottle County, Texas, District Clerk's Office, Auguste Dumont Declaration of Citizenship, May 27, 1899. At the current point in the narrative, Dumont and Crego's hog ranch was just east from where the Birds and McSwain were camped in northeastern Dickens County. The hog ranch, just across the county line in King County, became the spot where a post office was established. The community took the name of Dumont, and today Dumont is on Texas Farm Road 193.

8. Duck Creek crosses U.S. Highway 82 and Texas 114 three miles west of Dickens in Dickens County. In recent years, the Duck Creek Water Flood Control Project has placed two dams just north of the highway. Across the road on the south side is the Duck Creek Hunting Club for sportsmen who drive from large metropolitan areas to hunt dove, quail, and pheasant. According to Brune, Duck Creek is so named because flocks of ducks stopped at the water holes along the creek, which is a stream draining from the High Plains. Brune, *Springs of Texas,* p. 12.

9. The Western Trail had been opened in the late spring of 1876, leading past Fort Griffin to a new market at Dodge City, Kansas. Gard, *The Great Buffalo Hunt,* p. 221. Though Fort Griffin was almost seventy-five miles southeast of the Birds' headquarters, establishment of ranches in the Griffin area was probably very influ-

ential in the spread of the new business over the entire area to the west. According to Webb, the cowmen had, within five years following 1877, covered the Western Plains, and had taken the Panhandle and the arid and broken spaces drained by the Pecos River. Webb, *The Texas Rangers,* p. 425.

10. The year was 1880.

11. Chester White pigs are so named because of their white color and because the foundation stock for this breed of swine originally came from Chester County, Pennsylvania. H. B. Dawson, *The Hog Book,* pp. 11, 63.

Chapter Eight

1. The "foot of the plains" that the author refers to is most often called "the Caprock." Brune explains that this is the escarpment bordering the High Plains, "a calcareous stratum lying a few feet below the topsoils. . . . This formation blocked the erosional forces and formed the escarpments that brood over the adjacent lowlands." Brune, *Springs of Texas,* pp. 12, 162. People who live in the area settled by the author refer to the location of a place or a person above the escarpment as being "up on the Caprock." Although the author says that they headed for the Canadian Breaks, the nearest point of the Canadian River breaks would have been 150 miles from the Birds' settlement—far up into the Texas Panhandle. The breaks that the author mentions were more likely the rugged cliffs and canyons in picturesque Palo Duro Canyon. Inasmuch as the author states that they "struck one of the line camps on the Goodnight Range," the bear hunt was probably in what is now Armstrong County, southeast of Amarillo. The distance from the Birds' home settlement would have been about one hundred miles.

2. The time of the narrative was 1880. However, the actual Shoe Nail Ranch did not exist until F. P. Knott purchased fifty thousand acres of unappropriated public land in July 1883. The land, located in what would become Childress County, had previously been occupied, though not owned, by Bill and Tom Curtis and Tom Adkinson. They had grazed their cattle there for a few years beginning in 1879 before deciding to move farther west. C. B. McClure, "A History of the Shoe Nail Ranch," pp. 69–70.

3. According to Collinson, dugouts "were constructed by digging into a bank near water, with logs on the side for support. The top was covered with poles, mud, and soil and supported by a ridgepole. The average dugout was about ten by twelve feet, and two or three men could live comfortably in one. They were warm in winter and cool in summer. There was a fireplace in them, with a chimney, dug down. I lived in prairie homes [dugouts] half of my life—and spent my happiest days in them." Collinson, *Life in the Saddle,* pp. 121–122.

4. Colonel Charles Goodnight established his JA Ranch in Palo Duro Canyon in 1876. Headquarters were in southeastern Armstrong County. Harley True Burton, *A History of the JA Ranch,* p. 36. Goodnight's partner was John George Adair

of Ireland. While Adair provided the financing, Goodnight furnished the foundation herd and directed the ranch. The JA brand came from Adair's initials. J. Evetts Haley, *Charles Goodnight: Cowman and Plainsman,* pp. 295, 301.

5. Baylor County, of which Seymour is the county seat, had been organized just over a year previously—in 1879. *Texas Almanac, 1986–87,* p. 241.

6. There is no mention of John Harding in Britton's *The Early History of Baylor County,* which catalogs hundreds of early settlers, nor do the Baylor County records supply any documentation regarding him. Haley, letter, November 10, 1986.

7. The boy's first name was an abbreviation of the word *captain.* He was most likely named in honor of his grandfather, Joseph Bird, who had been a captain in the Confederate Army. Oma Dumont, Interview, April 12, 1963. The tombstone in the Paducah cemetery lists Capp *James* Bird, not Capp *Jay* as the author says here. His date of birth on the grave marker is listed as April 4, 1881, not March 1. J. Verne Dumont, Letter, Paducah, Texas, October 21, 1986. Capp Bird held the popular distinction of being the first white child born in King County, although he was actually born in Seymour, the Baylor County seat.

8. Like the Oxford ranch, the McCuin ranch is not on record. Haley, letter, November 10, 1986.

9. Williams says that John Farrar began running cattle with the JF brand in northeastern King County shortly after the buffalo herds were gone. (This would have been just north of the Birds' settlement, probably in 1878.) In 1888, Farrar branded 3,300 calves and sold out to Mabry, Crawford, and Glasgow of Graham for fifty dollars a head. Soon afterward, Glasgow sold his interest to his partners. The JF Ranch became the ranch of R. B. Masterson and sons in 1898. Williams, *The Big Ranch County,* p. 136. Today Farrar Creek appears on the map in northeastern King County. The sale of cows that the author is speaking of in 1881 must have been to John Farrar and not to Mabry, Crawford, and Glasgow, who came later.

10. In the days before fences, cattle were kept on the range by cowboys who rode out from the dugout camps each day. They would drive back all the cattle that were drifting off the range. Later when fences were built, it was the line rider's job to keep up all the fences on his part of the ranch. Harry H. Campbell, *Early History of Motley County,* pp. 30–31.

11. A Pitchfork brand was first registered in 1843 in the name of Norman Savage in Matagorda County on the Texas Gulf Coast. Gus L. Ford, *Texas Cattle Brands,* p. 11. This version of the pitchfork faced downward with no middle prong (⊓), but the later pitchfork faced upward with the prong added (⊔). Williams, *The Big Ranch Country,* p. 109. Whether Jerry Savage, who began the West Texas ranch in about 1880, originated his Pitchfork brand or whether he obtained the earlier brand from Norman Savage on the coast is not known. There is no evidence to link the two Savage men—Norman was a native Texan, and Jerry was Irish. According to Murrah, "In the late 1870's, . . . Jerry Savage drove 2,300 head through Fort Griffin, apparently to the headwaters of the Wichita [South Wichita River in east-

ern Dickens County]. These cattle bore a pitchfork brand." David J. Murrah, *The Pitchfork Land and Cattle Company: The First Century,* p. 3. In 1881 Savage sold his interests to J. S. Godwin and Dan B. Gardner. Godwin sold out to Gardner and his new partner, Eugene Williams of St. Louis, by May 1882. Ibid. In 1883 another St. Louis citizen, A. P. Bush, Jr., bought an interest in the ranch. In December of that year, the Pitchfork Land and Cattle Company was organized in St. Louis. D. B. Gardner was elected manager and held that position for the remaining forty-five years of his life. Gardner came to be known as "the grand old man of the Pitch-forks." Williams, *The Big Ranch Country,* p. 110. The Pitchfork Land and Cattle Company today has ranching operations in three states: "The home ranch, stretch-ing across 165,000 acres of central West Texas, is located eighty miles east of Lubbock along a fourteen-mile stretch of U.S. Highway 82. In Wyoming, the Pitchfork maintains a 35,000 acre steer ranch seven miles south of Laramie. The Pitchfork's newest operation is its four-thousand-acre Flint Hills Ranch, located twenty-seven miles southwest of Topeka, Kansas." Murrah, *Pitchfork,* pp. i–iii. The Pitchfork is still owned by the same Williams family of St. Louis that founded it. Ibid., p. iii. The Pitchfork Ranch headquarters are seventeen miles east of Dickens and fourteen miles west of Guthrie, just inside eastern Dickens County on U.S. Highway 82 and Texas 114. The eastern boundary of the Pitchfork Ranch in King County is approximately twenty miles west of the Birds' original settlement.

12. The Ross Ranch that the author refers to used R O S for its brand. In 1879, C. L. ("Kit") Carter established an open-range operation covering much of south-western Cottle County and spilling over into northwestern King County, south-eastern Motley County, and northeastern Dickens County. Ross Ranch headquar-ters were in Cottle County on South Buck Creek. Long and Long, interview, March 20, 1987. The ranch consisted of 40,000 acres of land and 15,000 cattle. It was named after Carter's wife's family, the Rosses. Anne Ross Carter was a sister of Sul Ross, the famous Indian scout who became governor of Texas in 1886. Lewis Nordyke, *Great Roundup,* pp. 51, 54, 56, 101. C. L. Carter was one of the founders and first president of the Stock Raisers Association of Northwestern Texas in Graham in 1877. According to Murrah, he was the first cattleman to bring livestock to what became Pitchfork country. Murrah, *Pitchfork,* pp. 1, 3. The Pitchfork Ranch began within months following the establishment of the Ross Ranch when Jerry Savage brought his Pitchfork-branded cattle into eastern Dickens and west-ern King counties. These two ranches bordered each other in northeastern Dickens County and northwestern King County, the Ross on the north and the Pitchfork on the south.

13. "Tongue River," or the South Pease as it is officially named, begins in south-western Motley County, flowing near the southern county line, and joins the Middle Pease in western Cottle County. Collinson describes the virgin range on Tongue River as having been unparalleled: "It was the favorite route to the Plains from the Indian Territory. Water was good; grass and wood were plentiful. There were deer in every thicket and antelope on every flat. Plums, currants, and grapes,

the finest that ever grew, were plentiful. . . . I have ridden horseback over most of the West since then, from Old Mexico to Canada, but I have never seen its equal as it was in those days." Collinson, *Life in the Saddle*, p. 121. Collinson surmises that "the old Comanche buffalo-eating Indian was the most savage" of all Indians in the northern tribes perhaps because "he hated to give up that country." Ibid. Campbell explains that when Collinson and Jim White camped near Roaring Springs in the area in 1896, "the land . . . was a dense thicket of cottonwood, walnut, grape vines, currant bushes, plum thickets. . . . Rocks, pitted with holes where [the Indians] ground their corn, can be seen throughout the area to this day." Campbell, *Early History of Motley County*, p. 36. Near the head of the Tongue River flow the natural Roaring Springs, a meeting place for people of different languages for ages past. The comingling of tongues is said to be the origin of the popular name for the river. Williams, *The Big Ranch Country*, p. 122. Collinson, however, has a different story: "This stream had been called 'Lengua Negra,' meaning Black Tongue, because so many buffalo had died there from a disease that caused their tongues to swell and turn black." Collinson, *Life in the Saddle*, p. 120. Campbell says the disease was also called "Lengua Prieta," meaning dark or black tongue, according to what S. R. Coggin told Collinson. Campbell, *Early History of Motley County*, p. 36. The Birds' camp on Tongue River would have been at the point where the river enters Cottle County from Motley County and flows northward for a few miles before reentering Motley County.

Chapter Nine

1. The author's family claims that her name was *Arrie* Ella, yet she named her first daughter *Arra* Jimmie, for herself (as she states in the narrative) and for her husband whose first name was James.

2. The time was late 1882.

3. Bill was one of Tom Bird's five brothers. The names of the author's husband's brothers and sisters appear in n. 18 of this chapter. According to the author at the beginning of chapter 13, Tom Bird's birthday was February 14. In *Blanco County Families for 100 Years,* Moursand says that Bird was born in 1848 (p. 19). The dinner party, therefore, was to celebrate Bird's thirty-fifth birthday in February 1883. The author would have been twenty-one.

4. John Abbott came to the Otta area, in southeastern Cottle County, around 1880. In 1882, Abbott married Lela Prewitt, daughter of the first postmaster at Otta. Their son, Louis C. Abbott, held the distinction of being the first white child born in Cottle County—October 21, 1884. John Abbott was killed at Otta by Bill Trumble on August 16, 1886. Carmen Taylor Bennett, *Our Roots Grow Deep: A History of Cottle County,* pp. 10–11.

5. The year was 1883.

6. Sul Carter was obviously named for his mother's brother, the famous Sul Ross who became governor of Texas.

7. Thorp Spring is in Hood County, about ten miles northwest of Granbury, Texas. In September 1873, Add-Ran Male and Female College was established by Addison and Randolph Clark. In 1890 ownership was transferred to the Disciples of Christ (Christian Churches), and it became Add-Ran Christian University. In 1895 the college moved to Waco, in 1902 it became Texas Christian University, and in 1910 it moved to its permanent location in Fort Worth. Webb, *The Handbook of Texas,* 1:7; 2:734.

8. The Murphys were neighbors of the author on two occasions: between 1883 and 1885, while J. T. Bird was employed on the Ross Ranch, and from 1889 to 1895, when the author and her two children lived on South Buck Creek. This Murphy family was apparently of no relation to Pat Murphy, who married Nora Bailey in 1894 (see Ch. 18, n. 11). Pat Murphy's granddaughter, Estelle Murphy Williams of Paducah, says that her grandfather came alone to Cottle County on horseback. As for the original Murphy family, the editor has found no further references.

9. Billy Pressley, according to Williams, spent twenty-five years on the Pitch-fork Ranch, arriving at the age of thirteen to work for D. B. Gardner. Serving as an assistant to wagon boss Press Goen, he became a valuable employee of the ranch. Gardner afforded the privilege to his employees of building up their own herds, an opportunity that both Pressley and Goen took advantage of to build "successful independent ranching careers." Williams, *The Big Ranch Country,* p. 111. Pressley was "genial" and "prank-loving," delighting in feeding his favorite black horse, Chub, biscuits from the chuck wagon. Ibid., p. 105. When Pressley left the ranch, Gardner allowed him to keep the horse—an act that brought the manager a great deal of credit. Ibid., pp. 105, 111. Because of excessive droughts on the ranch from 1898 to 1902, four or five windmills were built per year. Pressley Mill, one of the windmills, was named for Billy Pressley who had acquired the affectionate title of "Uncle Billy." Murrah, *Pitchfork,* p. 15. Pressley's work on the R O S Ranch and his residency with the Birds must have been between periods of employment on the Pitchfork.

10. James Abram Garfield, the twentieth president of the United States, was shot on July 2, 1881, by Charles Jewels Guiteau and died on September 19. *The Columbia Encyclopedia,* 3d ed., s.v. "James Abram Garfield." The author is mistaken about the year because the incident she relates happened two years after Garfield's assassination.

11. The Matador Ranch was organized in 1879 in Motley County as the Matador Cattle Company, Henry Harrison "Hank" Campbell, manager. In December of 1882, the ranch was sold to a Scottish syndicate, at which time it was renamed the Matador Land and Cattle Company. Campbell remained as manager until his resignation in 1891. The ranch continued to grow until 1950 when a breakup of the Matador ranges began, and all of the property was sold to various buyers. At its height, the total holdings of the Matador Land and Cattle Company exceeded one million acres. John and Colquet Warren, *The Matadors, 1879–1951,* pp. 27, 31; Campbell, *Early History of Motley County,* p. 28. Pearce states, "The career of the Matador

was unique in that this company survived to the middle of the twentieth century, though it experienced the same vicissitudes which drove other organizations of its kind into bankruptcy or into colonizing activities. That it persisted was due to four features: 'a knowledge of good land, a reliance on the best-bred cattle, an ample source of reserves, and a sound tradition of business management.'" William M. Pearce, *The Matador Land and Cattle Company*, p. 224. Pearce quotes J. Evetts Haley, *The Heraldry of the Range* (Canyon, Tex.: Panhandle-Plains Historical Society, 1949), p. 22.

12. Elizabeth ("Lizzie") Campbell (née Bundy) was known as the "Hostess of Motley County." She began her series of annual Christmas parties in 1883, and according to the hostess, the first big affair was a huge success. Campbell, *Early History of Motley County*, p. 59. As the time in the author's narrative was 1883, the Birds obviously attended Lizzie Campbell's first big Christmas party.

13. Round Mountain is eleven miles north of Johnson City in Blanco County on U.S. Highway 281.

14. The year was 1884. As the couple married in September 1877, the seventh anniversary was approaching.

15. Rister states, "In 1877 C. Bain and Company was operating a stagecoach service from Weatherford to Jacksboro, Fort Belknap, and Griffin, and return. . . . Two years later Frank Conrad advertised daily mail and passenger services (except Sunday) of stages to and from Albany, Graham, Fort Concho, Fort Elliott, and Mount Blanco." Rister, *Fort Griffin*, pp. 203–204. Of the five Fort Griffin connections above, the route to Fort Elliott in the eastern Texas Panhandle was north to Seymour, westward through Knox County and into eastern King County, northward to Otta in southeastern Cottle County, northwestward to Teepee City in eastern Motley County, and then north to Fort Elliott in Wheeler County. Bennett, *Our Roots*, p. 9. On December 16, 1881, the Texas Central Railway Company completed laying track from Ross (eleven miles north of Waco in McLennan County) to Albany, 177 miles to the northwest. The goal of the company was to reach the Panhandle where the line would connect with a line to Colorado. Because of overbuilding and ensuing financial difficulties, however, Albany remained the terminus for nineteen years. The community prospered from shipments of cattle, and "during the early 80's Albany claimed the distinction of being the buffalo bone shipping center of the world as the hunters gathered up the bones from the hunting grounds of 1874–78 north and west of Albany." Mrs. Clifton Caldwell and James Robert Green, "The Texas Central Company," pp. 2, 4. Tom and Ella Bird would have traveled south on the stagecoach from Seymour to Fort Griffin, where they would have taken another stage south to Albany. From there they would have taken the train southeast to Ross on the Texas Central, and from Ross they would have gone south on another line to Austin.

16. Baylor County showed a population growth from 715 to 2,595 between 1880 and 1890. *Texas Almanac, 1961–62*, p. 199.

17. Dr. L. T. Wilson came to Baylor County from Stanton, Virginia, in 1879. Britton, *Early History,* p. 110.

18. Moursand says that the names of the Bird brothers and sisters, in order of birth, are as follows: William, J. T., George W., Joseph Dorriss, Mattie, Mary, Theodosia E., Julia, Kate, Julius C., Susan Rebecca, and Frank E. Moursand, *Blanco County Families,* p. 20. The author names a "Martha," who most likely is "Mattie" in Moursand's list; "Dochia" would be Theodosia E.; "Sussie" would likely be "Susan Rebecca" (perhaps the author intended "Susie"). "Julia," named by Moursand, is omitted from the author's list; therefore, she must have been the one Bird offspring who was deceased.

19. Burnet, county seat of Burnet County, is twenty-five miles north of Round Mountain on U.S. Highway 281.

20. Some blacks lived on the Great Plains in the days of the earliest settlements. After the Civil War, they were employed as cowboys or as cooks on ranches, and they also served in large numbers in the U.S. Army. Later blacks found work as house servants and as porters on passenger trains. Frederick C. Luebke, ed., *Ethnicity on the Great Plains,* p. xxii.

21. Perhaps the Birds bought a hack and team because they had purchased a tombstone for their baby's grave, which was in Seymour. The author specifies that they went "by way of Austin and stopped over one day there to select a tomb for our baby's grave." If a tombstone could have been shipped from Austin to Seymour, a distance of about 240 airline miles, it surely would have been with great difficulty—involving train and stagecoach travel. It seems probable, then, that the family would have taken the tombstone with them.

22. The Birds most likely stopped in Seymour to place the tombstone, which they had bought in Austin, on Jimmie's grave.

Chapter Ten

1. The time was the winter of 1884–1885.

2. Otta, approximately twelve miles southeast of where Paducah now stands, was the location of the first post office in Cottle County. When the post office became official on December 22, 1879, on the land of Dudley M. Prewitt, a hog rancher, Prewitt was appointed postmaster. The frontier post office was named for Prewitt's wife—Otta Prewitt. John Abbott married the Prewitts' daughter, Lela, in 1882. Bennett, *Our Roots,* pp. 9, 10. Today the springs at the site of the former post office are on land owned by Homer Long, three miles northeast of the Chalk community. These springs start some two miles upstream from Long's house on the North Wichita River. The water becomes saltier downstream; however, cattle still can drink it. Brune, *Springs of Texas,* p. 137.

3. Three times in the 1920s, the author traveled in New Mexico, visiting her

sister Lucy's sons, the Fites, and her Aunt Martha Benson and her sons, named Bass (see chapters 23 and 24).

4. The Brazos, 840 miles in length, is the third largest river in Texas. Its three upper forks are the Double Mountain and Salt Forks (which merge in eastern Stonewall County) and the Clear Fork, which joins the main stream in Young County, just above Lake Possum Kingdom. *Texas Almanac, 1986–87,* p. 48.

5. Bessie Adell Bird was born on July 22, 1885.

6. George Brandt of Kansas City, along with others, built up the 3D Ranch (officially the Hesperin Land and Cattle Company). Around 1880, he first bought 40,000 acres in Cottle County for twenty-five cents per acre. Additional purchases to the west and north of the original land brought the ranch holdings to almost 100,000 acres, shaped as a giant L, in southeastern Cottle County. Later part of the land and all of the cattle were sold to W. Q. Richards. Eventually much of Richards' Moon and 3D ranch land was bought by Tom Burnett, son of Burk Burnett of 6666 Ranch fame. Williams, *The Big Ranch Country,* pp. 129–130. According to Tom Long, the 3D Ranch was sold and the brand was retired at the time of Mr. and Mrs. W. Q. Richards' divorce in 1915. Alma Gibson Long and Tom Long, interview with editor, Paducah, Tex., March 20, 1987. Today a portion of the former 3D Ranch makes up a portion of the Triangle Ranch (∇), owned by the great-granddaughter of well-known rancher Burk Burnett, Anne Windfohr of Fort Worth.

7. The time of this killing of the last buffalo was winter 1886.

8. John and Aaron Lasater came to King County from Jack County in the spring of 1877 along with Isom Lynn. Their purpose was to find more profitable ranching facilities. Sometime later the Lasaters went back to Jack County, but Isom Lynn remained and became the first white man to become a permanent settler of King County. Lottie Gibson, "Location, Resources and History," p. 6. Following the Lasaters and Isom Lynn, Tom and Ella Bird arrived in King County in December of that same year, 1877. Rock Corrals, built by the Lasaters, is in Big River Pasture, two miles east of Guthrie. Jane Huey, telephone interview, November 25, 1986. As for the Hensleys named by the author, Holden says that two Hensley brothers (first names unavailable) lived in a dugout "down Duck Creek four miles, at the mouth of a draw coming in from the west, still known as Spade River." William Curry Holden, *The Espuela Land and Cattle Company,* p. 34. Their brand was a spade and their headquarters was in, or near, the present town site of Spur. Ibid.

9. See chapter 8, n. 12, for a brief history of the Ross (R O S) Ranch.

10. When the Matador Cattle Company was established in 1879, the 50M brand was used. In December of that year, John W. Dawson of Fort Worth sold to the new ranch a herd of thirteen hundred cattle branded "V" on the right side. The V brand was retained to avoid rebranding the entire herd, which had come from South Texas. Campbell, *Early History of Motley County,* p. 29; Ford, *Texas Cattle Brands,* pp. 159–160; Pearce, *Matador Land,* p. 8.

11. The Double N Bar (NN) brand appeared in Dickens and Kent counties from 1881 to 1887, after which it was taken to Hale County. There is no record in Ford's *Texas Cattle Brands* of sale to the Matador Land and Cattle Company. The T41 brand began in Gonzales County in the 1870s. The Matador Land and Cattle Company purchased the T41 herd in 1880. As for the O brand, Ford records nothing about it in his discussion of the Matador Ranch area. Ford, *Texas Cattle Brands*, pp. 55, 117.

12. The Jingle Bob history has been well recorded by Collinson. In 1878, S. R. Coggin, of Brownwood, Texas, and Pitser Chisum, youngest brother of John Simpson Chisum of the Chisum Ranch on the Pecos River in New Mexico, came to Hank Smith's ranch in Blanco Canyon (the rock walls of the ranch house, which burned around 1940, still stand today at the intersection of Texas Farm roads 651 and 1063 in northern Crosby County). Collinson was staying there following his leaving the buffalo camp on Tongue River. Upon discovering that Collinson knew the area thoroughly, Coggin hired the former buffalo hunter to drive 8,000 cattle from the Chisum Ranch (the cattle were payment of a debt from Chisum to Coggin) to a good range in Texas. Collinson immediately chose his former camp site for the new ranch. The cattle, a fine herd of Shorthorns, sported an unusual identification feature: they were the only cattle known by a mark instead of a brand. Of course, like all cattle they had a brand, in this case, "a Rail on the ribs, a long straight bar on the left side (—)." Collinson, *Life in the Saddle*, p. 117. But it was the earmark that was unique: "To make this mark, the ear was split at the top and the two main leaders cut. This made the ear drop back and hang toward the neck," a feature that brought the label "Jingle Bob." Ibid. The drive to Texas involved two herds, one led by Collinson and the second by R. K. ("Bob") Wylie. Ibid., pp. 114–119. Pearce says that two camps were established early in 1879, one near Roaring Springs (at the head of Tongue River in southern Motley County) and the other near Teepee City (in northeastern Motley County). Pearce, *Matador Land*, p. 6. According to Collinson, "In May 1881, the Matador Land and Cattle Company bought the entire interest of the Jingle Bob herd from Coggin and Wiley, along with their horses and the land they had script on." Collinson, *Life in the Saddle*, p. 129. As for the Frying Pan brand (O—) connected by the author to the Jingle Bob herd, a Frying Pan brand was registered in Motley County in 1897, but cattle with this brand became a part of the Scarborough Ranch holdings in the Midland and Andrews counties area. Ford, *Texas Cattle Brands*, p. 158. The author may be confusing Chisum's Fence Rail brand with the Frying Pan.

13. Frank Collinson and his fellow buffalo hunters discovered a clear spring along Tongue River in the summer of 1876. They named the springs Roaring Springs. Campbell, *Early History of Motley County*, p. 20. It is located eight miles south of Matador in southern Motley County on Texas 70. Brune states, "Five kilometers [three miles] south of the town of that name are [*sic*] Roaring Springs. . . . Part of Coronado's army may have been camped here in 1541. When the buffalo hunters arrived in the 1870's, they found the poles of Comanche tepees still stand-

ing at Roaring Springs, probably abandoned a year or two earlier. In fact, this was the main camp of the Comanches in 1860." Brune, *Springs of Texas*, p. 338.

14. Jim Hall moved his Spur-branded cattle (⊃—) from his range near Richland Springs in San Saba County to government lands in northeastern New Mexico in 1877. In 1878 Hall purchased 1,500 head from Refugio County, Texas, cattle that were driven to Motley County by one of Hall's old hands, J. R. Beasley. Settling at the head of the Middle Pease River, Beasley bought for Hall, from a buffalo hunter, a claim with a dugout on it. This spot was the first headquarters of what would become the Spur Ranch. In 1879 Hall purchased approximately 800 cattle from his brothers in New Mexico and moved the herd to the new Motley County headquarters. When the cattle arrived, Hall moved his consolidated herd to Red Mud Creek in southwestern Dickens County, about ten miles southwest of the present town of Spur. In the fall of 1882 Hall sold all of his cattle—and the Spur brand—to Tom P. Stephens and Coleman Harris, who, the following spring, sold out to the Espuela Cattle Company. These holdings transferred to the Espuela Land and Cattle Company of Fort Worth in 1884, which became the Espuela Land and Cattle Company, Limited, of London in 1885. Holden, *Espuela Land and Cattle*, pp. 39–44. The principal investors of this company were Scotsmen, who sold out to the Swensons of New York in 1907. The new owners immediately began changing from the old Spur brand to their own 2M2 brand. The last herd of 20,000 Spur-branded cattle was sold to W. J. Lewis of Dallas in 1910. At the time of Williams's writing in 1954, the Spur brand was still being run on Lewis's ranch in Hall County. Williams, *The Big Ranch Country*, pp. 94–95. Ford records Lewis's account of the transaction: "'I bought all the cattle under the 'Spur' brand from the Swenson Bros. in 1910 and am still running the brand in Hall County. At that time there were about 20,000 cattle, counting the calves. Today [1936] there are about 2,000 Herefords on 55,000 acres.'" Ford, *Texas Cattle Brands*, p. 130. Whereas Holden says that the first headquarters of the Spur Ranch were established by J. R. Beasley at the head of the Middle Pease River, a location with which Tom Long of Paducah agrees, Williams states that the headquarters were at the head of the North Pease near the Quitaque Peaks. Alma Gibson Long and Tom Long, telephone interview, February 27, 1987; Williams, *The Big Ranch Country*, p. 93. These two peaks rise above the horizon in northwestern Motley County. The author concurs with Williams that the location was "on the headwater of the North Pease River about ten miles south of Quitaque Peaks."

15. For a brief history of the Pitchfork brand and the Pitchfork Ranch see chapter 8, n. 11.

16. Cowboy Sam Graves drove cattle bearing the Eight brand (OO) not the Scab Eight (8=8), from Jack County to King County, arriving June 19, 1882. The ranch was located in southeastern King County, in an area known as "Little Arizona," jokingly named by cattlemen who moved there after an exodus of other cattlemen to the free ranges of Arizona in the early 1880s. Sam Lazurus, the owner, hired Bud Arnett as manager. In 1883, Lazurus sold out to the Louisville Land and Cattle

Company, who later sold to S. B. ("Burk") Burnett in 1900. With the change in operation, the Eight cattle became a part of Burnett's now famous "6666" herd. Williams, *The Big Ranch Country,* pp. 22, 25–29; King County Historical Society, ed., *King County: Windmills and Barbed Wire,* pp. 26–27; Ford, *Texas Cattle Brands,* p. 176. The Scab Eight Ranch, which the author has confused with the ranch of the Eight brand, was in the Tongue River area between Cottle and Motley counties. "Scab Eight" was a term given the brand by cowboys because the brand often scabbed over and peeled off between the equal marks. Williams, *The Big Ranch Country,* p. 126. Headquarters of the Scab Eight were a string of dugouts on the head of Bluff Creek near the present Matador-Paducah highway at the Motley-Cottle county line. Campbell, *Early History of Motley County,* p. 54. Brune states, "Scab 8 Springs were 22 kilometers east of Matador on Highway 70, on O. J. Barron's Tongue River Ranch, managed by Taylor Martin. . . . According to Martin, the flow . . . could water 1,000 head of cattle at the old Scab 8 ranch headquarters. The springs have been dry since 1945." Brune, *Springs of Texas,* p. 338. In 1898 the 79,000-acre Scab Eight Ranch became the property of the Swenson Brothers Cattle Company. The cattle were branded with 2M2, and the name was changed to the Tongue River Ranch. Mary Whatley Clarke, *The Swenson Saga and the SMS Ranches,* p. 135. In 1981 the Swenson Land and Cattle Company sold the Tongue River Ranch to O. J. Barron, thus ending almost 75 years of Swenson ranching in Motley, Cottle, Dickens, and King counties.

17. See chapter 8, n. 9, for a brief history of John Farrar and his JF brand. No record exists of a King County Livestock Company.

18. The Moon brand ($\frown$) was registered in about 1865 in Fannin County, in northeast Texas, by Charlie Cannon from Bolivar, which is in Denton County. Ford, *Texas Cattle Brands,* p. 117. Apparently the author is mistaken about the Moon brand being trailed from Shackleford County one hundred miles to the southeast. In 1879, fourteen years later, Cannon was ranching on the North Wichita River, in southeastern Cottle County. Four years later Cannon lost his life in Seymour, and shortly afterward the Moon cattle were bought by Lindsay, Bedford, and Hinton and remained in Cottle County. The next owner was an Englishman named Maud, who was followed by a man named Grey that sold 60,000 acres to W. Q. Richards in 1902. Richards is the best remembered of all the Moon Ranch owners. Williams, *The Big Ranch Country,* pp. 128–129. Two or three years after Richards' death in 1922, the administrators of Richards' estate, O. L. Thomas and Judge A. J. Fires of Childress and Ben Tippen of Paducah, sold the ranch. Long and Long, interview, March 20, 1987. Richards had left $50,000 for construction of a hospital in Paducah and $2,500 for upkeep of the cemetery. Bennett, *Our Roots,* p. 96. In 1929, W. Q. Richards Memorial Hospital was built. The former Moon Ranch is now part of the Triangle Ranch in eastern Cottle County, owned by the great-granddaughter of well-known rancher Burk Burnett, Anne Windfohr of Fort Worth.

19. See n. 6 in this chapter for a brief history of the 3D Ranch.

20. Williams says that in the open-range days of the early 1880s ten to fifteen thousand head of cattle wore the OX brand at the junction of the two forks of the Pease in northeastern Cottle County. The brand was first used around 1875 in Denton County by George Merchant, who sold in three or four years to Cairns and Forsythe Brothers of Gainesville. The latter trailed the herds up to the forks of the Pease. The headquarters for the ranch was in Childress County north of the junction of the rivers. Supposedly the ranch house was the first house built in Childress County. Cairns apparently sold his interest to one of the Forsythe brothers, who ran the ranch until 1894 when he sold out to D. D. Swearingen and associates. The OX brand continued until 1930. A large piece of the ranch became the Portwood Ranch (in 1952), owned by W. H. Portwood of Seymour. Another part of the ranch (32,000 acres) became the YL Ranch, which was purchased in 1929 by Tom Burnett and added to his Triangle Ranch holdings. Williams, *The Big Ranch Country,* pp. 127–128, 202. Robertson and Robertson report that the OX Ranch was organized in 1882 and that it remained intact until 1905 when "much of the OX land was sold off for as low as 55 cents per acre." Pauline Durrett Robertson and R. L. Robertson, *Cowman's Country: Fifty Frontier Ranches in the Texas Panhandle, 1876–1887,* p. 123.

21. Though Texas cowmen asked for a lease act to permit them to lease the public domain, if the state wouldn't sell them the lands, the legislature passed instead the Land Board Act of 1883. Haley, *Charles Goodnight,* p. 383. Haley, quoting in part from the legislation, explains that it "provided for the competitive sale of as many as seven sections to the individual; that ranch lands 'may be leased . . . for not less than four cents per annum' for not more than ten years; and that leases were to be let competitively upon such terms as the State Land Board . . . might designate." Ibid., p. 384. Early the following year, however, the board gave permission "for county surveyors to receive bids for both sale and lease of public lands." Ibid. The competitive features of leasing were seen to be "inapplicable" because the ranges were already filled with cowmen who had bought parts of their ranges, built tanks, and fenced their grassland. Ibid.

22. Few fences had existed in Texas before the invention of barbed wire because of a scarcity of wood and stone. When the new wire began to appear on the ranges, the small cowmen opposed its use, because they usually lacked money to buy land and fence it—the open range was their only hope. Opposition turned to fury when these open-range cowmen discovered fencers enclosing land they neither owned nor leased. Appeals to legislators and the governor were ignored, and, as a result, the fence cutters' war of 1883 ignited. Many of the cutters formed bands, some of them with names such as Owls, Javelina, and Blue Devils. They usually worked at night, destroying wiring and posts and leaving warnings against rebuilding the fences. Occasionally the destruction included pasture burnings. Finally, on January 8, 1884, Governor John Ireland, who had avoided the issue, called a special session of the legislature. Fence cutting and pasture burning became felonies, and fencing public land or land belonging to others became a misdemeanor. Enforce-

ment of these laws eventually diminished the fence troubles, but as late as 1888, ranchmen in Navarro County had their fences cut by a group of cowmen with small operations. The era of the open range ended with fencing, and its end led to the development of the great Texas ranches. Gard, *Rawhide Texas,* pp. 75–77. John Gibson, a well-known rancher of Cottle and King counties for many years, helped to fence the Moon Ranch, the Eight Ranch, the 3D Ranch, and the Pitchfork Ranch in 1883 and 1884. Gibson stated that barbed wire was expensive at that time. Fencers used bois d'arc and cedar posts, and the workers earned twenty dollars per mile of fencing. Bennett, *Our Roots,* p. 16.

23. The time was the winter of 1885–1886, not 1884–1885 as the author states.

24. On December 31, 1885, the "Great White Ruin" roared into the northern states and devastated the range lands from the Dakotas to the Rio Grande. Nordyke, *Great Roundup,* p. 156. Cattle, horses, people—everything unprotected—died. Nordyke says, "Cattle crashed off bluffs, walked straight into bogs, piled up in ditches. . . . Nearly every waterhole and lake was filled with cattle that drowned, froze or were trampled to death there. . . . Everywhere that there was an east-west fence, cattle stacked up against it and died, some of them still standing." Ibid., p. 157. After the wind and snow ceased, cattle that had survived in their march southward were no better off. Waterholes were frozen and the grass was covered with snow and ice. Many of the cattle died of starvation, and others fell to lobo wolves thirsting for warm blood. Ibid., p. 158.

25. The term *cowboy* originated in 1766 in Dutchess County, New York. It was a term given by patroons (owners of manor farms) to Samuel Munro and his followers, who organized raids against the manor farms as resisters to manorial oppression in behalf of dispossessed tenants. These raiders took "pigs, chickens, horses, and cows." Charles Zurhorst, *The First Cowboys and Those Who Followed,* p. 29. As the cow population on the manor farms decreased, the patroons coined the disparaging term "cow-boy" to refer to Munro and his rebels. In the early 1770s the term became synonymous with the words "robber" and "bandit." Opportunists committed frequent acts of violence and robbery in the colonies, falsely identifying themselves as cowboys and members of the Sons of Liberty, which had become the head of Munro's efforts. Munro's cowboys and their descendants eventually carried their name and their characteristics to the West. Ibid., pp. 29–30. Soule offers a different origin for the term. After the battles for Texas independence at the Alamo and San Jacinto, some young men "drifted into west Texas near the Rio Grande and Mexico and lived as best they could." Gardner Soule, *The Long Trail: How Cowboys and Longhorns Opened the West,* p. 27. The longhorn cattle in the area, which had formerly been ranched by Spaniards and Americans, had returned to the wild. These young men hunted the "night-prowling, night-foraging longhorns," eating the beef and using the leather for their clothing. Ibid. Led by Ewen Cameron, a group of them were known as Cameron's Cowboys. Eventually all of these men came to be called "a new name: the cowboys." Ibid.

26. *Sut Lovingood: Yarns Spun by a "Nat'ral Born Durn'd Fool,"* by George Wash-

ington Harris, was published in 1867. It is considered a masterpiece of frontier humor. Donald McQuade, ed., *The Harper American Literature,* p. 2209. *Peck's Bad Boy and His Pa,* by George Wilbur Peck, was published in 1882. Peck attracted more readers than any other writer of literature about humorous bad boys than Mark Twain. Alleen Pace Nilsen and Kenneth L. Donelson, *Literature for Today's Young Adults,* pp. 516–517.

27. As cattle rustling became widespread, the cowmen saw a need to organize for action. On February 15 and 16, 1877, under a now-famous old oak tree in Graham, the Stock Raisers Association of Northwestern Texas was founded by forty men. The first president was C. L. ("Kit") Carter. Nordyke, *Great Roundup,* pp. 17, 51, 96. The association hired "brand inspectors" to examine cattle in shipping pens and in trail herds passing through the country. These experts could detect evidence of brand changing or blotting. Whitlock, *Cowboy Life,* p. 147. Carter established the Ross (R O S) Ranch two years later, in 1879, in adjoining corners of Cottle, Motley, Dickens, and King counties.

Chapter Eleven

1. A "willow tail" (the author says "'willer tail'") is a horse, usually a mare, which has a loose, long, coarse, heavy tail—not an indication of good breeding. Adams, *Western Words,* p. 177.

2. Mr. Carr became the author's neighbor three years later in 1889, when she moved south to the Buck Creek area, near the Ross Ranch headquarters. Lorene Carr of Paducah lives on the original Carr land, ten miles southwest of Paducah on Texas Farm Road 2278. The grandparents of her husband Cecil, Mr. and Mrs. T. M. ("Tom") Carr, were the neighbors the author refers to in her text. Both the grandparents and the parents (Mr. and Mrs. T. W. Carr) of Cecil Carr are buried in Buck Creek Cemetery. Lorene Carr, Interview, Paducah, Texas, March 20, 1987. Cecil Carr died in October 1979.

3. Adams says that when a calf was killed, the tongue, liver, heart, lights (lungs), kidneys, sweetbreads, and brain were chopped up into small bits and stewed slowly in an iron kettle. Some people might throw in potatoes, tomatoes, or anything else that was handy. If the eater could tell what was in it, it was not a first-class stew. One cowboy, according to Adams, remarked, "'You throw ever'thing in the pot but the hair, horns, and holler.'" Adams, *Western Words,* p. 150. The longer it cooked, the better it was. If the cowboy wished to be polite, he called it son-of-a-gun stew, but if no delicate ears were present, he called it by its true fighting name—son-of-a-bitch stew. Ibid., p. 150.

4. *Bronc peeler* is another name for a rider of the range string, a string composed of wild and semiwild horses that fight every time they are saddled. Every ranch that raises its own horses has some that have never felt the saddle. Ibid., pp. 19, 132.

5. The gathering of buffalo bones began in Texas before the slaughter of the

animals was completed. The bones were hauled to cities with carbon works where they were prepared for use in refining sugar (the calcium phosphate neutralized the acid of the cane juice). Old bones were ground into meal for sale as fertilizer, and the most choice ones went into bone china. The horns provided material for buttons, combs, and knife handles. Gatherers received six to eight dollars a ton until the market was glutted, when they sometimes received as little as four dollars. The bone boom seldom lasted more than two or three years in any one section of the country. Gard says "Texas railroads shipped more than half a million tons of buffalo bones. Even at six dollars a ton, that meant more than three million dollars for the gatherers." Gard, *The Great Buffalo Hunt*, pp. 296, 300, 303–304. Sometimes the bone fields became battlefields because of the competition among pickers. To subdue these "bone wars," the pickers invoked the hide hunter's unwritten law—one picker was not to enter "another's territory or molest any of his things. . . . Bone law recognized the right of discovery, pre-emption, and priority to a reasonable area, often a stand where hide hunters had killed buffaloes for a day's skinning." Ralph A. Smith, "The West Texas Bone Business," p. 125.

6. The new home was in western Cottle County, north of present U.S. Highways 62 and 70 connecting Paducah and Matador.

7. Louis Abbott, son of John Abbott, writes in a letter to Carmen Taylor Bennett on January 4, 1969: "'I was born October 21, 1884 and the tragedy of which Mrs. Ella Bird Dumont speaks occurred on August 16, 1886. My father was warned against going to the spring because Trumble was known to be in the vicinity, but I, being just 22 months old, insisted on going with him and in order to please me he led me by the hand to the spring. While dipping up water from the spring and holding me by one hand, the shots were fired by Trumble from ambush. My father was unarmed.'" Bennett, *Our Roots*, p. 11.

8. Although cramps, painful spasmodic contractions of muscles, most commonly occur in the limbs, they may also affect certain internal organs. "The cause of these painful seizures," according to one medical dictionary, "resides in the nervous system, and operates either directly from the great nerve centres, or, as is generally the case, indirectly by reflex action, as, for example, when attacks are brought on by some derangement of the digestive organs." *Black's Medical Dictionary*, 34th ed., s.v. "cramp." Alma and Tom Long suggest that perhaps Tom Bird's cramps could have been chronic appendicitis. The appendix might have ruptured causing peritonitis. Long and Long, letter, February 24, 1987.

9. The year was 1886. Capp would have been five years old, not seven, and Bessie would have been fourteen months old.

10. Quanah, Texas, was established in Hardeman County in 1884, just across the Red River from the southwestern portion of the Indian reservation of the town's namesake—Quanah Parker. Southeast of the town are conical, flat-topped hills, the largest of which is Medicine Mound, where Comanche warriors sought sacred visions for generations. When the Quanah, Acme and Pacific Railway Company was chartered in the early 1900s, Quanah Parker invested $40,000. The railroad

(the QA&P) stretched westward from the town of Quanah through Cottle and Motley counties to Floydada in Floyd County. Neeley, *Quanah Parker and His People,* p. 169. In 1890, Quanah had a population of 1,500 people. Webb, *The Handbook of Texas,* 2:422–423. The author is writing about the winter of 1886–1887. She states later, on the eve of her departure for Quanah with Mrs. Bailey, that Quanah was "about fifty miles away."

11. Groesbeck Creek has both a north and a south fork, which join and empty into the Red River in Hardeman County.

12. Thomas William White was nicknamed "Willie."

Chapter Twelve

1. The John Baileys were very early settlers west of Paducah. Long and Long, letter, February 24, 1987.

2. Catfish Creek begins in east central Cottle County and drains to the north into the South Pease River. Webb, *The Handbook of Texas,* 1:309.

3. According to Q. Bailey of Paducah, the youngest son of Mr. and Mrs. John Bailey, the baby on the Quanah trip was Myrtle. Five or six older children were left at home. Bennett, *Our Roots,* p. 17.

4. Brune corroborates the author's statement that the rain was partially to blame for the decomposition of the tombstone: "As gypsum is quite soluble, water moving through it tends to dissolve out caverns." Brune, *Springs of Texas,* p. 271. Geraldine Daughtry of the current Quanah Historical Commission states that no record of Tom Bird exists with the local funeral director, and the location of the grave is unknown. In the early 1970s a massive cleanup of the cemetery destroyed both hand-carved wooden markers and stone markers, an act that today's Historical Commission regrets. Geraldine Daughtry, letter, Quanah, Tex., February 6, 1987. Until the editor's correspondence with Daughtry, no one in Quanah was aware that such a distinguished Texas Ranger, buffalo hunter, and rancher as J. T. Bird was buried in the local cemetery.

5. A *swag* is a low place. Adams, *Western Words,* p. 160.

6. Hidebugs are "*Dermestes ladarius* larvae (also known as 'bacon beetles,' 'larder beetles,' and 'hide beetles')" that "attack furs, hides and stored meat and cheese. There are 731 species, occurring worldwide." *The Oxford Dictionary of Natural History,* s.v., "Dermestidae." Belonging to class Insecta and order Coleoptera, they are a family of black or brown small beetles, often with a pattern of fine hair or scales. Ibid.

7. *Slather* means a large quantity, a good deal, much. *A Dictionary of Americanisms,* s.v. "slather." The author's *slathered* would likely mean to go into something with great force.

8. Bennett reports a conversation that she had with Q. Bailey about his sister Myrtle and the antelope. It seems that the baby's (Myrtle's) cries were what attracted the antelope herd to the travelers. If the baby had stopped crying, the herd

might have run away. Ella Bird, trying to draw a bead on the animals, reportedly said, "'For goodness sake, Mrs. Bailey, let the baby cry until I can kill some of these antelope!'" Bennett, *Our Roots*, p. 19.

9. The year was 1887.

10. The *Nogal Nugget*, a Democratic weekly newspaper printed in English, came from Nogal, New Mexico, in Lincoln County. It began in August 1887, and in 1889 it was moved to Lincoln, New Mexico, taking the new name of The *Liberty Banner*. It ceased publication in April 1891. Porter A. Stratton, *The Territorial Press of New Mexico 1834–1912*, pp. 279–280. As the time in the narrative is 1887, the year The *Nogal Nugget* began, the author must have been a charter subscriber to the newspaper. Most likely Tom Bird subscribed during his visit to New Mexico in search of a home for his family in the mountains. We can assume that Lincoln County was an area he was considering.

11. *Chocy* is probably an English corruption of the Spanish *choza*, meaning a hut or a cabin.

12. Childress is the county seat of Childress County, on U.S. Highways 62, 83, and 287, just north of Cottle County where the author lived. Childress County increased from 25 to 1,175 people from 1880 to 1890. *Texas Almanac, 1961–62*, p. 199.

13. As late as 1903, Dr. J. N. Albert signed birth and death certificates in Childress County. The courthouse and records burned in 1891, so no additional information is available. Winona Furr (District and County Clerk of Childress County), letter, November 24, 1986.

14. The year was 1888.

15. According to Webb's *The Handbook of Texas*, there was no town in Motley County in 1891 when the county was organized (2:156). Traweek concurs, saying that the first activity upon organization of the county in 1891 was instrumentation of plans to build a courthouse for the county. The town of Matador grew up around this building. Eleanor Mitchell Traweek, *Of Such As These: A History of Motley County and Its Families*, p. 16. As the time in the author's narrative is 1888, Matador was nonexistent. The man who could have built the hack top probably lived thirty-five miles from the author on the immense Matador Ranch.

16. Crouch says, "No social gathering in the country ever compared to the reunion on the Clear Fork where several hundred persons put up tents for a week's encampment that attracted visitors from over the state. Here politicians announced their platforms and denounced their opponents, and bands vied with each other. Families found this general meeting the time and place for their own reunions; clubs and organizations met here." Crouch, *A History of Young County*, p. 77.

17. "Uncle Charles" (Benson), the brother of the author's mother, had rescued the author, her mother, her sister, and her half-brother in Memphis at the end of the Civil War. Crouch makes no reference to Charles Benson as a citizen of Graham in her *A History of Young County, Texas*.

18. George W. Black came to Young County in 1876. He first made his home in Tonk Valley where he organized a Baptist church. On April 13, 1880, he and two

other ministers organized a church in Graham: "Reverend Black served as third and fifth pastor of this church, holding a long pastorate each time." Crouch, *A History of Young County,* pp. 177–178. The author is writing of the effect of her grandmother's death on the people of Graham. At the time of her death, the grandmother was no longer Mrs. Benson but was named Michener. Oma Dumont, interview, April 12, 1963.

19. Edgar Rye, as quoted by Adams, corroborates the author's opinion of cowboys, stating, "'Nowhere on God's footstool were women and children safer than under the protecting care of the cowboys. They never failed to respond to an appeal for help when the lives and homes of the early settlers were in danger. With his pony and arms the cowboy placed his life at their service and boldly marched to victory or death.'" Ramon Adams, ed., *The Best of the American Cowboy,* p. 28.

20. The author wrote her manuscript in 1927 and 1928, so Sul Carter's death must have been in 1926 or 1927. Carter had been foreman of the former Ross (R O S) Ranch in Cottle, King, Motley, and Dickens counties, the ranch that was owned by his father, C. L. ("Kit") Carter.

Chapter Thirteen

1. At the time of Capp Bird's death, November 6, 1957, the small carved Bible and Capp's old violin were given to his oldest son, Capp, Jr. The latter died during the 1970s in New Mexico. Current location of the Bible and the violin are unknown. Oma Dumont, interview, April 12, 1963; J. Verne Dumont, letter, October 21, 1986.

2. This vase, which is extremely heavy, is all that remains in the Dumont family of the author's carvings. J. Verne Dumont, the author's grandson, has the vase in his home. As for the other pieces, some were stolen and some were destroyed in the storm that blew away the Birds' home in 1895 (see chapter 18).

3. The CV brand in northwestern Cottle County is probably the same CV first used by Claiborn Varner in Somervell County, southwest of Fort Worth. In 1856, young Charlie Goodnight and his stepbrother, Wes Sheek, contracted with Varner for 430 head of cattle to be kept on shares for ten years. Eight years later, in 1864, Goodnight and Sheek bought Varner's entire CV stock, paying seven dollars per head in gold. Sometime between 1865 and 1867, the CV cattle were traded to a Comanchero, José Pieda Tafoya, in the Quitaque country (in Briscoe County at the site of present-day Quitaque). Haley, *Charles Goodnight,* pp. 13, 112, 190. Tafoya usually traded dry goods and ammunition to the Indians for rustled cattle. Webb, *The Handbook of Texas,* 2:425. The Goodnight-Sheek transaction with Tafoya was, no doubt, a more legitimate trade. Inasmuch as the CV Ranch mentioned by the author was only about thirty-five miles east of the Quitaque area, Tafoya must have sold the CV cattle to landowners who named their ranch for the brand. The CV Ranch in northwestern Cottle County became a part of the Hughes brothers' Mill Iron Ranch following the establishment of the latter. J. B. Brothers, interview,

Paducah, Tex., May 3, 1963. This larger Mill Iron spread, incorporated in 1881, spilled over into Childress, Cottle, Hall, and Motley counties. Lee Gilmore, "The Mill Iron Ranch," p. 57. Today the community of Cee Vee, with its post office, is on Texas Farm Road 1440 in northwestern Cottle County.

4. The year was 1888.

5. Teepee Creek received its name because it was once a favorite camping place for Indians. Teepee City, on Teepee Creek, began as a trading post, established in 1875 by Charles Rath and Lee Reynolds. Shortly afterward the post was taken over by S. N. Armstrong and a fellow named Sharp. Here was the post office for the Pease River Valley. Armstrong operated a hotel and saloon—with dance hall girls—along with the post. Old-timers reported later that there were two rooms: one for the saloon and the other for the hotel, where everyone bunked together. Frank Collinson told Harry Campbell in an El Paso interview that Rath and Reynolds intended to start the trading post but that they stayed only about two weeks. Collinson said that Armstrong and Sharp, who must have come with them, actually established the post. Armstrong stayed from 1875 until his death. Today a stone marker on the west side of the creek is a reminder of the early post office. Campbell, *Early History of Motley County*, pp. 12–13, 35, 49; Williams, *The Big Ranch Country*, pp. 124–125; Traweek, *Of Such As These*, p. 46. Traweek cites the inscription on the stone marker: "'Camp of early buffalo hunters. Only settlement west of Henrietta, north of Fort Griffin and south of Fort Elliott (now Mobeetie) 1875–1880. Headquarters of Texas Rangers under Captain G. W. Arrington at intervals 1879–1881. Abandoned about 1886. First white child born in Motley County was Nora Cooper, born here in 1882. S. N. Armstrong, pioneer merchant, buried near this site.'" Traweek, *Of Such As These*, p. 46. The monument was erected by the state of Texas in 1936. Ibid. The location of Teepee City is fourteen airline miles east-northeast of Matador or eighteen miles by car, over paved, graveled, and dirt road. From the Matador-Paducah highway, the location is nine and one-half miles northeast. Teepee City was four miles from the Motley-Cottle county line, and the author was living in Cottle County near Tongue River next to the eastern border of the Matador Ranch; therefore, the distance from her home to Teepee City would have been ten or eleven miles, not five as she says in the text.

6. Virginia Gober was a sister to W. Q. Richards of the 3D and Moon ranches. She and her husband Joe came to Cottle County before T. J. Richards, another brother, arrived and began his large-scale ranching business. Long and Long, letter, February 24, 1987. Joe Gober, first sheriff of Cottle County (from 1892 to 1898) was a close friend of Tom Bird's in earlier years, a friendship that Gober discusses in a personal letter to the author. Obviously Gober had requested that the author give him Tom Bird's famous rifle: "In regard to the gun, I did not know just how much Capp and you appreciated this gun. I wonder if I was the last man to kill a deer with it? As you know, after Tom gave you the gun, he hunted very little, if any, with it. He used to let me have it when I hunted with him. The last hunt we were on, I killed a deer. . . . There were very few people [who] knew what close

friends Tom and I were. . . . I hope you and Capp fully understand me. I merely wanted the gun to refresh some memories of that past. I did not know you were writing the life of yourself and Tom. I know I can have one of the first that comes out." Joe Gober to Ella Bird Dumont, February 14, 1933, Ella Bird Dumont Collection, Panhandle-Plains Historical Museum, Canyon, Tex.

7. Buck Creek, which crosses U.S. Highway 83 seven miles south of Paducah, branches only a few yards west of the highway into North Buck Creek and South Buck Creek. The latter stream stretches westward through southwestern Cottle County. Four branches of South Buck Creek cross Texas Farm Road 2278 between one mile and three miles north of the community of Delwin. Here was the location of the author's new home in 1889, and here also were the headquarters of the Ross Ranch, Sul Carter, foreman.

8. The year was 1889.

9. J. W. ("Bud") Arnett served as the only manager (foreman) of the Eight Ranch. When Burk Burnett acquired the ranch in 1900, Arnett continued to run the ranch for many years. Williams, *The Big Ranch Country*, p. 27. The name of Jeffers is not included in a list, "Old 8 Cowboys," from 1887. King County Historical Society, ed., *King County: Windmills and Barbed Wire*, p. 51. Campbell speaks of Claud Jeffers, who was a bronc rider for over thirty years on the Matador Ranch and who later became a wagon boss. Campbell, *Early History of Motley County*, p. 64. Perhaps Claud Jeffers is the man for whom the author made the fawn-skin vest.

Chapter Fourteen

1. The year was 1889.

2. For an explanation of *chocy*, see chapter 12, n. 11.

3. Benjamin, county seat of Knox County, is located on the divide between the South Wichita and Brazos Rivers (commonly referred to as "The Narrows"). The town was begun in August 1884, and, after becoming a center of cattlemen's activities, was made county seat upon organization of the county in 1886. Webb, *The Handbook of Texas*, 1:147. At the time that Tom and Ella Bird first passed through The Narrows in 1877, and for six and one-half years afterward, there was no town in this area.

4. According to Crouch, about two thousand Indians moved to the Brazos Indian Reservation in Young County in 1854: "Caddo, Anadarko, Waco, and Tonkawa Indians each had their own villages." Crouch, *A History of Young County*, p. 21. However, Price and Rathjen state, "Indians who now lived on reservations saw no reason why their place of residence should change their ancient habits of raiding and, in one way, they found an unanticipated advantage in their new homes—they could raid adjacent frontiers and retreat to sanctuary and government support on their reservations." Price and Rathjen, *The Golden Spread*, p. 45. After the reservation failed to restrain the tribes, the land was opened for preemp-

tion by settlers in 1873: "The name Tonkawa clung to the western part of the reserve which had been the home of the Tonkawa tribe. A ridge runs through this valley and on each side settlements were made, thus designating Upper Tonk and Lower Tonk, . . . merely a distinction of location for those attending a church meeting or a picnic." Crouch, *A History of Young County,* p. 94. The entire area was referred to as "Tonk Valley." Ibid.

5. Eliasville, the southernmost town in Young County, was named for Elias DeLong, who built the first store there. Ibid., pp. 95–96. Today Eliasville is on Texas Farm Road 701.

6. The Reverend G. W. Black had married Tom Bird and Ella Elgar twelve years earlier, in 1877.

7. Charles Benson, the author's maternal uncle, had rescued Ella, her mother, her sister, and her oldest stepbrother in Memphis following the Civil War.

Chapter Fifteen

1. The time was fall 1889. The author built her home on Buck Creek in southwestern Cottle County. In *Our Roots Grow Deep,* Bennett states: "All of the earliest settlers at Buck Creek lived in dugouts, but as life improved for them, they built houses. The first nice house built in the county was built by the Sul Carters in 1888. It stood for many years just east of the crossing at Buck Creek" (p. 117).

2. The first store in Paducah, the Carroll Brothers General Store, housed the post office when it was moved from Otta to Paducah. Vent Carroll was appointed postmaster. *Paducah Post* (May 21, 1936), sec. 2, p. 3.

3. The U.S. Post Office had been established at Otta in December 1879. Bennett, *Our Roots,* p. 10. The year in the author's narrative was 1889. From the author's home on South Buck Creek, Otta would have been ten to twelve miles east, not four miles as she says.

4. A list of cowboys on the Eight Ranch in 1887 does not include a Lon Caruth. King County Historical Society, *King County,* p. 51.

5. Charles David Bird was born on October 21, 1866, in Canton, Georgia. As a cowboy in Dickens and Motley Counties, he worked one year (1884) on the Pitchfork Ranch and fifteen years (1885–1900) for the Matador Land and Cattle Company. In 1900 he became self-employed, operating his own ranch of 10,240 acres, twenty miles southeast of Matador. Later Mr. Bird acquired another ranch of 5,200 acres seven miles west of Spur in Dickens County. In later years Charlie Bird served as president, director, and chairman of the board of the First State Bank of Matador until his death, February 22, 1961, at the age of 94. He is buried in the Matador cemetery. Charles A. Bird (Grandson of Charles D. Bird), letters, Midland, Tex., February 11 and 23, 1987. Charlie D. Bird served as a pallbearer at the author's funeral in 1943.

6. Gard explains that cowboys would sometimes travel two hundred miles to attend a dance, which might last for three days. As there usually were not enough

women to go around, the men had to take turns dancing. Women would bring their children if there was no one to leave them with, and the mothers would take turns watching the little ones. The dances usually began about sundown and lasted until sunrise. One early settler recalled, "'We danced the schottische, waltz, glide, polka, and all kinds of square dances.'" Gard, *Rawhide Texas,* pp. 109, 111.

7. For a discussion of the gyp rock vase, see chapter 13, n. 2.

8. Charlie Davidson, who, with his brothers Tom, Bob, Morgan, and Floyd, was a King County cowboy, settled on land on the North Wichita River in northern King County. This land was later owned by Allen Dwayne Goodwin. Long and Long, letter, February 24, 1987.

9. J. J. McAdams's original ranch headquarters were near the center of Cottle County. According to Tom Long, McAdams never held title to this land. He obtained the land for a horse and a saddle from a man named Breckenridge. Long and Long, interview, March 20, 1987. In *Our Roots Grow Deep,* Bennett says that McAdams held "Winchester claim" to his land (p. 21). It was McAdams who offered the site for the county seat (Paducah) in 1892. Webb, *The Handbook of Texas,* 2:324. Bettie B. McAdams Gafford, granddaughter of J. J. McAdams, reports that McAdams later moved fifteen miles east to the Cottle and Foard county line, establishing the McAdams Hat Ranch in 1898. Following McAdams's death in 1921, Tom Burnett bought the ranch. Today the land is part of the Triangle Ranch, owned by Burnett's granddaughter, Anne Windfohr of Fort Worth. Bennett, *Our Roots,* pp. 190–191. The year in the author's narrative is early 1890, two years before Paducah was organized.

10. The author was approaching her twenty-ninth birthday in 1890.

11. Farming began in Cottle County in 1889, according to Walter Liedtke, Sr., of Paducah. His father, F. W. Liedtke, moved there from Canada in that year, buying some land from a Mr. West and homesteading a large portion, also. Walter Liedtke, Sr., interview, April 10, 1963.

12. *Park's Floral Magazine* (1871–1925), of Livonia, Pennsylvania, led the flower journals in circulation through most of the 1890s. Both it and *Vick's Illustrated Monthly,* which was generally thought to be of a higher class, originated with seed houses, although by 1900 *Vick's* was claiming that it was "unconnected with any seed house or nursery." Frank Luther Mott, *A History of American Magazines,* 4:342.

13. The year was 1890.

14. Garret Augustus Hobart, a U.S. lawyer and politician, became vice president of the United States in 1897 when William McKinley became the twenty-fifth president. *Random House Dictionary,* s.v. "Hobart" and "McKinley." The election of these men to their high offices was seven years after the year of the author's narrative, 1890.

15. According to her grandson, J. Verne Dumont, the author had a cactus garden at her home in Paducah. It contained over 400 varieties of cacti from all over the United States. The garden was kept in a brick dugout, which had six feet of stand-

ing room. Above the ground, around the dugout, was a two-foot wall of bricks. The dugout had a glass-paned roof that slanted to the south. Therefore, the cacti survived even in the bitter wintertime. J. Verne Dumont, telephone interview, February 21, 1987.

Chapter Sixteen

1. The year was 1890. Speaking of the school, Bennett states: "It is to the Carter family [of the Ross Ranch] that I give chief credit for the establishment of what I consider to be the first publicly-supported school in Cottle County which was opened in 1891. Possibly there were private or subscription schools in other communities by that time, but documentary evidence indicates that Buck Creek was the first to use state funds in its operation. The name of the school at that time was Ryan and it retained this name until it was moved to the crossing on Buck Creek itself." Bennett, *Our Roots,* p. 116. According to the author's narrative, the year of the first school at Buck Creek was 1890, but Bennett states that it was 1891.

2. The expression "p's and q's" has several origins: (*a*) an admonition among pedagogs to their young students to note the right-handed knob of the letter *p* and the left-handed knob of the *q*; (*b*) a warning to apprentice printers who might become confused in choosing type because the face of a type letter is just the reverse of the printed character; (*c*) a chalking up of the amount of pints (*p*'s) and quarts (*q*'s) a customer consumed in an evening at the alehouse—a slip on the part of the barmaid might ruin a man's evening if he were overcharged; (*d*) an admonition of French dancing masters to young gentlemen, to mind their *pieds* and *queues* (feet and pigtails); (*e*) a warning to a man of the fifteenth through seventeenth centuries to avoid soiling his jacket (pee) with the grease or flour from his pigtail (queue). Charles Earle Funk, *A Hog on Ice,* pp. 199–200.

3. Capp Bird was nine years old in 1890, the actual year in the narrative; Bessie ("Baby") was five years old.

4. Larry Carter was the son of Sul Carter, foreman of the Ross Ranch, and the grandson of C. L. ("Kit") Carter, owner of the ranch and founder of the Stock Raisers Association of Northwestern Texas. J. Verne Dumont, Family Papers and Photographs. The handwriting on the photographs is unidentified.

5. The original Steel Dust, foaled in 1843 in Illinois, was brought to Lancaster, Texas, from Kentucky in 1846 by Mid Perry. Steel Dust was a blood bay, standing over fifteen hands and weighing 1,200 pounds. The horse died in the same vicinity (south Dallas County) in 1864. American Quarter Horse Association, *Stud Book and Registry,* p. 22. Steel Dust first gained fame as a quarter horse racer and then as a sire. His colts came to be in demand as cow ponies and as winning racers. Wayne Gard, *The Fabulous Quarter Horse: Steel Dust,* pp. 13–14, 32, 36. Naturally, the name Steel Dust came to be a popular name for a horse.

6. *Mavericking* is the act of hunting down and branding unbranded calves. In the West it became a synonym for *stealing.* Adams, *Western Words,* p. 98.

7. Sir Henry Morton Stanley was, of course, the famous adventurer and journalist who was commissioned by the *New York Herald* to find the great explorer David Livingstone, the Scottish missionary and explorer from whom no word had come from Africa for quite some time. Stanley accomplished this mission on November 10, 1871, and subsequently made three more journeys to Africa. Published accounts of Stanley's four trips to Africa include *How I Found Livingstone* (1872), *Through the Dark Continent* (1878), *In Darkest Africa* (1890), and *The Exploration Diaries of H. M. Stanley* (edited by Richard Stanley and Alan Neame, 1962). *The Columbia Encyclopedia,* 3d ed., s.v. "David Livingstone" and "Sir Henry Morton Stanley." The title given by the author in her text is one that she is inaccurately recalling from memory.

8. The courthouse in Childress and the records burned in 1891. No one today recalls what hotels were in Childress in 1890. Furr, letter, November 24, 1986.

9. W. Q. Richards became the owner of the 3D cattle and part of the 3D land sometime during the 1890s. Williams, *The Big Ranch Country,* p. 130.

10. Henry H. Campbell managed the Matador Land and Cattle Company from 1879 to 1891. His farewell address at the annual Christmas dance in 1891 has become famous. His son, Harry Campbell, quotes the account of Max Bentley of the *Western Weekly:* "'His [Campbell's] farewell address to his cowboys is a true picture of Henry Campbell. Those of the Matador Ranch who knew him best say his speech is a noble document which should live forever in the annals of the West.'" Campbell, *Early History of Motley County,* p. 65. Shortly after beginning the speech, Campbell choked up, and he handed the speech to his wife, Lizzie, to complete. Bentley continued: "'His speech predicted a new era of things in the West. He foresaw the era in which we are living today. He described the approach of an age of specialization in which no man might hope to stay alive without study and hard work. He counseled the cowboys not to go on with their careless life in the saddle with no thought of the future. He advised them to acquire their own land, to marry, raise families and become the backbone of the era on whose threshhold Henry Campbell knew they were standing.'" Ibid. The entire address appears in the conclusion of Campbell's book, and it is mentioned again by the author in chapter 18. Following his departure from the Matador Ranch, Henry H. Campbell established the Campbell Ranch in southwestern Motley County in 1891. The ranch is operated today by the grandsons of Henry Campbell—Harold H. Campbell and Hal Vance Campbell.

11. The town of Kirkland was named for J. C. Kirkland, an early settler. Webb, *The Handbook of Texas,* 1:967. Today the town is nine miles southeast of Childress on U.S. Highway 287.

Chapter Seventeen

1. The year was 1891.

2. Charlie Work, an early settler of the region, occupied land in southern Cottle

County and northern King County, near the North Wichita River. The "Work Place," as it is frequently called by current owner Burnet Richards, begins one and one-half miles north of the North Wichita River on the west side of U.S. Highway 83 between Guthrie and Paducah. Long and Long, letter, February 24, 1987.

3. Twenty-one is the number of feet that a swift running horse makes in a leap when running. Ibid. "Sailing by me on twenty-one" is the expression the author applies to a yearling that sped by her.

4. Pottsboro is in Grayson County, just north of Sherman on Texas Farm Road 120 in Northeast Texas. According to Webb, A. A. Neff was county surveyor during the organization of Paducah in January 1892. Webb, *The Handbook of Texas*, 2:324.

5. Cottle County, along with some twenty other West Texas counties, was created from Fannin County in 1876. It was named for George Washington Cottle, an Alamo hero. Paducah, which was chosen as the county seat over Cottle, a small settlement on Salt Creek southeast of the Paducah site, was organized on January 11, 1892. Grace Jones Piper, interview, Paducah, Tex., March 20, 1987. The new county seat was established near the center of Cottle County on the site of the J. J. McAdams Ranch. Sixteen town fathers cast the deciding votes after McAdams offered the land. The town was named for Paducah, Kentucky, the home of the new community's county surveyor, A. A. Neff, and the county attorney, R. E. Avant. Webb, *The Handbook of Texas*, 2:324. Longtime Cottle County resident Bonnie Davis states that where Paducah now stands, J. J. McAdams, A. A. Neff, John Carroll, G. Backus, Lal Backus, and S. J. Bailey once lived. *Paducah Post* (May 21, 1936), sec. 2, p. 3. Elfie B. Carlock, widow of the former longtime owner and editor of the *Paducah Post*, Ed Carlock, stated in 1963 that the first Paducah newspaper, the *Paducah Times*, began in 1893 under Vent Carroll's editorship, and the paper was later published by Oran Kelley. After Kelley a Mr. Butler owned the newspaper. Elfie B. Carlock, interview, Paducah, Tex., April 14, 1963. In May 1906, the *Paducah Times* became the *Paducah Post*. Bennett, *Our Roots*, preface. Ed Carlock purchased the business in 1908. Carlock, interview, April 14, 1963. In addition to the Carroll Brothers General Store, a second store was opened by C. H. Scott in 1893. Webb, The *Handbook of Texas*, 2:324. Bonnie Davis adds that one of the first general countrywide dances in Paducah took place in Mr. Scott's newly constructed grocery store—on the evening prior to the day that he moved in. *Paducah Post* (May 21, 1936), sec. 2, p. 3. Davis records also that a one-room school building, located at the far southeast corner of the town section, was used as the courthouse until 1893, when the new courthouse was built. *Paducah Post* (May 21, 1936), sec. 2, p. 8. Kenneth Tooley, editor of the *Paducah Post* in the early 1960s, said that near the turn of the century J. H. Doolen held Sunday School every Sunday at 3 p.m. in the local saloon. The first separate post office, away from the Carroll Brothers General Store, was at the rear of the old First State Bank building. The First Baptist Church was organized about 1898, with W. P. Grogan as minister. Kenneth Tooley, interview, Paducah, Tex., April 15, 1963. Grogan was the minister who married Ella

Bird and Auguste Dumont in 1895. Incorporation of Paducah came in 1910 with a
population of 1,350. Webb, *The Handbook of Texas,* 2:324.

6. The Reverend Robert Jameson, known as "Uncle Bob," was a Methodist
pastor in Cottle County from 1903 to 1906. In 1906, he moved to Matador in
Motley County and was pastor there for four years. Traweek, *Of Such As These,*
pp. 276–277. As the time in the narrative is 1892, the author is probably confused
about the first pastor's name and is remembering "Uncle Bob" Jameson who arrived later.

7. Webb says that A. A. Neff was Cottle County surveyor in 1892. Webb, *The
Handbook of Texas,* 2:324. The author states that he was part of the Neff family she
had known in Young County in 1875. Her first teacher had been Mrs. M. H. Neff.
In the narrative, the author states that Miss Ola Neff was the daughter of her "dear
old teacher," yet the author implies that Ola Neff is also the daughter of the
Mr. Neff who was organizing Paducah. Confusion comes from the initials of Mrs.
M. H. Neff in Young County and A. A. Neff in Cottle County. It is possible that
A. A. Neff and Ola Neff were brother and sister, both the children of Mrs. M. H.
Neff, the author's former teacher.

8. J. D. Short's and Ola V. Neff's signatures appear on report cards from
Paducah Academy for both Capp and Bessie Bird. These cards are dated November, December, January, and February 1894 and 1895. The two students received
perfect marks of excellence. Library Files, Ella Bird Dumont Collection, Panhandle-
Plains Historical Museum, Canyon, Tex.

9. The year was 1893.

10. When Judge and Mrs. J. W. Woodley moved to Paducah in 1895, they found
that the "little red court house, the temple of justice which was the pride of the
pioneers in those days," had just been built. *Paducah Post* (May 21, 1936), sec. 2,
p. 8. At this time, according to Bonnie Davis's *Paducah Post* article, the only store
and post office were operated by Auguste Dumont. He and W. Q. Richards had
bought out the Carroll brothers, and Dumont later bought out Richards's interest.
When the mail hack came in each weekday from Childress, this was the gathering
place of the populace, numbering fifty or sixty people. The main attraction of the
town was the hotel owned by a Mr. Culberson. It had four bedrooms. Ibid. No
mention appears here of C. H. Scott's general store in Paducah, the second such
store in the community, which is reported to have opened in 1893 (see n. 5 above).

11. The year was 1894.

12. The original Virginia Dare was the first white child of English parents born
in America on August 18, 1587. Her parents, Ananias and Ellinor Dare, were members of Sir Walter Raleigh's Roanoke Island Colony on the North Carolina coast,
which was established in 1585. When the next expedition arrived at the location of
the colony sixteen years later, in 1591, the settlers were all gone. The exact fate of
Virginia Dare is unknown. *The Columbia Encyclopedia,* 3d ed., s.v. "Virginia Dare."
Virginia Dare: A Romance of the Sixteenth Century, by Miss E. A. B. Shackelford,
was a 207-page novel published by Thomas Whittaker in New York in 1892. Though

the work is now obscure, a copy of it is in the Library of Congress collection of American fiction. Lyle H. Wright, *American Fiction: 1876–1900*, p. 485. In addition, a folktale centers on the fate of Virginia Dare. According to this tale, the Indians on Roanoke Island in the early 1600s marveled at the sudden appearance of a milk-white doe. She was not only extremely beautiful, she was clever enough to elude all arrows and traps. The Indians, therefore, organized a hunt, inviting the best archers from far and wide to participate. One of the archers, named Wanchese, had been to England and had returned with a silver arrow given to him by the queen. She had told him it would kill even the bearer of a charmed life. The hunt proceeded and Wanchese followed the white doe to the beach. He shot her through the heart with his silver arrow. At the moment the white doe died, she looked into Wanchese's eyes and whispered, "Virginia Dare." *American Folklore and Legend*, p. 31. Since Baby gave her reading in 1894, it is likely that she was reading from the folk legend and not from the romance novel, which had been published only two years previously.

13. "Raining like forty" refers to the forty days and nights of rain in the Book of Genesis. Since there was little literature available other than the Bible, early settlers used many biblical comparisons. Long and Long, letter, Feburary 24, 1987.

14. John Marlin of New Haven, Connecticut, first made Ballard breech-loading carbines and metallic cartridge derringers. His own Marlin rifle replaced the Ballard firearms and were celebrated for their strength, easy workmanship, and simplicity of action. A. Merwyn Carey, *American Firearms Makers*, p. 74; Edward S. Farrow, *American Small Arms*, p. 217.

Chapter Eighteen

1. Campbell states in *Early History of Motley County* that "a man named Austin, a part-time farmer and line rider for the Matador Ranch" built the second hotel in Matador (p. 44). A two-story structure called "The Southern," it served as a courthouse when the latter burned, according to Campbell, and it also was used later as a Masonic meeting place. Ibid.

2. Whiteflat was originally a line camp of the Matador Ranch. Today the community is eight miles north of Matador on Texas Highway 70.

3. Several families named Moore settled in early-day Matador, but the author most likely is speaking of John L. and Lou Gibson Moore who came to Motley County in 1886 or 1887. Mrs. Moore became a close friend of Lizzie Campbell and assisted the latter in entertaining the cowboys of the area—especially at the famous Matador Ranch Christmas dances. John Moore served as a mail carrier on horseback in Motley County, until he was appointed sheriff. Mrs. Moore became famous as a fashionable milliner of Matador. Traweek, *Of Such As These*, pp. 313–314. Lou Gibson Moore was an aunt of Lottie Gibson, Alma Gibson Long, and Merrick Gibson of Paducah and of J. J. Gibson of Guthrie. Long and Long, letter, February 24, 1987. Mr. and Mrs. McDonald originally did laundry for the cowboys on

the Matador Ranch. It was in their home in Matador that the first wedding occurred (in 1891) after organization of the county. Campbell, *Early History of Motley County,* pp. 45–46, 48.

4. H. P. Cook, who came to Cottle County in 1890, states in the February 18, 1937, issue of the *Paducah Post* that the drought was in 1892, 1893, and 1894, not 1895 as the author implies. According to Grace Jones Piper, Cook wrote: "'Why, it didn't rain enough in those three years to wet my shirt through my coat!'" Grace Jones Piper, letter, Paducah, Tex., February 26, 1987. Haley, however, speaks of the "memorable drought of 1893 to 1895, which practically depopulated the country." Haley, *Charles Goodnight,* p. 383.

5. The year was 1895.

6. Lewis E. Fite moved to San Antonio in 1919 and entered the real estate business. He is credited with developing the Jefferson area of the city and the northwest part of the city as well. Fite was a founder of Methodist Hospital in San Antonio, serving afterward as chairman of the board. He was also prominent in many religious, civic, and educational activities, one of which was serving on the board of regents for Southwestern University in Georgetown, Texas. Fite married Kathleen Roots, now in her eighties, who lives today in San Antonio near her one daughter, Betty Fite Thorne. L. E. Fite died in 1981 at the age of 86. Kathleen R. Fite, telephone interview with Ruth Stephens, February 8, 1987.

7. Tackett Mountain is in southwestern Young County. It is named for the Reverend Pleasant Tackett who lived on Fish Creek near the mountain, along with his wife and three sons in the 1860s. Crouch, *A History of Young County,* p. 34.

8. Fairview later came to be called Valley View. Today an empty schoolhouse marks the spot, five miles west of Paducah, just off the combined U.S. Highways 62 and 70.

9. Jack Luckett first worked for H. H. Campbell when the latter was manager of the Matador Ranch and continued to work on the ranch after Murdo Mackenzie took over as head. Luckett became wagon boss. In 1902 when he married, he moved into Matador where he built the first cotton gin. He then entered the mercantile business, eventually becoming the owner of Matador Mercantile Company. Traweek, *Of Such As These,* p. 293.

10. As the year was 1895, Baby (Bessie Adell) would have been ten years old, not eight. Capp's age of fourteen here is correct.

11. After Nora Bailey married Pat Murphy, they had two daughters, Mae Belle Murphy Nixon and Estelle Murphy Williams. The latter lives today in Paducah. Long and Long, letter, February 24, 1987.

Chapter Nineteen

1. *Play parties* are social events at which old-fashioned games are played, and *candy breakings* are gatherings of young people to make candy, especially molasses candy. *A Dictionary of Americanisms,* s.v. "play party" and "candy breaking."

2. A. Dumont had written his proposal six years before, in 1889.

3. *Snide* is an adjective, meaning, among other things, sneaky and under-handed. *Dictionary of American Slang,* 2d supplemented ed., s.v. "snide." The author uses the term as an infinitive here, meaning "to sneak out" or "to back out."

4. Henrietta is the county seat of Clay County in north central Texas, on U.S. Highway 287, seventeen miles east of Wichita Falls. Graham is approximately seventy miles south and a bit west of Henrietta.

5. Webb states in *The Handbook of Texas:* "The Fort Worth and Denver City Railway Company was chartered in 1873, by citizens of Fort Worth, Texas, to build toward Denver, Colorado" (1 : 634). General Grenville M. Dodge, who had been in charge of constructing the Union Pacific end of the transcontinental railroad and who had built the Texas and Pacific from Fort Worth to Sierra Blanca, offered and was hired to build the 110 miles to Wichita Falls. Fort Worth soon became one of the largest cattle-shipping points in the state. Webb, *The Handbook of Texas,* 1 : 634.

6. In 1938, the author wrote in additional notes to her manuscript that she still had every article of her second wedding trousseau—the hat, veil, gloves, shoes, and hose—all in good shape. When her son Elgar found the trousseau after her death, however, it was in such bad condition that he burned it. Oma Dumont, interview, April 12, 1963.

7. Wharton states that A. Dumont became known as "The Father of Cottle County." Wharton, *Texas under Many Flags,* p. 139.

8. The first permanent stone jail, built on the present site of Paducah's Veterans Administration Building, had an appropriation of $12,000 in May 1893. Piper, letter, February 26, 1987.

9. "Belle Mahone," by J. H. McNaughton, reads as follows:

> Soon beyond the harbor bar, Shall my bark be sailing far,
> O'er the world I wander lone, Sweet Belle Mahone.
> O'er thy grave I weep good-bye, Hear, O hear my lonely cry,
> O without thee what am I, Sweet Belle Mahone?
>
> Lonely like a withered tree, What is all the world to me?
> Life and light were all in thee, Sweet Belle Mahone.
> Daisies pale are growing o'er, All my heart can e'er adore
> Shall I meet thee never more, Sweet Belle Mahone?
>
> Calmly, sweetly slumber on, (Only one I call my own!)
> While in tears I wander lone, Sweet Belle Mahone.
> Faded now seems ev'rything, But when comes eternal spring,
> With thee I'll be wandering, Sweet Belle Mahone.
>
> *Chorus:*
> Sweet Belle Mahone! Sweet Belle Mahone!
> Wait for me at Heaven's gate, Sweet Belle Mahone.

Joe Mitchell Chapple, ed., *Heart Songs Dear to the American People,* pp. 328–329.

10. The marriage certificate, dated December 28, 1895, was signed by Fred M. Campbell, county clerk. The marriage was performed on December 29 by W. P. Grogan, Baptist minister, and Campbell entered the marriage in the county records December 30. The wedding ceremony was on a Sunday morning at 11:30 a.m. in the Paducah Baptist Church. J. Verne Dumont, Family Papers and Photographs.

Chapter Twenty

1. Baby (Bessie Adell) would have turned eleven the July 22 following the wedding of the author and A. Dumont on December 29, 1895.

2. Capp Bird continued to play his violin in later years, and he was considered to be quite talented. Pearl Swint, interview, Paducah, Tex., April 9, 1963.

3. The year was 1896.

4. The author always kept a lush flower garden in Paducah, which brought her the admiration of the townspeople.

5. Lena Doolen later married G. Y. Bowman and moved to Dallas in the early 1920s. Long and Long, letter, February 24, 1987.

6. The year was 1897.

7. Capp was now sixteen and Baby was twelve.

8. This was the winter of 1897–1898.

9. Mr. and Mrs. W. Q. Richards's only child died as an infant and was buried in Quanah, probably because the parents had taken the baby there for better medical treatment. The couple divorced in 1915. W. Q. Richards, who died on September 30, 1922, is buried beside his sister, Virginia Gober, in the Paducah cemetery. May Canon Richards died October 16, 1923, and is buried by the side of her infant child in Quanah. Long and Long, letter, February 24, 1987; Piper, letter, February 26, 1987.

10. J. M. "Uncle Bud" Barron, born circa 1870, married Addie Brooks on December 20, 1890, at Thornton, in Limestone County. Wharton, *Texas under Many Flags,* p. 134. The couple came to Cottle County on April 1, 1896, settling seven miles south of Paducah. Six children were born, three of whom lived to adulthood: Elmo, Willie (also called Bill), and Jewel. Arbie (named in the author's text) died at age seven, and two others died at younger ages. Piper, letter, February 26, 1987.

11. The Campbell home belonged to Fred M. Campbell, county clerk, who had signed the Dumonts' marriage certificate. Mrs. Campbell had made the author's wedding dress and had directed the Dumonts' wedding dinner. In the text, the author says that the Campbell place was their permanent home in Paducah. Actually the location was permanent, but the author built a new house on the spot eighteen years later, in 1916.

12. The first official school building in Paducah, locally referred to as "the little blue school," was built in 1898 or 1899 where today's Alamo School stands. It was four blocks southwest of the Dumonts' home. This first school later burned and

was rebuilt. Alma Gibson Long says that she started to school there in 1917. Long and Long, letter, February 24, 1987. The building was eventually moved to the northeast side of Paducah, taking the name of Dunbar School. In 1909 D. A. ("Dave") Goodwin donated six acres of land for the site of a new school building, which was built in 1910 at a cost of $25,000. It was five blocks west of the Dumonts' home. Known merely as "the school" until the redbrick high school was constructed south of it in 1924, it was then named Goodwin School after D. A. Goodwin to distinguish the two buildings. The older structure became a junior high school. Piper, letter, February 26, 1987.

13. Canyon, county seat of Randall County, on Interstate 27, sixteen miles south of Amarillo in the Texas Panhandle, was first called Canyon City. It was named for Palo Duro Canyon. Webb, *The Handbook of Texas,* 1:291.

14. According to the headstone on Auguste Elgar Dumont's grave, he was born February 12, 1900. Chronological time in the author's narrative should be 1899, but it is likely that she combined two years inadvertently. Though the author refers to this son as Elgar, as he grew up he was called "Frenchie," a nickname referring to the French blood that he inherited from his French-Canadian father.

15. Around 1900 the J. M. Barrons bought a home in Paducah at what is now 904 12th Street. Later this one-story house was moved one and one-half blocks west to 1314 Easley. This house has been designated a Texas Historical Landmark. The plaque on the front of the house reads: "Gober-Barron-Williford House. Late Victorian structure; has fine glass and gingerbread trim. Built 1896 and lived in by first (1892–1898) Cottle County sheriff Joe L. Gober. At that time, many people lived in dugouts. Building materials had to be hauled from railroad towns of Childress and Quanah. (Paducah acquired railway line in 1909.) Gober home sold to J. M. Barron, who was county's third sheriff. Since 1941, it has been owned by the J. H. Williford family. Recorded Texas Historic Landmark—1962. Texas State Historical Survey Committee." In 1910 the Barrons built a large two-story house on the site of their original home. Today, Alma and Tom Long live in the restored Barron two-story house. Long and Long, telephone interview, February 27, 1987. The J. M. Barrons' granddaughter, Fern Barron Tippen, daughter of Elmo Barron, lives today on the west side of Paducah.

16. Charles Benson was the maternal uncle of the author who had rescued the author's pregnant mother and her three children, Lucy, Ella, and Thomas, in Memphis at the end of the Civil War. He took them back to the home of the author's grandmother in Mississippi.

17. Dickens, county seat of Dickens County, was organized in 1891. *Texas Almanac, 1986–87,* p. 276. Dickens City, as the author calls it, is on U.S. Highway 82 and Texas 114, approximately forty airline miles southwest of Paducah.

18. Capp would have been eighteen or nineteen years old.

19. The Mr. Collinson for whom the author made the beaded vests was surely the well-known Frank Collinson of Jingle Bob cattle fame. In *Life in the Saddle,* Collinson states that around the turn of the century, after the Jingle Bob cattle had

been sold to the Matador Land and Cattle Company, he entered a cattle partner-
ship with R. B. Masterson in King County (p. 222). As the time in Mrs. Dumont's
narrative is near "the turn of the century," Frank Collinson must be the ranchman.
The Masterson Ranch, still in business today, is approximately twenty-five airline
miles southeast of Paducah in northeastern King County. The great-grandson of
R. B. Masterson, Bill Masterson, now runs the ranch. At the time of publication of
Life in the Saddle (1963), Collinson's son, Ralph Collinson, lived in Amarillo. Collinson, *Life in the Saddle*, p. xi.

20. The sewing machine used special needles for sewing leather that were three-
or four-sided, as well as regular needles for sewing fabric. Oma Dumont, interview, April 12, 1963. No source consulted revealed the meaning of the term *bacinet*.
Grace Rogers Cooper's *The Sewing Machine: Its Invention and Development* (Washington: Smithsonian Institution, 1976) and Brian Jewell's *Veteran Sewing Machines:
A Collector's Guide* (New York: A. S. Barnes, 1975) list hundreds of manufacturers
and names of sewing machines in the nineteenth and twentieth centuries—but no
bacinet. The term could have denoted a type of special machine or one with special
attachments. This seems likely because the author does not capitalize *bacinet*.
Henry Campbell's son, Harry, wrote of the author's talents: "Mrs. Dumont of
Paducah had a very important part in the early days. When the cowboys wanted an
extra special vest, or gloves, they relied on her to fill the bill and she never failed
them. D. C. Keith once said she only had to look at hands and could make gloves
to fit perfectly, without any measurements. She made some very beautiful buckskin
vests for the cowboys. She was a very gifted woman and made many things from
gypsum rock, which is found in Cottle County." Campbell, *Early History of Motley
County*, p. 41.

21. Capp Bird was noted for experimenting with electrical devices. He made the
first telephone, phonograph, and radio in Cottle County. Coils for transmitters
were made by winding copper wire by hand around oatmeal cartons, and condens-
ers were made by using waxed paper and tinfoil. Before World War I, Capp made
and operated a wireless station. At the beginning of the war, he picked up a strong
wireless signal and reported it to the government, which located a strong German
station near the border in Mexico. Capp did not have a license to operate the set he
had made, and the government ordered him to dismantle it. He was not prose-
cuted, however, because of the help he had given in finding the German station. A
young man named Brent Daniels, who was employed by the U.S. Bureau of Standards in Amarillo, tried to enlist Capp's talents for his organization, but his attempts were futile. Oma Dumont, interview, April 12, 1963.

Chapter Twenty-One

1. The year is not clear at this point, because the author seems to be fusing
years together without clear distinctions between them. From the coming events in
the narrative, it is safest to assume that the year was 1903.

2. Kelley was Oran Kelley, who followed Vent Carroll as editor of the *Paducah Times*. Carlock, interview, April 14, 1963. Ora Winton later married the Tommy spoken of here—Tom M. Drummond—who became a prosperous rancher, farmer, and businessman in Cottle County. Tom Drummond came to Cottle County in 1898 at the age of twenty. His family engaged in stock raising in Cottle and King counties, but Drummond later disposed of the stock and kept the land for cotton farming. Drummond was prominent in the oil industry, in the lumber business, and in real estate. He formed the Drummond-Crump Lumber Company with James A. Crump in Paducah. Ora Winton and Tom Drummond were married April 17, 1907. They had three children. Wharton, *Texas under Many Flags,* pp. 150–151. Until her death in July 1985, Corinne Drummond Martin, the only daughter of Tom and Ora Drummond, continued to farm the land fifteen miles southwest of Paducah, which her grandfather, William Z. Drummond, had bought in 1898. No record exists of the Mitchel named in the text.

3. Thornton, Texas, on Texas Farm Roads 1246 and 2749 in Limestone County, southeast of Waco, grew from a population of 182 in 1880 to 675 by 1915. Webb, *The Handbook of Texas,* 2:776.

4. Why Mrs. W. Q. Richards would have been living in Quanah in 1903 is not known. Her baby died in 1897 and was buried in Quanah, but the Richardses did not divorce until 1915. The author speaks of Mrs. Richards here as if the rancher's wife were a permanent citizen of the town forty miles northeast of Paducah.

5. The author had last been to Young County in 1895, eight years earlier.

6. Sister Superior of St. Mary's Academy indicates in a letter of September 7, 1903, that she is sending a catalog and that the school is opening on the following day. She states: "We trust if you decide to place your daughter with us, you will do so at the earliest possible date." Library Files, Ella Bird Dumont Collection, Panhandle-Plains Historical Museum, Canyon, Tex. Bessie Bird would have been eighteen years old at the time.

7. Pyrography is the process of burning designs on wood or leather with a heated tool.

8. Elgar would have been four years old on February 12, 1904.

9. Belton, the county seat of Bell County, is on Interstate 35 approximately 60 miles north of Austin. In 1904, Belton had a population of 3,700. Webb, *The Handbook of Texas,* 1:144.

10. Marble Falls, in Burnet County, is on U.S. Highway 281 eleven miles north of Round Mountain.

11. In *Blanco County Families for 100 Years* Moursand says that Joseph Bird was elected county judge of Blanco County in 1890 and 1892, when he was sixty-nine and seventy-one years of age, respectively (pp. 19–21). By 1904, the time of Baby's visit, Joseph Bird would have been eighty-three years of age. His political career was most likely already over. The author must be remembering his tenure as county judge twelve to fourteen years earlier. Joseph Bird's first wife, Eliza Dorriss Bird, died May 27, 1896. Bird then married Martha A. Gill, the widow of the Meth-

odist preacher in Blanco. Joseph Bird died on August 15, 1909, at the age of 88. Moursand, *Blanco County Families*, p. 20.

12. Fannie Cage was one of six living brothers and sisters of Addie Barron. The latter was the youngest girl. Wharton, *Texas under Many Flags*, p. 134.

13. Hunter Goodwin was a daughter of D. A. ("Dave") Goodwin, who gave the land for the new school in 1910. Long and Long, letter, February 24, 1987.

14. Bessie Bird had died sometime during the night, so the townspeople realized on Sunday that the body would have to be buried before Monday. At the graveside some people held lanterns, while others held tapers. J. Verne Dumont, Family Papers and Photographs (unidentified handwriting). Bessie Bird had turned nineteen the month before her death.

Chapter Twenty-Two

1. According to Lottie Gibson of Paducah, Addie Barron persuaded the author to wear colors in the 1930s and early 1940s. Lottie Gibson, interview, Paducah, Tex., March 20, 1987. The author states that the date she is writing this part of her memoirs is twenty-four years after Bessie Bird's death. Bessie died in 1904, so the time of writing would be 1928. The date on page one of the original typed copy of the manuscript is February 1, 1927; therefore, the author must have spent two years in composing her memoirs—1927 and 1928.

2. The year was 1905.

3. The year was 1906.

4. Pearl Fessenden was the daughter of the author's younger half-sister, Claudie Bellamy, who married Al Fessenden. Pearl was later to marry Albert Swint in Paducah and to live there for many years. Oma White was the daughter of Lewis E. White, the author's half-brother who was born in Mississippi after his father's death in Memphis at the end of the Civil War. Oma Dumont, interview, April 12, 1963. The author and her sister Lucy had named their new half-brother Lewis after their own father, Lewis Steptoe Elgar. (See chapter 1.).

5. The year was 1907.

6. The first train, a freight, pulled into Paducah in 1909, and on Christmas Day of that year, the first passenger train arrived. Elma Rutledge, unmarried yet to Walter Chalk, was on the passenger train. *Paducah Post* (May 21, 1936), sec. 2, p. 3. (After living in Paducah for many years, Elma Chalk later became a prominent citizen of Lubbock.) During the same year, 1909, Bud Barron drove the first home-owned automobile, a Winton Six, into town. Ibid.

7. Elgar would have been nine or ten at this point.

8. Pearl Fessenden and Albert Swint married on March 5, 1911. They lived for many years just one block east of the author's home in Paducah, and they are buried in the Paducah cemetery. Oma Dumont, interview, April 12, 1963.

9. According to the chronology of the narrative, the year was 1913. A typed note discovered in family papers states that Auguste Dumont served as postmaster

at Paducah from December 4, 1895, until February 4, 1915. At the time of the narrative, he would have been postmaster for eighteen years, not twenty-one as the author states. According to a letter in the Dumont family records from J. T. Sluder, assistant attorney general of Texas, Dumont also was serving as county treasurer of Cottle County in 1908. J. Verne Dumont, Family Papers and Photographs.

10. Oma White and Melvin Woodley married on December 28, 1913. Oma Dumont, interview, April 12, 1963.

11. Francis E. McGaughey had been Auguste Dumont's partner in a hog ranch near Otta in 1885. (See Chapter Ten.)

12. An original certificate for a patent of 160 acres of land on the waters of the Salt Fork, tributary of North Wichita River (two and one-half miles southwest of Paducah), was issued to Auguste Dumont on July 31, 1900. The certificate was registered by Arthur Lile, Cottle County clerk. It had originally been signed on July 23 by Joseph D. Sayers, governor of Texas. Library Files, Ella Bird Dumont Collection, Panhandle-Plains Historical Museum, Canyon, Tex. Today this land is farmed by Randell Bockleman, stepson of J. Verne Dumont, in Paducah.

13. Stradley became postmaster in Paducah. He had two children, Forest and Sue. Long and Long, letter, February 24, 1987.

14. Auguste Dumont died on April 8, 1915. Oma Dumont, interview, April 12, 1963.

Chapter Twenty-Three

1. The year was 1916. At the time of Auguste Dumont's death in 1915, the author was approaching her fifty-fourth birthday, Capp had just turned thirty-four, and Elgar was fifteen.

2. According to Wharton, Elgar Dumont completed Tyler Commercial College on June 19, 1919, and went to work for the Ford Motor Company's agency in Paducah as a bookkeeper. Wharton, *Texas under Many Flags,* p. 139. The agency belonged to John Carroll, whose children were Bill, "Toad," Joe, and Mozelle. Mozelle Carroll married Gordon Davis, a city manager of Paducah. Long and Long, letter, February 24, 1987.

3. The watch chain made from the author's hair for her son Elgar is now in the possession of Elgar's son, J. Verne Dumont, in Paducah.

4. At this point in the narrative, the author writes about a trip to New Mexico in the summer of 1920 to visit her Fite relatives. Lewis White, her stepbrother, and his daughter Lizzie accompanied her, but the author does not state whether Capp or Elgar went along. Among the highlights were visits in the cities of Las Vegas, Santa Fe, and Roswell and in the communities of La Luz, Cloudcroft, and Hope in south-central New Mexico. This material is omitted because it is mostly a travelogue.

5. Elizabeth Benson Elgar White Bellamy died in the spring of 1922. Oma Dumont, interview, April 12, 1963.

6. The author backs up one year from the year of her mother's death. Mr. Bellamy died in 1922. Elgar was twenty-one in 1921.

7. Elgar Dumont and Oma Irons were married on April 16, 1922. Oma Dumont, interview, April 12, 1963. Oma's friend was the former Anna Mae Williford who had married Wylie Ellis. They later moved to Houston. Long and Long, letter, February 24, 1987.

8. The time was summer 1922. Capp would have been forty-one years of age. Wharton says that Oma Smith was the daughter of C. S. Smith, a Paducah blacksmith. Wharton, *Texas under Many Flags*, p. 137. Oma Smith was much younger than Capp. She later abandoned him and their two young boys, Capp Jay, Jr., and Tommy. Long and Long, letter, February 24, 1987.

9. The Star name was used by two different companies for an early automobile, but both seem to have died a quick death, along with twenty-two hundred other makes of cars. Among the numerous industry songs of the automobile may be found the title "In a Nifty Star." Floyd Clymer, *Treasury of Early American Automobiles*, pp. 205, 210; Rudolph E. Anderson, *The Story of the American Automobile*, p. 236.

10. Capp Jay Bird, Jr., born in 1923, became known as "Junior" Bird. As an adult, he moved to New Mexico (exact location is unknown to the Dumont family), where he died in the late 1960s or early 1970s. J. Verne Dumont, interview with the editor, Paducah, Texas, October 11, 1986. His one daughter, Jamie Carol, was born in the mid-1950s. Oma Dumont, interview, April 12, 1963. The Dumont family has no information about Junior Bird's daughter.

11. The year was 1924.

12. Twenty-one pages of narrative in the original manuscript are devoted to a day-by-day account of the author's visit in the Los Angeles area. While she was there, Mrs. Dumont visited primarily with her son Capp and his wife, but she also spent a considerable amount of time with Mrs. G. Backus and the former Miss Lura Halley. She was able to visit once again with her old friend Ola Neff. This long passage has been omitted because it is primarily a travelogue.

13. Quanah, Texas, was for many years the junction of the Fort Worth and Denver Railroad and the Quanah, Acme, and Pacific (QA&P) Railroad. Travelers to Paducah would go to Quanah and take the QA&P passenger train to Paducah. When the editor's mother attended Clarendon College in Donley County around 1915 or 1916, she took the QA&P train northeast to Quanah, spent the night, and traveled northwest to Clarendon the next day on the Fort Worth and Denver line.

14. Elgar Dumont became postmaster on December 10, 1924, for a four-year term, and he was reappointed for a second term in 1928. Oma Dumont, interview, April 12, 1963.

15. Thomas Telsa ("Tommy") Bird was born December 31, 1924. He was a Marine veteran of World War II. He died January 20, 1946, as a result of an accidental gunshot wound. Two children survived him, one by each of two marriages. Ibid. The Dumont family has no information on the location of Tommy Bird's family.

16. The apartment house was built on lots behind the author's home in 1925. Ibid. The structure no longer exists.

Chapter Twenty-Four

1. Elgar and Oma Dumont moved into the apartment house in the spring of 1926. Oma Dumont, interview, April 12, 1963.

2. The Campbell Ranch is approximately sixteen miles west-southwest of Matador. Long and Long, interview, March 20, 1987. Traweek explains, "H. H. Campbell lived in the original half dugout which was built on this location by the Dutchman who gave Dutchman Creek its name. Later, Harry Campbell, son of H. H. Campbell, added two more rooms, hauling cement for this structure from Childress with a wagon and team. The cement was mixed by hand and poured from five gallon buckets to make walls which are a foot thick. Ultimately other rooms were built. . . . Today the house is a modern and attractive split level ranch home. Perhaps the room with the greatest charm is the kitchen, built on the lowest level where the dugout used to be." Traweek, *Of Such As These,* p. 209. Today Harold Campbell, son of Harry Campbell and grandson of H. H. Campbell, lives on the ranch with his wife, Grace. The second son of Harry Campbell, Bundy, now ranches in Motley County and lives in Matador with his wife, Lucretia. Hal Vance Campbell, the youngest son of Harry Campbell, lives with his wife, Betty Jean, on the western edge of Motley County above the Caprock, on land that originally belonged to Vance's grandfather. In addition to three sons, Harry Campbell had one daughter, Erin Campbell Shearer, who was an older stepsister of Harold, Bundy, and Vance. Ibid.

3. According to Meador, Mrs. Henry Campbell served as postmistress of Motley County for a quarter of a century. Douglas Meador, interview with editor, Matador, Tex., June 11, 1963. Mrs. Campbell's son Harry says that his mother was noted for three things: her daintiness; her mode of dress; and her interest in city, state, and national affairs. Campbell quotes Mr. Jim Gibson of Paducah who states: "'I used to go to see Mrs. Campbell after she was old and blind. . . . I never saw Mrs. Campbell that I did not marvel at her brilliant mind.'" Campbell, *Early History of Motley County,* p. 62. Lizzie Campbell died in 1931 at the age of 81. Meador, interview, June 11, 1963.

4. Mrs. Sul Carter, whose husband was named for his uncle Sul Ross, had been a neighbor and longtime friend of the author from her days on the R O S Ranch. Mrs. Carter's daughter had married Jim Eblen of Paducah and had borne three sons. Long and Long, letter, February 24, 1987.

5. Here the author writes of another trip to New Mexico in 1927. Elgar, Oma, little J. Verne, and the author's stepbrother Lewis White accompanied her. Once again they visited Fite relatives—sons of the author's sister, Lucy: Flennoy Fite in Hope, New Mexico; Tom Fite and the family of Charlie Fite (deceased) in Cloud-croft; and Burton Fite at the state college "just out of Mesilla Park" (now New Mexico State University in Las Cruces). They also went to El Paso and spent a Sunday in Juarez sight-seeing. Finally, in the Sacramento Mountains the author saw her elderly Aunt Martha Benson Bass (her mother's sister) and Aunt Martha's

sons (the author's cousins), Lon and Charles Bass. The account is omitted because it primarily describes scenery and family gatherings.

6. Ed Carlock purchased the *Paducah Post* in 1908 from a Mr. Butler. Carlock, interview, April 14, 1963.

7. Elgar Dumont moved his family into the stucco home on June 1, 1927. Oma Dumont, interview, April 12, 1963.

8. Phillip Eugene Dumont was born on September 3, 1927. J. Verne Dumont, telephone interview, Feburary 21, 1987.

9. Phillip Eugene died on May 7, 1928, of whooping cough and complications from the disease. Oma Dumont, interview, April 12, 1963.

BIBLIOGRAPHY

Adams, Ramon F. *Western Words: A Dictionary of the Range, Cow Camp, and Trail.* Norman: University of Oklahoma Press, 1944.

———, ed. *The Best of the American Cowboy.* Norman: University of Oklahoma Press, 1957.

American Folklore and Legend. Pleasantville, N.Y.: Reader's Digest Association, 1978.

American Quarter Horse Association. *Stud Book and Registry.* Fort Worth: American Quarter Horse Association, 1941.

Anderson, Rudolph E. *The Story of the American Automobile.* Washington, D.C.: Public Affairs Press, 1952.

"Ballads and Songs Collected by the Missouri Folk-Lore Society: 'The Dying Californian,'" *The University of Missouri Studies: A Quarterly of Research,* ed. H. M. Belden, 15(1)(January 1, 1940): 350–351.

Barsness, Larry. *Heads, Hides and Horns: The Compleat Buffalo Book.* Fort Worth: Texas Christian University Press, 1985.

Bennett, Carmen Taylor. *Our Roots Grow Deep: A History of Cottle County.* Floydada, Tex.: Blanco Offset Printing, 1970.

Bigham, Jim Bob. Interview with editor. Paducah, Tex. October 11, 1986.

Bigham, Verlon. Interview with editor. Lubbock, Tex. October 11, 1986.

Bird, Charles A. (Grandson of Charles D. Bird). Letters to editor. Midland, Tex. February 11 and 23, 1987.

Black's Medical Dictionary. 34th ed. Totowa, N.J.: Barnes and Noble Books, 1984.

Branch, E. Douglas. *The Hunting of the Buffalo.* New York: D. Appleton, 1929.

Britton, Sarah Ann. *The Early History of Baylor County.* Dallas: Story Book Press, 1955.

Brothers, J. B. Interview with editor, Paducah, Tex. May 3, 1963.

Brune, Gunnar. *Springs of Texas,* vol. 1. Fort Worth: Branch-Smith, 1981.

Burke, Lee. "I. Wilson Knives." *The American Blade* 2 (July/August 1975): 38–42.

Burton, Harley True. *A History of the JA Ranch.* Austin: Von Boeckman-Jones, 1928.

Byrd, A. J. *History and Description of Johnson County and Its Principal Towns.* Marshall, Tex.: Jennings Brothers, 1879.

Caldwell, Mrs. Clifton, and James Robert Green. "The Texas Central Company." A Report from the Old Jail Art Center, Albany, Tex. Typescript, n.d.

Campbell, Harry H. *Early History of Motley County*. San Antonio: Naylor, 1958.

Carey, A. Merwyn. *American Firearms Makers*. New York: Thomas Y. Crowell, 1953.

Carlock, Elfie B. Interview with editor. Paducah, Tex. April 14, 1963.

Carr, Lorene. Interview with editor. Paducah, Tex. March 20, 1987.

Chapel, Charles Edward. *Guns of the Old West*. New York: Coward-McCann, 1961.

Chapple, Joe Mitchell, ed. *Heart Songs Dear to the American People*. Cleveland: World, 1950.

Clarke, Mary Whatley. *The Swenson Saga and the SMS Ranches*. Austin: Jenkins, 1976.

Clymer, Floyd. *Treasury of Early American Automobiles*. New York: McGraw-Hill, 1950.

Collinson, Frank. *Life in the Saddle*. Edited by Mary Whatley Clarke. Norman: University of Oklahoma Press, 1963.

The Columbia Encyclopedia, 3d ed. New York: Columbia University Press, 1963.

Cottle County, Texas. District Clerk's Office. Auguste Dumont Declaration of Citizenship. May 27, 1899.

Crockett, James Underwood. *Trees*. New York: Time-Life Books, 1972.

Crouch, Carrie J. *A History of Young County, Texas*. Austin: Texas State Historical Association, 1956.

Daughtry, Geraldine. Letter to editor. Quanah, Tex. February 6, 1987.

Dawson, H. G. *The Hog Book*. Chicago: Breeder's Gazette, 1911.

A Dictionary of Americanisms on Historical Principles. Ed. Mitford M. Mathews. Chicago: University of Chicago Press, 1951.

Dictionary of American Slang. 2d supplemented ed. Ed. Harold Wentworth and Stuart Berg Flexner. New York: Thomas Y. Crowell, 1960.

Dorland's Illustrated Medical Dictionary. 25th ed. Philadelphia: W. B. Saunders, 1975.

Dumont, Ella Bird. Collection. Panhandle-Plains Historical Museum, Canyon, Tex.

Dumont, J. Verne. Family Papers and Photographs. Paducah, Tex.

———. Interview with editor. Paducah, Tex. October 11, 1986.

———. Letter to editor. Paducah, Tex. October 21, 1986.

———. Telephone interview with editor. February 21, 1987.

Dumont, Oma. Interview with editor. Paducah, Tex. April 12, 1963.

Encyclopedia Britannica. 14th ed. Chicago: Encyclopedia Britannica, 1961.

Exley, Jo Ella Powell. *Texas Tears and Texas Sunshine: Voices of Frontier Women*. College Station: Texas A&M University Press, 1985.

Farrow, Edward S. *American Small Arms*. New York: Bradford, 1904.

Fenton, James I. "The Lobo Wolf: Beast of Waste and Desolation." *Pandhandle-Plains Historical Review* 53 (1980): 57–70.

Fite, Kathleen R. Telephone interview with Ruth Stephens. February 8, 1987.

Ford, Gus L. *Texas Cattle Brands*. Dallas: Anne Johnston Ford, 1958.

Funk, Charles Earle. *A Hog on Ice*. New York: Harper and Brothers, 1948.

Furr, Winona (District and County Clerk of Childress County). Letter to editor. Childress, Tex. November 24, 1986.

Gard, Wayne. *The Fabulous Quarter Horse Steel Dust.* New York: Duell, Sloan and Pearce, 1958.

———. *The Great Buffalo Hunt.* New York: Alfred A. Knopf, 1959.

———. *Rawhide Texas.* Norman: University of Oklahoma Press, 1965.

Gibson, Lottie. Interview with editor. Paducah, Tex. March 20, 1987.

———. "Location, Resources and History." In *King County: Windmills and Barbed Wire,* ed. the King County Historical Society. Quanah, Tex.: Nortex Press, 1976.

Gillett, J. B. "'Slick' Clements Was a Good Marksman." *Frontier Times* 1(February 1924): 17–18.

———. *The Texas Ranger: A Story of the Southwestern Frontier.* Yonkers-on-Hudson, New York: World Book Company, 1927.

Gilmore, Lee. "The Mill Iron Ranch." *Panhandle-Plains Historical Review* 5 (1932): 57–66.

Griggs, William C. "The Battle of Yellowhouse Canyon in 1877." *West Texas Historical Association Year Book* 51(1975): 37–50.

Haines, Francis. *The Buffalo.* New York: Thomas Y. Crowell, 1970.

Haley, Amy (District and County Clerk of Baylor County). Letter to editor. Seymour, Tex. November 10, 1986.

Haley, J. Evetts. *Charles Goodnight: Cowman and Plainsman.* Norman: University of Oklahoma Press, 1949.

Holden, William Curry. *The Espuela Land and Cattle Company.* Austin: Texas State Historical Association, 1970.

Hornecker, Martin. *Buffalo Hunting on the Texas Plains in 1877.* Geneseo, Ill.: Geneseo Republic, 1929.

Huey, Jane. Telephone interview with editor. November 25, 1986.

King County Historical Society, ed. *King County: Windmills and Barbed Wire.* Quanah, Tex.: Nortex Press, 1976.

Knight, Oliver. *Fort Worth: Outpost on the Trinity.* Norman: University of Oklahoma Press, 1953.

Ledbetter, Barbara A. Neal. "Fort Belknap, 1880–1890." Typescript, 1961.

———. *Fort Belknap: Frontier Saga.* Burnet, Tex.: Eakin Press, 1982.

———. Letter to editor. Graham, Tex. December 22, 1986.

Lee, Ernest, ed. "A Woman on the Buffalo Range: The Journal of Ella Dumont." *West Texas Historical Association Year Book* 40 (October 1964): 146–167.

Liedtke, Walter, Sr. Interview with editor. Paducah, Tex. April 10, 1963.

Long, Alma Gibson, and Tom Long. Interview with editor. Paducah, Tex. March 20, 1987.

———. Letters to editor. Paducah, Tex. December 17, 1986; February 24, 1987.

———. Telephone interview with editor. Paducah, Tex. February 27, 1987.

Luebke, Frederick C. *Ethnicity on the Great Plains.* Lincoln: University of Nebraska Press, 1980.

McClure, C. B. "A History of the Shoe Nail Ranch." *Panhandle-Plains Historical Review* 11(1938): 69–83.

McQuade, Donald, ed. *The Harper American Literature,* vol. 1 New York: Harper and Row, 1987.

Matthews, Sallie Reynolds. *Interwoven: A Pioneer Chronicle.* College Station: Texas A&M University Press, 1982.

Mayer, Frank H., and Charles B. Roth. *The Buffalo Harvest.* Denver: Sage, 1958.

Meador, Douglas. Interview with editor. Matador, Tex. June 11, 1963.

A Memorial and Biographical History of Johnson and Hill Counties, Texas. Chicago: Lewis, 1892.

Mott, Frank Luther. *A History of American Magazines.* Vol. 4, *1885–1905.* Cambridge: Harvard University Press, Belknap Press, 1957.

Moursand, John S. *Blanco County Families for 100 Years.* San Antonio: John S. Moursand, 1958.

Murrah, David J. *The Pitchfork Land and Cattle Company: The First Century.* Lubbock: Texas Tech University Press, 1983.

Neeley, Bill. *Quanah Parker and His People.* Slaton, Tex.: Brazos Press, 1986.

Newcomb, William W. *The Indians of Texas.* Austin: University of Texas Press, 1961.

Nilsen, Alleen Pace, and Kenneth L. Donelson. *Literature for Today's Young Adults.* 2d ed. Glenview, Ill.: Scott, Foresman, 1985.

Nordyke, Lewis. *Great Roundup.* New York: William Morrow, 1955.

Oliver, John W. *History of American Technology.* New York: Ronald Press, 1956.

The Oxford Dictionary of Natural History. Oxford and New York: Oxford University Press, 1985.

The Oxford Dictionary of Quotations. 2d ed. London: Oxford University Press, 1952.

Paducah Post. May 21, 1936.

Pearce, William M. *The Matador Land and Cattle Company.* Norman: University of Oklahoma Press, 1964.

Piper, Grace Jones. Interview with editor. Paducah, Tex. March 20, 1987.

———. Letter to editor. Paducah, Tex. February 26, 1987.

Preece, Harold. *Lone Star Man.* New York: Hastings House, 1960.

Price, B. Byron, and Frederick W. Rathjen. *The Golden Spread.* Northridge, Calif.: Windsor, 1986.

The Random House Dictionary of the English Language. Ed. Jess Stein. New York: Random House, 1966.

Rathjen, Frederick W. *The Texas Panhandle Frontier.* Austin: University of Texas Press, 1973.

Rattenbury, Richard. "A Winchester for All Seasons." *Man at Arms* 8 (September/October 1986): 10–14.

Rister, Carl Coke. *Fort Griffin on the Texas Frontier.* Norman: University of Oklahoma Press, 1957.

———. *The Southwestern Frontier, 1865–1881.* Glendale, Calif.: Arthur H. Clark, 1928.

Roberts, Captain Dan W. *Rangers and Sovereignty.* San Antonio: Wood Printing and Engraving, 1914.

Roberts, Mrs. D. W. *A Woman's Reminiscences of Six Years in Camp with the Texas Rangers.* Austin: Von Boeckman-Jones, 1928.

Robertson, Pauline Durrett, and R. L. Robertson. *Cowman's Country: Fifty Frontier Ranches in the Texas Panhandle, 1876–1887.* Amarillo: Paramount, 1981.

Sellers, Frank. *Sharps Firearms.* North Hollywood, Calif.: Beinfeld, 1978.

Smith, Ralph A. "The West Texas Bone Business." *West Texas Historical Association Year Book* 55 (1979): 111–134.

Smyres, Louise Patton. Telephone interview with Donna Gene Reardon. October 14, 1986.

Soule, Gardner. *The Long Trail: How Cowboys and Longhorns Opened the West.* New York: McGraw-Hill, 1976.

Stratton, Porter A. *The Territorial Press of New Mexico 1834–1912.* Albuquerque: University of New Mexico Press, 1969.

Streeter, Floyd Benjamin. "The Millett Cattle Ranch in Baylor County, Texas." *Panhandle/Plains Historical Review* 22 (1949): 65–83.

Sweet, William Warren. *Religion on the American Frontier: The Baptists 1783–1830.* New York: Cooper Square, 1964.

Swint, Pearl. Interview with editor. Paducah, Tex. April 9, 1963.

Taack, La Fonda (District and County Clerk of Young County). Letter to editor. Graham, Tex. July 16, 1986.

Texas. Texas Water Development Board. Ox Yoke Creek Quadrangle Map, King County, 1981.

Texas Almanac and State Industrial Guide, 1986–87. Dallas: A. H. Belo, 1985.

Texas Almanac, 1961–1962. Dallas: A. H. Belo, 1961.

Texas Ranger Muster Rolls, Companies B and D, Frontier Battalion, 1874–1877. Texas State Archives, Austin.

Texas Ranger Muster Rolls, Company A, Minute Men, 1872–1874. Texas State Archives, Austin.

Texas Ranger Muster Rolls, Company D, Frontier Battalion, 1874–1876. Texas State Archives, Austin.

Tilghman, Zoe A. *Quanah, The Eagle of the Comanches.* Oklahoma City: Harlow, 1938.

Tooley, Kenneth. Interview with editor. Paducah, Tex. April 15, 1963.

Traweek, Eleanor Mitchell. *Of Such As These: A History of Motley County and Its Families.* Quanah and Wichita Falls: Nortex, 1973.

Vernon's Annotated Revised Civil Statutes of the State of Texas, vol. 12A. Kansas City: Vernon Law Book Company, 1960.

Warren, John, and Colquet Warren. *The Matadors, 1879–1951.* Matador, Tex.: John Warren, 1952.

Webb, Walter Prescott. *The Texas Rangers.* New York: Houghton Mifflin, 1935.

————, ed. *The Handbook of Texas.* 2 vols. Austin: Texas State Historical Association, 1952.

Wharton, Clarence R. *Texas under Many Flags,* vol. 4. New York: American Historical Society, 1930.

Whitehouse, Eula. *Texas Flowers in Natural Colors.* Austin: Texas Book Store, 1936.

Whitlock, V. H. (Ol' Waddy). *Cowboy Life on the Llano Estacado.* Norman: University of Oklahoma Press, 1976.

Williams, J. W. *The Big Ranch Country.* Wichita Falls, Tex.: Terry Brothers, 1954.

Wright, Lyle H. *American Fiction: 1876–1900.* San Marino, Calif.: Huntington Library, 1966.

Wright, Muriel H. *A Guide to the Indian Tribes of Oklahoma.* Norman: University of Oklahoma Press, 1951.

Zurhorst, Charles. *The First Cowboys and Those Who Followed.* New York: Abelard-Schuman, 1973.

INDEX

Thompson, Mr. (cowboy on North
Central Plains), 58
Thornton, Tex., 125–126, 202n.10 (Ch.
20), 205n.3
Thorp Springs, Tex., 49, 177n.7
Three D Ranch, 56, 57, 95, 180nn.6, 7,
185n.22
Throckmorton County, Tex., 14,
20–22, 159n.13
Tongue River, 46, 48, 56, 68, 175–
176n.13, 181nn.12, 13
Tongue River Ranch, 183n.16
Tonkawa (Tonkaway) Indians, 154n.8,
156n.20, 192n.4
Tonk Valley, 81, 113, 193n.4
Trail herds, 61
Triangle Ranch, 180n.6, 183n.18,
184n.20, 194n.9
Trumble, Bill, 62–63, 176n.4
Turney, Mr. and Mrs. (Paducah, Tex.),
146
Tyler Commercial College, 139, 207n.2
Typhus, 151n.3

Veal's Station, 8, 154n.9
"Virginia Dare," 102, 198–199n.12

Waco Indians, 154n.8, 156n.20, 192n.4
"Wait for Me at Heaven's Gate, Sweet
Belle Mahone," 116, 201n.9
Walker, George, 75
Walker, Mr. and Mrs. (on wagon train
to Texas), 3
Weatherford, Tex., 155n.15, 178n.15
Weatherly family (Benjamin, Tex.), 81
Webb, Mr. (Cottle County, Tex.), 62
Wells, Mr. (Cottle County, Tex.),
62–64
Western Trail, 172n.9
Wheeler County, Tex., 178n.15
White, Elizabeth Benson Elgar (au-
thor's mother). *See* Bellamy, Eliza-
beth Benson Elgar White

White, Ercell, 140
White, Hugh, 105
White, Lewis E. (author's step-
brother), 2–3, 6, 81, 135, 206n.4
White, Lizzie (author's niece), 137, 140
White, Mr. and Mrs. (Blanco County,
Tex.), 12
White, Oma (author's niece), 135–136,
206n.4, 207n.10
White, Thomas William ("Willie"; au-
thor's stepbrother), 2–3, 8, 65,
188n.12
White, Thomas Buckle (author's step-
father), 2
White, Tom, 71
Whiteflat, Tex., 105
Wichita Indians, 156n.20
Wilson, Dr. L. T., 52, 179n.17
Winchester '73 Rifle: awarded to J. T.
Bird, 11, 157–158n.6; Comanche at-
tempt to trade for, 27–29, 169n.28;
used by author in antelope hunt, 85
Windfohr, Anne Burnett, 180n.6,
183n.18, 194n.9
Winter of 1885–1886 ("The Great
White Ruin"), 58, 185n.24
Winton, Ora, 125, 130, 134, 135, 205n.2
Woodley, Judge and Mrs. J. W.,
198n.10
Woodley, Melvin, 137, 207n.10
Work, Charlie, 97, 196–197n.2
Work, Mr. and Mrs. (Dallas, Tex.),
113–114
Wylie, R. K. ("Bob"), 56, 181n.12

Yager, Mr. and Miss (Johnson County,
Tex.), 8
Yarbrough, Mr. (King County, Tex.),
39, 43
Yellowhouse Canyon (Yellowhouse
Draw), 35, 171–172n.4
YL Ranch, 184n.20
Young County, Tex., 10, 155n.17, 156n.18